The Politics of Appropriation

The New Cultural History of Music

SERIES EDITOR Jane F. Fulcher

SERIES BOARD
MEMBERS: Celia Applegate
Philip Bohlman
Kate van Orden
Michael P. Steinberg

Enlightenment Orpheus: The Power of Music in Other Worlds
Vanessa Agnew

Voice Lessons: French Mélodie in the Belle Epoque
Katherine Bergeron

Songs, Scribes, and Societies: The History and Reception of the Loire Valley Chansonniers
Jane Alden

Harmony and Discord: Music and the Transformation of Russian Cultural Life
Lynn M. Sargeant

Musical Renderings of the Philippine Nation
Christi-Anne Castro

The Sense of Sound: Musical Meaning in France, 1260–1330
Emma Dillon

Staging the French Revolution: Cultural Politics and the Paris Opera, 1789–1794
Mark Darlow

Music, Piety, and Propaganda: The Soundscapes of Counter-Reformation Bavaria
Alexander J. Fisher

The Politics of Appropriation: German Romantic Music and the Ancient Greek Legacy
Jason Geary

JASON
GEARY

The Politics of Appropriation
German Romantic Music and the Ancient Greek Legacy

UNIVERSITY PRESS

Oxford University Press is a department of the University of Oxford.
It furthers the University's objective of excellence in research, scholarship,
and education by publishing worldwide.

Oxford   New York
Auckland   Cape Town   Dar es Salaam   Hong Kong   Karachi
Kuala Lumpur   Madrid   Melbourne   Mexico City   Nairobi
New Delhi   Shanghai   Taipei   Toronto

With offices in
Argentina   Austria   Brazil   Chile   Czech Republic   France   Greece
Guatemala   Hungary   Italy   Japan   Poland   Portugal   Singapore
South Korea   Switzerland   Thailand   Turkey   Ukraine   Vietnam

Oxford is a registered trademark of Oxford University Press
in the UK and certain other countries.

Published in the United States of America by
Oxford University Press
198 Madison Avenue, New York, NY 10016

© Oxford University Press 2014

All rights reserved. No part of this publication may be reproduced, stored in a
retrieval system, or transmitted, in any form or by any means, without the prior
permission in writing of Oxford University Press, or as expressly permitted by law,
by license, or under terms agreed with the appropriate reproduction rights organization.
Inquiries concerning reproduction outside the scope of the above should be sent to the Rights
Department, Oxford University Press, at the address above.

You must not circulate this work in any other form
and you must impose this same condition on any acquirer.

Publication for this book was supported by the AMS 75 PAYS Endowment of the American
Musicological Society, funded in part by the National Endowment for the Humanities and the Andrew
W. Mellon Foundation.

Library of Congress Cataloging-in-Publication Data
Geary, Jason.
The politics of appropriation : German romantic music and the ancient Greek legacy / Jason Geary.
   pages cm.
(New cultural history of music series)   Includes bibliographical references and index.
ISBN 978–0–19–973611–9 (hardback)
1. Dramatic music—Germany—19th century—History and criticism.
2. Greek drama (Tragedy)—Appreciation—Germany.   I. Title.
ML1729.4.G43 2013
781.5'520943—dc23
2013015336

9 8 7 9 6 5 4 3 2 1
Printed in the United States of America
on acid-free paper

To Helen, Ethan, and Aiden, my joy and inspiration

CONTENTS

Acknowledgments ix
Abbreviations xi

Introduction 1

CHAPTER ONE Ancient Greece and the German Cultural Imagination 10

CHAPTER TWO Mendelssohn's *Antigone* and the Rebirth of Greek Tragedy 28

CHAPTER THREE The Reception of *Antigone* and the Aesthetics of Appropriation 79

CHAPTER FOUR The Growth of a Genre: Taubert's *Medea* and the Greek Stage Revival in Berlin 99

CHAPTER FIVE Mendelssohn and Oedipus in the Age of Christianity 135

CHAPTER SIX Lachner and the Emergence of a New Athens 168

CHAPTER SEVEN The Wagnerian Turn 197

CHAPTER EIGHT Epilogue: The Decline of a Genre 227

Notes 235
Bibliography 253
Index 263

ACKNOWLEDGMENTS

Although I can never hope to acknowledge all of those colleagues, family members, and friends who have played a part in shaping the outcome of this book, there are certain individuals without whom this work would be virtually unthinkable in its present form. Let me begin by singling out my dissertation advisor, James Hepokoski, who offered unyielding support when this project was in its infancy and from whose keen scholarly insight I continued to benefit even after I had finished my thesis and this project had begun to take shape in new and unexpected ways. Others who took time out of their busy schedules to read and comment on portions of this manuscript and to whom I extend my warmest thanks include Roland John Wiley, R. Larry Todd, Douglass Seaton, Patrick McCreless, and Leon Plantinga. Many thanks go also to my colleagues at the University of Michigan, who offered support and encouragement along the way.

I would also like to thank the many institutions whose financial assistance has been crucial to the completion of this book. I am deeply grateful for the support I received from the University of Michigan, particularly for the generous funding from the office of Lester Monts, senior vice provost for Academic Affairs, which helped pay for a research trip to Germany in 2008 and was also used to defray costs incurred during the process of compiling the manuscript. I am also thankful for the year I was able to spend devoting nearly all of my energies to this project as a member of the School of Historical Studies at the Institute for Advanced Study in Princeton, New Jersey. My colleagues there were a source of great knowledge and inspiration, and I am especially grateful to Heinrich von Staden for his support. I am equally appreciative of the financial assistance I received at various times from the

German-American Fulbright Commission, Yale University, and the University of Michigan School of Music, Theatre & Dance.

I would like to thank those libraries and archives that provided me with access to their manuscript collections, including the Mendelssohn Archiv at the Staatsbibliothek zu Berlin—Preußischer Kulturbesitz, the Landesarchiv Berlin, the Bodleian Library at Oxford University, and the Bayerische Staatsbibliothek in Munich. I am especially grateful to the Universitätsbibliothek Leipzig for permission to include unpublished material in this book. I would also like to thank the many staff members and librarians at these institutions, whose helpfulness and expertise were critical factors in the completion of this project. Special thanks goes to Peter Ward Jones at the Bodleian Library for his warm generosity and for his willingness to help with deciphering especially challenging passages of handwritten text from unpublished correspondence.

The editorial team at Oxford University Press has been an invaluable source of support during the process of writing this book. Thanks go to the executive editor for music publications, Suzanne Ryan, for her patience and wise counsel, and to Adam Cohen for his willingness to field my many inquiries concerning the more mundane aspects of preparing a manuscript for publication. I am also grateful to the series editor, Jane Fulcher, a colleague and friend who has lent her continued support to this project.

Finally, I would like to extend a special, heartfelt thanks to those of my family members who have been so supportive of me over the years, including, but by no means limited to, my parents, my siblings, my late grandmother Vollie, who proudly claimed to be my "number-one fan," and my two young sons, Ethan and Aiden, who help me keep things in perspective. But, above all, my eternal gratitude goes to my wife Helen, who has patiently and lovingly endured all of the time and energy spent completing this work.

Portions of chapter 2 of this book previously appeared as "Reinventing the Past: Mendelssohn's *Antigone* and the Creation of an Ancient Greek Musical Language," *Journal of Musicology*, Vol. 23, No. 2 (Spring 2006), 187–226. A short section of chapter 5 is taken from my essay "Converting the Pagans: Mendelssohn, Greek Tragedy, and the Christian Ethos," in *Mendelssohn Perspectives*, eds. Nicole Grimes and Angela Mace (Farnham, UK: Ashgate, 2012), 163–76; and portions of chapter 6 represent an expansion of material that first appeared as "Incidental Music and the Revival of Greek Tragedy from the Italian Renaissance to German Romanticism," in *Ancient Drama in Music for the Modern Stage*, eds. Peter Brown and Suzana Ograjensek (Oxford: Oxford University Press, 2010), 49–62. I am grateful to all parties involved for permission to reprint these materials.

ABBREVIATIONS

D-B   Staatsbibliothek zu Berlin—Preussischer Kulturbesitz, Berlin, Germany
D-Mbs   Bayerische Staatsbibliothek, Munich, Germany
GB-Ob   Bodleian Library, Oxford University, Oxford, UK
GS   *Gesammelte Schriften* (complete edition of Richard Wagner's writings; see bibliography for full reference)
MA   *Mendelssohn Archiv* (Staatsbibliothek zu Berlin)
PW   *Prose Works* (complete translated edition of Richard Wagner's writings; see bibliography for full reference)

The Politics of Appropriation

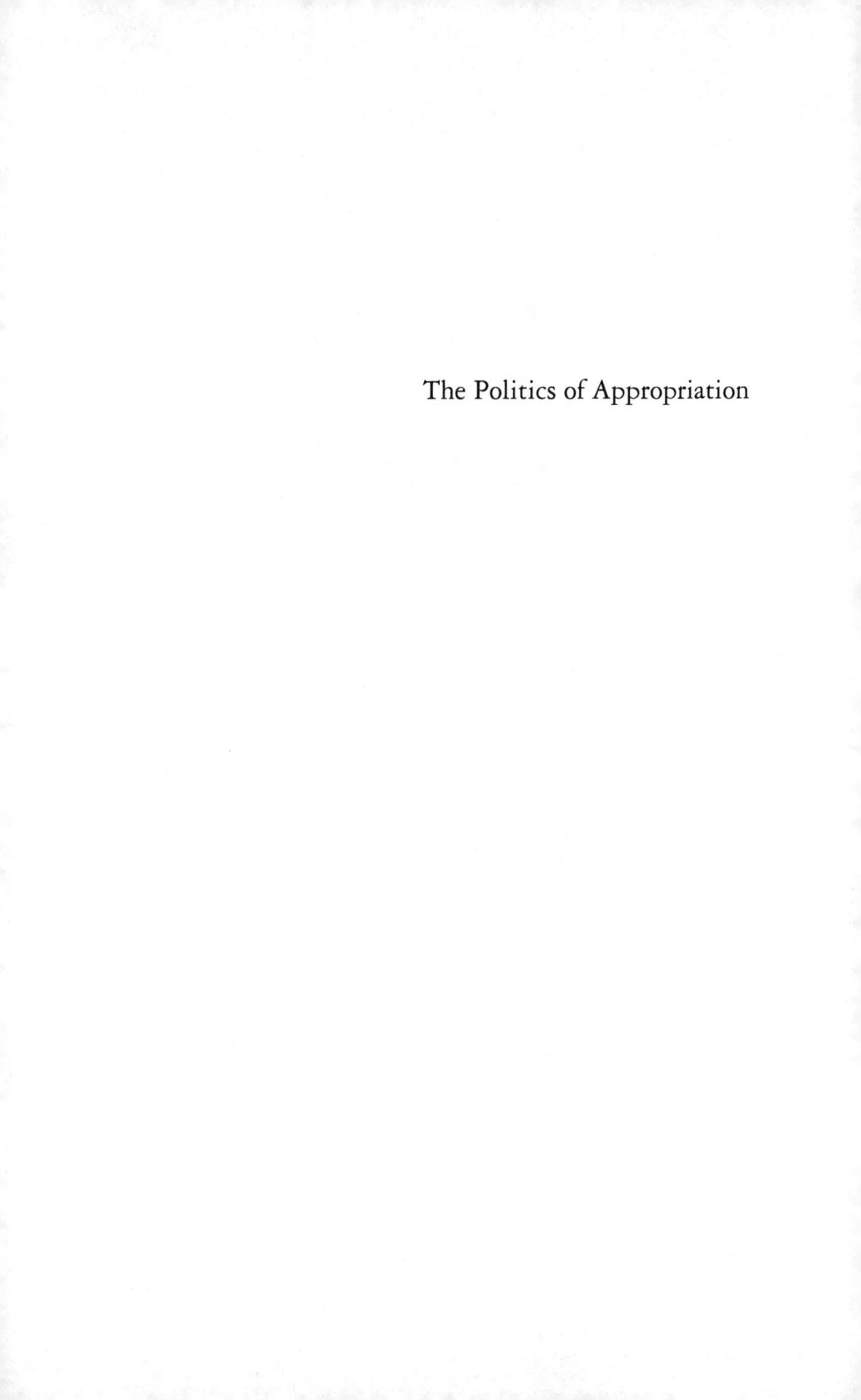

Introduction

IN 1844, THREE years after the highly successful production of Sophocles' *Antigone* at the Prussian court, King Friedrich Wilhelm IV ordered the creation of a bronze medallion to commemorate the event.[1] On one side, Antigone is shown burying her slain brother, along with smaller engravings of Ludwig Tieck, who oversaw the production, and Felix Mendelssohn, who composed the music for it. On the other side is a depiction of Sophocles with the date of the court premiere and a Greek inscription by the philologist August Böckh paraphrasing the epitaph thought to have adorned Sophocles' tombstone: "Gaze upon the eternal Sophocles, who won first prize in the art of tragedy, the most revered of art forms."

That the Prussian king would go to such lengths to commemorate this event suggests both its extraordinary impact and its groundbreaking nature. This retrospective gesture also points to a personal desire aimed at capitalizing on the lasting success of a production that he himself had commissioned. As the king explained to his brother-in-law, Prince Johann of Saxony, this medallion celebrated nothing less than the German resurrection of ancient tragedy.[2] Looking back on the singular event that it commemorated, we can point to this bronze medallion as a symbol of the fruitful manner in which artistic, intellectual, and political spheres combined to give expression to a German fascination with Greek antiquity that formed a vital part of an emerging cultural and national identity.

The importance of Greece for Germany of the nineteenth century has long been acknowledged. The idea of a singular German devotion to the Greeks dating back to the mid-eighteenth century and spanning much of the nineteenth has been a commonplace among scholars at least since the publication in the 1930s of seminal works by E. M. Butler and Walther Rehm.[3] This research, along with that of more recent scholars, has highlighted the degree to which German artists and intellectuals of the period looked to ancient Greece as both a model of aesthetic beauty and a touchstone of humanity.[4] But whereas the influence of Greece on literature, art, architecture, and philosophy has been well established, considerably less attention has been given to the intersection of German music and Hellenism over the course of the nineteenth century. Moreover, scholars who have dealt with this topic have focused almost exclusively on Richard Wagner's interest in Greek tragedy and its connection to his operas. Such a limited focus, however, effectively ignores the trend of combining music and Greek tragedy that began with the 1841 Prussian court production of *Antigone* and that continued in some fashion throughout the remainder of the century.

Widely perceived as the first genuine revival of Greek tragedy on the German stage, the Mendelssohn-Tieck *Antigone* inspired a host of similar performances and thus contributed to a larger European revival of ancient drama. Among these performances were two highly visible ones that occurred at the Prussian royal court in Berlin and that clearly aimed to build on the success of the Mendelssohn-Tieck *Antigone*: an 1843 production of Euripides' *Medea* with music by the court composer Wilhelm Taubert and a staging of Sophocles' *Oedipus at Colonus* in 1845 with music by Mendelssohn. Not to be outdone, the Bavarian court in Munich also became an important site of such theatrical experimentation, mounting a production of *Antigone* in 1851 with Mendelssohn's by-then celebrated music, followed in 1852 by Sophocles' *Oedipus the King* featuring a score by the court composer Franz Lachner.

Though all of these productions were (eventually) presented in public or semi-public forums, their courtly origins underscore the degree to which the German revival of Greek tragedy was inextricably linked to the royal courts of Berlin and, to a lesser extent, Munich. This connection in turn points to how many rulers of the time were quick to exploit the legacy of ancient Greece for the advancement of their own political agendas. It is certainly no accident that the two courts at which these productions of Greek drama took root were the same ones behind such grand neoclassical buildings as Karl Friedrich Schinkel's Altes Museum in Berlin and Leo von Klenze's Glyptothek in Munich, both completed in 1830.

The purpose of this book is to investigate this revival of Greek tragedy within a broad cultural framework of German Hellenism. It explores above all the role of music in a complex web of sometimes competing cultural, political, and artistic aims that converged in the groundbreaking productions mentioned above and in similar ones inspired by these efforts. In addition, this study reassesses Wagner's appropriation of the Greeks in light of these developments and considers the trajectory of these two distinct paths relative to changing perceptions of ancient Greece. This book thus provides a detailed exploration of the fruitful intersection of music and Hellenism in Germany from the mid-to-late nineteenth century.

The broad cultural resonance of the ancient dramas staged in Germany in the 1840s and '50s ultimately reflects an enduring German veneration of Greek antiquity. One aspect of this Hellenism, which emerged from the late Enlightenment, was a belief that Germany represented the sole heir to the classical Greek legacy. Though the French or British might boast of strong neoclassical traditions, only the Germans possessed a genuine spiritual affinity with the Greeks and were thus capable of reaching the heights once attained by the ancients, or so the argument went. Such thinking mirrored the growing sense of cultural superiority shared by many Germans of the time—a notion that went hand in hand with Germany's self-appointed task of redeeming the modern world through its universal, civilizing culture. These ideas in turn contributed to the formation of a German national identity defined by the collective consciousness of a shared cultural heritage that, to some extent, compensated for the lack of a politically unified state. As I show in chapter 1, a critical element of this burgeoning identity was the appropriation of ancient Greece, which occurred in the form of neoclassical art and architecture, literary works inspired by Greek models, and the rise of disciplines such as classical philology and archaeology. Also included in this appropriation were those staged productions of Greek tragedy in which music contributed to the sense of an "authentic" re-creation.

Such productions therefore offer a window onto the nature of an appropriation fraught with aesthetic, social, and political concerns. In chapter 2, for example, I argue that Friedrich Wilhelm IV looked to Greek tragedy as a way of revitalizing Berlin's cultural life in hopes of gaining public support for a monarchy intent on recapturing aspects of a more glorious (German) past. Somewhat paradoxically, the court productions of ancient drama commissioned by the king were defined in part by an attempt at Christianizing the text at hand. This effort, which reflects a general desire among German Hellenists to reconcile ancient Greek civic, religious, and artistic ideals with the Christian values of a modern age, was embodied above all in the music composed for these productions, as the discussion in chapter 5 of Mendelssohn's allusions to the Protestant chorale and to Handel's *Messiah* in his *Oedipus at Colonus* illustrates most clearly.

Indeed, a central task of this book is to consider the music for such productions relative to the political and social concerns surrounding their commission and performance. Michael P. Steinberg in particular has opened the door to this avenue of inquiry concerning the Mendelssohn-Tieck *Antigone*.[5] Steinberg argues that the play's essential theme of the state versus the individual not only resonated with ongoing debates over the role in society of an increasingly centralized state but may also have evoked Mendelssohn's anxieties about his parents' decision to abandon Judaism in the face of a Christian-oriented power structure. Working within a relatively limited scope, however, Steinberg says very little about the actual music, except to suggest that its "rhetorically understated" nature may be a reflection of Mendelssohn's own ambivalence toward Friedrich Wilhelm's conservative Prussian regime. My aim is to engage with the sociopolitical issues arising out of the commission, performance, and reception of Greek tragedy staged with music in nineteenth-century Germany, interrogating the score as a site of meaning that reflects elements of the play, the overall nature of the production, and the broader cultural context in which such productions were conceived.

Thus I will show in chapter 2 that, although Mendelssohn ultimately decided in favor of a "modern" compositional language for the music of *Antigone*, he nonetheless employed strategies meant to suggest certain defining elements of Greek tragedy, including its poetic meter and the unison chanting thought to have been characteristic of its delivery. This approach can be seen as a response to the production's goal of faithfully re-creating antiquity, which itself is an expression of a characteristically nineteenth-century impulse to recover the past in its truest form. But even as the "ancient" dimension of Mendelssohn's music is informed by the general historicist impulse of the 1841 court production, the "modern" one draws upon familiar stylistic and topical references that reverberate with the sentiments of German nationalism and cultural pride inherent in the king's decision to stage Greek tragedy in the first place. Mendelssohn's *Antigone* thus highlights the intersection of artistic, cultural, and political spheres as viewed through the prism of a powerfully symbolic ideal of Greece. It also affirms the notion that, however autonomous an artistic field may appear on the surface, it always remains on some level subject to pressures of an economic and political sort.[6]

Chapter 3 traces the reception of *Antigone*, placing particular emphasis on the public performances that occurred in Leipzig and Berlin in 1842. These performances were important for establishing the widespread influence of the Mendelssohn-Tieck *Antigone* throughout Germany and abroad. Along with the Prussian court premiere, they also raised a host of aesthetic issues surrounding the revival of ancient drama on the modern stage, a discussion of which occurs in the third chapter. It also becomes clear to what extent the success of such productions was dependent upon Mendelssohn's score, which went on to serve as a model for similar compositions.

Chapters 4 and 5 follow the development of reviving Greek tragedy in Berlin and include a discussion of Taubert's music for *Medea* and Mendelssohn's score for *Oedipus at Colonus*, respectively. Chapter 6 then shifts the focus to the Bavarian court in Munich by exploring the performance of Sophoclean tragedy in light of King Maximilian II's own political and cultural ambitions. These performances included fully staged productions of *Antigone* and *Oedipus at Colonus* with Mendelssohn's music, as well as Sophocles' *Oedipus the King* with newly composed music by Franz Lachner. Not unlike those at the Prussian court, such undertakings are to be understood both within the context of German Hellenism and also as part of the king's efforts to reform the city's cultural life. In the case of Maximilian II, these efforts essentially represented a continuation of the attempt by his father, Ludwig I, to transform Munich into a "New Athens."

Ultimately, my objective is to show how the music written for these productions, while characterized by the same historicizing impulse as Mendelssohn's *Antigone*, is nonetheless informed by—and informs—the broader cultural resonances of each individual tragedy and the unique circumstances surrounding its performance. In addition to affirming the significance of such productions in nineteenth-century Germany, chapters 4, 5, and 6 reveal the extent to which contemporary observers viewed the accompanying music as the product of a newly emerging genre replete with its own conventions and stylistic parameters. Along with *Antigone*, these works of incidental music present a rich tapestry woven from the strands of political stagecraft, an abiding Hellenism, and mounting concerns with fashioning a German identity—all the while shedding light on a little known chapter in the history of German Romantic music.

To be sure, this body of music has received growing scholarly attention in recent years, much of it from two German academics working independently of one another. Since the late 1970s, the esteemed philologist Hellmut Flashar has published a series of articles and book chapters on Mendelssohn's music for Sophoclean tragedy, culminating in a forty-four-page volume issued in 2001 by the philological-historical division of the Saxon Academy of Sciences.[7] More recently, theater historian Susanne Boetius completed a monograph that, in addition to discussing Mendelssohn's music, also addresses other Greek tragedies set to music around this time.[8]

Flashar's earliest publications on the topic coincided with a performance of Mendelssohn's *Antigone* in 1979 marking the sesquicentennial of the German Archaeological Institute. Issued in honor of this occasion was a sumptuous volume on *Berlin und die Antike* that included an essay by Flashar discussing Mendelssohn's music for Sophoclean drama.[9] The revival of Mendelssohn's work and the scholarship surrounding it helped open the door to a critical reevaluation of a largely forgotten corner of his output. This trend paralleled a larger postwar reassessment of Mendelssohn's music and, in the case of *Antigone*, breathed new life into a work that had been routinely touted as one of the composer's best around the time of his death in 1847.

Yet as valuable as the scholarship produced by Flashar and Boetius has been, it has tended to shy away from discussion of the music in favor of exploring the circumstances surrounding its composition. Boetius, for example, has performed painstaking archival work involving the manuscript sources of *Antigone* and *Oedipus at Colonus*. Her research has revealed much insight into the genesis of these compositions, identifying the origins of textual variants and uncovering two slightly different versions of Mendelssohn's *Antigone*, one featured at the work's premiere and the other heard in subsequent productions. Yet she often treats this endeavor as an end in itself by not then illuminating the music on the basis of such findings. Flashar, too, eschews discussion of the music in all but a superficial sense. Moreover, his efforts to place Mendelssohn's incidental music in its larger context tend to downplay or altogether ignore the ideological dimension of Friedrich Wilhelm's interest in Greek tragedy.

In all fairness, neither Flashar nor Boetius is a musicologist, and so their lack of attention to the music is understandable. But because this music played such a crucial part in the "authentic" revival of Greek tragedy, it is necessary to consider both its specific nature, as well as its relationship to the cultural and political aims behind its creation. This study not only provides the first English-language account of this trend as a cultural, theatrical, and musical phenomenon, but places a distinct emphasis on the music as it builds upon prior efforts to illuminate the external factors that shaped these works. Indeed, even the handful of publications in English that treat this subject in any meaningful way, including Steinberg's work, have tended to avoid a robust consideration of the music. Two notable exceptions include R. Larry Todd's insightful though brief discussion of Mendelssohn's incidental music in his recent biography of the composer and Douglass Seaton's exploration of the relationship between the music of *Antigone* and the play's poetic meter, which I further develop in chapter 2.

Finally, my book expands the general scope of previous research by considering settings of Greek tragedy beyond those of Mendelssohn and by asking how these works fit into the German musical landscape of the mid-nineteenth century. Thus, in chapter 7, I make a connection with Wagner that has yet to be adequately acknowledged. There I argue that Wagner's obsession with the

Greeks around 1850 must be understood in light of the developments outlined above, in particular the extraordinary popularity enjoyed by Mendelssohn's *Antigone* and the production for which it was conceived. Repeatedly invoking Greek antiquity as a model of art and humanity, Wagner's series of influential reform essays call for the advent of a *Gesamtkunstwerk* that would combine the "purely human" arts of music, poetry, and dance with the plastic arts to create something like a modern-day embodiment of ancient Greek tragedy. What he really had in mind, of course, was his own radical conception of opera, or as it has come to be known, music drama.

Scholars have traditionally viewed Wagner's emphasis on Greece as simply the culmination of a personal lifelong interest, overlooking or at best downplaying the extent to which he was responding to—and reacting against—the recent trend of staging Greek tragedy with music. On several occasions in his writings, Wagner makes negative, mostly implicit reference to this development in self-conscious opposition to the sort of musico-dramatic work that he envisioned. For example, he dismisses the 1841 *Antigone* as an "artistic white lie" rooted in an aesthetic of "slavish restoration." These remarks reflect Wagner's universal rejection of such productions (and the music therein) as misguided attempts at *re-creating* Greek tragedy in opposition to his own aim of *reinventing* it on wholly modern, Germanic terms, arising not from a royal commission but from the spirit of the *Volk*.

Wagner effectively sought to undermine the claims of historical authenticity attributed to such productions. He did so by portraying them as symbols of an outdated and naïve late-Enlightenment belief in the ability to recover the past in its original form. The implication of this stance is clear, namely that his proposed aim of capturing the essence of Greek antiquity is somehow indicative of the relativism espoused by adherents of a rising historicist outlook. Yet for all of his efforts to distance himself from productions such as the Mendelssohn-Tieck *Antigone*, Wagner's use of Greek tragedy as an aesthetic construct upon which to build his operatic reforms stems from the same German tradition of appropriating Greek antiquity in the name of cultural and artistic regeneration. Like Friedrich Wilhelm IV, Wagner understood the power of this trope to give legitimacy to artistic endeavors of an experimental sort.

Scholars of Wagnerian opera, rather than focusing on the cultural implications of Wagner's Greek obsession, have typically searched for connections between the plots and characters of Greek tragedy and those of the music dramas. Yet, even from this perspective, an understanding of Wagner's Greeks in light of the Mendelssohn-Tieck *Antigone* proves instructive, because he appears to have been concerned with reclaiming ownership of *Antigone*'s mythic plot—first by presenting a detailed analysis of the Oedipus myth in *Opera and Drama* that stresses Antigone's role in redeeming mankind and then by borrowing elements from Sophocles' play for his own retelling of the Nibelung saga in the *Ring* cycle. Thus chapter 7 will point to several striking but as yet largely unacknowledged parallels between these two narratives, challenging the nearly exclusive focus that scholars have placed on the tragedies of Aeschylus as source material for the *Ring*.

Ultimately, Wagner's rejection of the 1841 *Antigone* constitutes an attempt to delegitimize Mendelssohn's effort at reconciling modern music with ancient drama. He goes about this task by attacking the very aesthetic premise upon which Mendelssohn's effort rests, namely the idea of "authentically" re-creating Greek tragedy. In Wagner's mind, this approach inevitably results in a stale and artificial imitation of the original. Tellingly, such criticism echoes Wagner's anti-Semitic attacks around this time on Mendelssohn and other Jewish composers. Wagner's basic claim was that, as members of a foreign race alienated from the European cultures into which they had assimilated, Jews were incapable of *creating* true art but were adept at *imitating* it in a superficial and trivial manner.[10] Thus in the case of Mendelssohn, who had succeeded in mimicking the formal language of J. S. Bach, Wagner derides all that he perceives as imitation of the most artificial sort, and the music to *Antigone* is simply another case in point. Just as Wagner's anti-Semitic diatribes can be seen as an attempt to exclude Mendelssohn from the highest ranks of German composers, so too his denunciation of the 1841 *Antigone* challenges the very right of this Jewish musician to appropriate the ancient Greek legacy in the name of German Romantic music. It is also clear that Wagner's goal of staking an exclusive claim on the Greek cultural heritage stems not only from his opposition to the aesthetic embodied by the Mendelssohn-Tieck *Antigone*; it stems as well from an anxiety born of the realization that the German revival of Greek tragedy—not unlike the ongoing revival of Bach—was coming at the hands of Germany's foremost Jewish composer.

This book concludes with a brief epilogue that explores the general decline of staging Greek tragedy with music by considering the later nineteenth-century reception of Mendelssohn's *Antigone*. The downfall of this trend can be ascribed largely to shifting attitudes toward classical antiquity. Such views were themselves shaped by Wagner and by Friedrich Nietzsche, who at one time was counted among the most fervent of the composer's disciples. In his seminal *Birth of Tragedy* (1872), Nietzsche bolstered Wagner's claims for a German *Gesamtkunstwerk* in the mold of Greek tragedy. This work challenged the prevailing view of antiquity by underscoring its Dionysian aspects and singled out Wagner's music dramas as modern-day representatives of classical tragedy. It was in this climate that the music written to accompany staged revivals of Greek tragedy came to be seen as outmoded and largely blind to the Dionysian element of ancient culture.

By drawing a line from the mid-century revival of Greek tragedy to Wagner's theoretical and practical use of the Greeks, this study offers a vivid portrait of the reception of ancient Greece in German music of the mid-to-late nineteenth century. Of course, this portrait excludes the centuries-old practice of adapting Greek literature and mythology for the operatic stage, and also ignores countless solo, chamber, and orchestral works that somehow engage with the ancient Greek tradition. The rationale for this decision concerns the nature of the stage music discussed, which essentially straddles the line between opera and incidental music in the conventional sense.

In contrast to most works of incidental music, which generally consist of music that is independent of the script, the music considered in this book comprises mainly choruses and other set numbers that were integrated into the body of the original play and were intended to be rendered musically. Thus the composer's task somewhat resembles the process of setting an opera libretto to music, with the resulting work likely to include arias (or aria-like passages) and choruses. The word "incidental" in the label reserved for this music should be understood to mean "occurring as a result of something" and not, as is often the case, denoting something secondary or subordinate in nature. Indeed, compositions such as Mendelssohn's *Antigone* constitute a distinct subgenre of incidental music with roots dating back to 1585, when Andrea Gabrieli set the choruses for a performance of Sophocles' *Oedipus the King* at the Teatro Olimpico in Vicenza.[11] In Germany of the mid-nineteenth century, such works were vital to the success of the productions previously mentioned and thus served as a driving force behind the broader revival of Greek tragedy on the European stage.

By highlighting the link between German Romantic music and German Hellenism, this book underscores the persistent influence of ancient Greece on Germany of the nineteenth century. It further reveals that the Greeks appealed equally to artists and rulers with widely varying and at times competing agendas. The nexus of art and politics exemplified in the revival of Greek tragedy demonstrates in vivid fashion the extent to which music is shaped by forces external to the work itself, while the reassessment of Wagner shifts what has traditionally been a biographical understanding of his interest in the Greeks to a more richly contextual one. Attesting as they do to Germany's fruitful relationship with Greek antiquity, the musical and theoretical works explored in this book are themselves a testament to the manifold ways in which music both shapes—and is shaped by—the culture in which it exists.

CHAPTER ONE | Ancient Greece and the German Cultural Imagination

TO GERMANS LIVING around the turn of the nineteenth century, ancient Greece symbolized a world of beauty, perfection, and unity with nature. It thus stood in stark contrast to a modern world plagued by disharmony and alienation. As Friedrich Schiller asked with great rhetorical flare in his *Letters on the Aesthetic Education of Man* (1793–94): "What modern individual could step forward and compete, man against man, with an individual Athenian for the prize of humanity?"[1] At the heart of Schiller's dichotomy between ancient and modern was a belief that Greece had attained the pinnacle of artistic beauty and individual morality. This idea had gained widespread currency among German intellectuals in the late 1700s and continued to shape the German cultural imagination well into the nineteenth century. Even for those who appeared to side with the moderns in what amounts to a German version of the seventeenth-century French *Querelle des Anciens et des Modernes* or the English "Battle of the Books," Greece offered a compelling model for the contemporary vision of a future utopian ideal.[2] Thus Goethe seemed to capture the spirit of an age when he urged: "Let each man be a Greek in his own way. But let him be one nonetheless!"[3]

Many Germans of this period sensed a unique cultural affinity with the ancient Greeks. Such an affinity seems to have been taken for granted by Hegel when he proclaimed in his *Lectures on the History of Philosophy*: "At the name of Greece, the educated European, and we Germans in particular, feel at home."[4] From the time that it emerged as a formative influence in the mid-eighteenth century, German Hellenism presented itself as an alternative to the Roman-inspired classicism characteristic of France. In this way, Greece played an important role in shaping a national identity defined by the growing awareness among Germans of a shared cultural heritage—one that owed a considerable debt to the legacy of Greek antiquity.[5] Nowhere was this connection more obvious than in the Weimar Classicism of Goethe and Schiller, which represented the pinnacle of German literature and came to symbolize the redemptive power of German culture as a whole. Such observations suggest the allure of Greece and help begin to answer several questions central to this study. Why did Friedrich Wilhelm IV include Greek tragedy as part of his plan to reform cultural life in Berlin? Why did the Mendelssohn-Tieck *Antigone* resonate so powerfully with contemporary Germans? And why did Wagner look to Athenian tragedy as a model for his envisioned artwork of the future?

The present chapter provides a framework for addressing such questions by exploring the significance of ancient Greece for Germany in the mid-eighteenth to the mid-nineteenth century. This task entails an investigation of the ideological construct that went by the name of Greece and served a multitude of purposes and competing agendas. As Friedrich Schlegel keenly noted in one of his *Athenaeum* fragments, "Everyone has found in the ancients what he needed or wished, above all himself."[6]

Drawing from a rich body of scholarship, this account considers three more or less distinct phases of German Hellenism with the aim of identifying common themes while highlighting the changing nature of Germany's obsession with the Greeks.[7] The first phase concerns the eighteenth-century rediscovery of Greece and the establishment of a Greek ideal. This model, shaped largely by the pioneering art historian Johann Joachim Winckelmann (1717–68), was born of a belief that the Greeks had lived in complete harmony with nature and had attained an artistic perfection worthy of emulation. The second phase involves a consolidation of this ideal in the decades leading up to 1800 at the hands of figures such as Goethe, Schiller, and Wilhelm von Humboldt, each of whom nonetheless questioned aspects of Winckelmann's Greece. The third phase, which also took root in the late eighteenth century but extended well into the nineteenth, represents a more fundamental challenge to the Greek ideal. This transformation came about through the advent of Romanticism and the increasing emergence of a historicist view of Greece, which developed in part from the rise of classical philology as a rigorously academic discipline. Yet as we shall see, this challenge did little to undermine the significance of ancient Greece as a cultural trope. The result is a rich chapter in German cultural and intellectual history woven from the multiple strands of Hellenism that emerged in the early nineteenth century, of which both the revival of Greek tragedy with music and the Wagnerian effort to devise a *Gesamtkunstwerk* in the mold of Attic drama are compelling examples.

Winckelmann and the Invention of Greece

Winckelmann is generally credited with ushering in a new era of German Hellenism that dawned in the mid-1700s.[8] In his seminal work of 1755, *Gedanken über die Nachahmung der griechischen Werke in der Malerei und Bildhauerkunst* (*Reflections on the Imitation of Greek Works in Painting and Sculpture*), Winckelmann rejected Baroque aesthetic values and boldly proclaimed that "the only way for us to become great, and indeed—if this is possible—inimitable, is by imitating the ancients," by which he meant the Greeks.[9] For Winckelmann, ancient Greece was a sunny, joyful society whose artistic and moral superiority was unsurpassed in human history. At a time when most Germans looked to France for cultural inspiration, Winckelmann pointed to Greece as the original source of taste and refinement: Greek art, through its "noble simplicity and tranquil grandeur," had transcended even the beauty of nature and thus provided the only genuine model for the modern age.[10] Winckelmann attributed the normative quality of the Greeks to their harmony with nature, which originated with a mild climate under fair skies and manifested itself in a vigorous physical regimen combined with unrestrictive clothing that allowed artists to fully appreciate the natural beauty and contours of the superior Greek body.

Winckelmann's veneration of Greece, though not unprecedented, stood out in the face of a European classicism whose focus had traditionally been Rome. During the Middle Ages, the classical tradition had waned but never completely faded from view. Although a careful distinction between Greek and Roman culture was not always maintained, a number of factors, including the rise of Christianity, the more widespread knowledge of Latin, and the greater accessibility of Roman materials, combined to relegate ancient Greece to a position of secondary importance.[11] This disparity only intensified with the revival of classical learning that occurred in the Renaissance, during which time ancient Rome generally provided the model for humanist aspirations.

Winckelmann's elevation of Greece signaled a decisive break with the prevailing tradition of Latin humanism. In his eyes, Rome was essentially a derivative culture—a notion reflected in his claim that "an ancient Roman statue will always stand in the same relation to a Greek original as Virgil's Dido...does to Homer's Nausicaa."[12] Winckelmann underscored this belief in Greek supremacy in his groundbreaking *Geschichte der Kunst des Alterthums* (*History of Ancient Art,* 1764–67), the most original aspect of which concerned its approach to ancient art as a succession of distinct stylistic periods. He claimed that such periods arose from the unique social and political conditions of a given historical moment, and that they reflected an organic process of development, maturity, and decline. On the basis of this thinking, Winckelmann drew a connection between the superiority of Greek art and the unique political freedom enjoyed by the Greeks, thereby suggesting a vital link between the political existence of a nation and its aesthetic achievements.[13]

Such a historicist outlook, however, also introduced a fundamental paradox into Winckelmann's view of Greece. Simply put, how could modern artists be expected to successfully imitate the Greeks if Greek art was determined by a unique set of historical circumstances? Critics were quick to highlight this conundrum, though Winckelmann himself never fully addressed the issue and appears not to have dwelt on it.[14] Indeed, this very contradiction lies at the heart of Winckelmann's legacy to German Hellenists of the late eighteenth and early nineteenth century, for whom ancient Greece came to represent a yearned-for ideal that remained forever out of reach.

Winckelmann's views on Greece profoundly influenced his contemporaries, including such leading figures as Gotthold Ephriam Lessing (1729–81) and Johann Gottfried Herder (1744–1803). The former penned his celebrated aesthetic treatise *Laocoön* (1761) largely in response to Winckelmann's essay on imitation. There Winckelmann had claimed that the ancient Greek sculpture of Laocoön offered instructive proof of Greek art's superiority to that of the Romans. The nobility of the Greek soul, he argued, was reflected in the depiction of the dying priest who, even in the grips of unimaginable pain, held his mouth open only slightly and displayed a relatively serene expression. Moreover, this portrayal contrasted starkly with that of Virgil's *Aeneid*, in which the same figure is described as crying out in great anguish.[15] And though Lessing rejected Winckelmann's claim, arguing that it failed to take into account a fundamental distinction between the visual and literary arts, nowhere did he challenge its underlying assumption of Greek moral and artistic superiority.

For his part, Herder revealed Winckelmann's influence through his frequent characterization of Greece as the glorious youth of mankind's development. Herder acknowledged that the Greeks represented artistic perfection and the absolute fulfillment of humanity, but his firmly historicist stance eventually led him to reject Winckelmann's call for imitating the ancients. It was pointless to imagine a return to the golden age of Greece insofar as that period was a direct reflection of its distinct cultural, political, and geographical attributes. As he mused in a tribute to Winckelmann published in 1781: "Where did you go, childhood of the ancient world—sweet, beloved, youthful naiveté in imagery, plastic works, and in character? You are gone, with your dream full of pleasant truth; and no voice, no ardent desire of those who love you, can awaken you from out of the dust."[16] Herder viewed Greece as a model to be emulated, rather than imitated, and in this way helped give rise to the notion that the true path to re-creating Greek antiquity lay not in replicating its artistic forms but in capturing its spirit through modern creative endeavors.

So pervasive was Winckelmann's influence that it appears to have had an impact on some composers of the late eighteenth century. Discussing the music of Christoph Willibald Gluck (1714–87) with reference to the "noble simplicity" that Winckelmann had identified as the essence of Greek art became fairly common even during the composer's lifetime.[17] Gluck, of course, was at the forefront of an operatic reform aimed at achieving a more cohesive bond between music and drama by, among other things, ridding the genre of excessive melodic ornamentation. His first reform opera, *Orfeo ed Euridice*, premiered in Vienna in 1762 with a libretto by the classically minded Raniero de Calzabigi (1714–95) and featured a vocal line whose simplicity offers a musical analogue to the Winckelmannian aesthetic of ancient art. The graceful C-major melody with which Orfeo expresses grief at the loss of his bride in the aria "Che farò senza Euridice" bears a parallel of sorts to what Winckelmann, in the sculpture previously discussed, saw as Laocoön's expression of a noble and dignified soul even as he suffered tremendous physical torment.[18]

In his preface to the published score of *Alceste* (1769), Gluck used language remarkably similar to that of Winckelmann when he noted in regard to this work: "I further believed that the greater part of my task was to seek a beautiful simplicity, and I have avoided a display of difficulty at the expense of clarity."[19] Though both men were in Rome in 1756, it seems unlikely that the two would have met, especially considering that Winckelmann was still fairly unknown at the time. To the extent that Gluck's music reveals the influence of Winckelmann, it is a reflection of changing aesthetic tastes in Germany (and elsewhere in Europe) that owed a great deal to Winckelmann's rediscovery of ancient Greece. Gluck further capitalized on this wave of classicism following his move in 1773 to Paris, where he achieved stunning success with the operas *Iphigénie en Aulide* (1774) and *Iphigénie en Tauride* (1779), both adapted from Euripides.

A crucial element of Winckelmann's Hellenism was its implicit challenge to French neoclassicism. Represented above all by the works of Pierre Corneille (1606–84) and Jean Racine (1639–99), this brand of classicism was generally acknowledged among European intellectuals as the most legitimate successor to the Greco-Roman tradition. Yet with its tacit assertion of a uniquely German access to the Hellenistic past, Winckelmann's appropriation of the Greeks undermined the French claim to the classical legacy. It also provided a basis for the general rejection of influential critics such as Johann Christoph Gottsched (1700–66), whose *Versuch einer critischen Dichtkunst für die Deutschen* (*Attempt at a Critical Poetics for the Germans*, 1730) advocated a German literary and theatrical practice modeled on seventeenth-century French neoclassicism. Lessing, for instance, took direct aim at Gottsched in his *Briefe, die neuste Literatur betreffend* (*Letters Concerning the Most Recent Literature*, 1759). In the seventeenth letter, Lessing complained that Gottsched's objective was not to improve contemporary German theater so much as to replace it with a new, French version "without inquiring whether or not this Frenchified theater was appropriate to the German way of thought."[20] So whereas Gottsched had dismissed Shakespeare as a barbarian, Lessing touted him as a model for German poets, claiming that his plays had come closer to the spirit of antiquity than even those of Corneille. Clearly hoping to undercut the primacy of French neoclassicism, Lessing maintained that, apart from the *Oedipus* of Sophocles, no dramatic works had more powerfully stirred human emotion than the tragedies of Shakespeare.[21]

Roughly a decade later, Herder issued a similar rejection of French neoclassicism by condemning its slavish imitation of Greek tragedy and its blind allegiance to the Aristotelian unities.[22] Because the defining characteristics of Attic drama stemmed from the specific nature of the Greek world and not from some adherence to pre-established rules, it was futile for any Northern European nation to model its own dramatic practice on that of the Greeks. Like Lessing, Herder pointed to the example of Shakespeare. He argued that the playwright had successfully created a national literary tradition based on the social attitudes and historical experiences unique to England. French drama, on the other hand, possessed nothing of this essential quality, leaving Herder to conclude: "It is an effigy outwardly resembling Greek drama, but the effigy lacks spirit, life, nature, truth—that is, all the elements that move us."[23] Thus if German poets hope to create a viable tradition of their own, they must avoid imitating the ancients in the same lifeless fashion and must instead embrace the means by which the Greeks established a theater born of their own distinctive national character.

The rejection of French neoclassicism represents a key element of German Hellenism. Underlying the views of Winckelmann, Lessing, Herder, and others is a firm belief that, whereas other European cultures practiced a watered-down form of classicism, Germany alone held the key to unlocking the true essence of the ancient Greek spirit. It is undoubtedly for this reason that, as Suzanne Marchand points out, German Hellenists tended to de-emphasize their dependence on a centuries-old humanist tradition and downplay or simply ignore the intermediary function of Rome. Such a perspective ultimately laid the groundwork for a German national self-identification with the Greeks that relied in no small part on the Hellenists' distorted view of themselves as "rediscoverers of a lost Arcadia."[24]

Weimar Classicism and the Greek Ideal

Winckelmann's idealized image of Greece shaped German views of Greek antiquity throughout the late eighteenth century and well into the nineteenth.[25] Most prominent of the many German poets who took up the mantle of Greece in the wake of Winckelmann were Johann Wolfgang von Goethe (1749–1832) and Friedrich Schiller (1759–1805). As chief representatives of Weimar Classicism, both of these men were noticeably influenced by Winckelmann. For Goethe, Winckelmann's ideal of Greece had been affirmed by the poet's Italian sojourn from 1786 to 1788, during which he reported being greatly moved by ancient ruins and the extraordinary beauty of the Italian landscape. As Goethe explained, suggesting a parallel between his own experience and that of the classically inspired Renaissance architect Palladio (whose treatise he had recently read), "The revolution that is going on in me, is that which has taken place in every artist who has studied Nature long and diligently and now sees the remains of the great spirit of antiquity; his soul wells up, he feels a transfiguration of himself from within, a feeling of freer life, higher existence, lightness and grace."[26] Goethe's verse revisions of his earlier *Iphigenie auf Tauris*, undertaken in Rome during the winter of 1786–87, marked the beginning of an artistic rebirth defined by the impulse to create literary works rooted in a classical aesthetic. As one scholar has put it: "The new version represents, in form and content, the triumph of classical restraint over the monstrous threat of the Tantalid curse."[27] Indeed, Iphigenie's longing for home, together with her opening claim in which she confesses to "seeking the land of the Greeks with my soul," offers a fitting parallel to Germany's yearning for the return of ancient Greece.

Although Goethe adapted both Greek and Roman models, the poet's Italian experience cemented his view of Greece as a truer embodiment of the classical spirit. Like Winckelmann, Goethe ultimately came to view Roman art as a diluted version of the Greek original. Yet as he revealed in the *Italienische Reise*, published in 1816, his first encounter with an actual Greek ruin left him feeling somewhat alienated. Accustomed to seeing Roman architecture,

Goethe found the Doric temples at Paestum, the site of an ancient Greek settlement south of Naples, to be "oppressive, even terrible," but noted that within an hour he had come to terms with the "severe style" of the Greeks.[28] On his return trip through Paestum, he seems to have fully reconciled himself to the Greek aesthetic, commenting: "It is the final, and I would like to say, most splendid idea that I will now take, complete and whole, with me back to the north."[29] For Goethe, ancient Greece had come to represent an ideal that held the promise of stimulating a German cultural and artistic rebirth, much as it had inspired a renewal of the poet's own creative enterprise. But, like Winckelmann, Goethe turned down the chance to visit the land that he so admired. This decision suggests that for him, as for many other Germans of the time, the significance of Greece resided less in its historical reality than in a carefully crafted image of moral and aesthetic perfection.

The years following Goethe's return to Weimar in 1788 marked his most intense period of engagement with the Greeks. His Hellenism at this time was fueled in no small part by a close personal and professional relationship with Schiller. Both independently and collaboratively, the two men embarked on a campaign to establish classical principles as a guiding force in German arts and letters; thus appeared such works as Goethe's Homerian epic *Hermann und Dorothea* (1797) and Schiller's *Braut von Messina* (1803), a tragedy replete with Greek chorus. They also published theoretical works in newly founded journals including Schiller's *Die Horen* (1795–97) and Goethe's *Die Propyläen* (1798–1800), the former concerned with literary matters and the latter dedicated to fostering neoclassicism in the visual arts.

Like Goethe, Schiller espoused a view of Greece shaped by the influence of Winckelmann. In his celebrated poem "Die Götter Griechenlands" (1788, rev. 1800), Schiller lamented the passing of the ancient gods and gave poetic voice to the intense longing for Greece felt by many Germans of the time.[30] The initial stanzas evoke the glory of a lost world filled with joy and beauty—a world in which the gods were more humane and mankind more divine. The remainder of the poem, however, reminds us that this glorious past has given way to the cold austerity of a northern temperament and that, try as we might, the golden age of Greece can never fully be recovered. Schiller encapsulated this yearning for the ancient world in lines that appear virtually unchanged in both versions of the poem:

Schöne Welt, wo bist du?—Kehre wieder,
Holdes Blütenalter der Natur!
Ach, nur in dem Feenland der Lieder
Lebt noch deine goldne Spur.

> Beautiful world, where are you? Come back
> You flowering age of nature!
> Ah, only in the fairyland of song
> Does your golden trace still live on.

Schiller further highlighted the disparity between ancient and modern in a series of essays that appeared in *Die Horen*. Of these, the most influential were *Briefe über die ästhetische Erziehung des Menschen* (*Letters on the Aesthetic Education of Man*, 1793–94) and *Über naive und sentimentalische Dichtung* (*On Naive and Sentimental Poetry*, 1795–96). In both cases, Schiller revealed a fascination with the Greeks that reflected his disenchantment with the present age. He described a modern world that, in contrast to ancient Greece, was beset by the division of labor and the fragmentation of the individual. Indeed, the notion of a splintering modern self was a defining outlook of late eighteenth-century German Hellenism. As Goethe explained in an 1805 essay written in honor of Winckelmann:

> Man may achieve much through the purposeful application of isolated faculties, and he may achieve the extraordinary by combining several of his capacities; but he can accomplish the unique, the totally unexpected, only when all his resources are uniformly united within him. The latter was the happy lot of the ancients, especially of the Greeks in their best period; fate has assigned the two former possibilities to us moderns.[31]

Similarly, Schiller described the Greeks as wholly unified beings who were content with their own humanity and thus felt no compulsion to seek nature in external objects. By contrast, he claimed that "we [moderns], in discord with ourselves and unhappy in our experience of humanity, have no more urgent interest than to flee out of it and to remove such an unsuccessful form from our eyes."[32] His essay *Über naive und sentimentalische Dichtung* relies on this dichotomy to posit the existence of two basic types of poet: the "naïve," an embodiment of harmonious unity who imitates nature in an objective and instinctive fashion and is more characteristic of antiquity; and the "sentimental," who imitates merely the idea of nature and thus assumes the more typically modern stance of self-consciously reflecting on humanity's alienation from nature and the resulting loss of unity.[33] Although Schiller appears to side with the ancients, he ultimately envisions a return to Greek unity, albeit in a modern guise. Accompanied by the overall progress of civilization and an increased aesthetic consciousness, this return will occur on a higher plane and will mark the advent of a stage of humanity surpassing even that of the Greeks.

The influence of Weimar Classicism on German culture of the late eighteenth century helped to consolidate the notion of Greece as an ideal of beauty and humanity. Although Goethe and Schiller acknowledged the impossibility of a return to Greece, they placed tremendous faith in the power of a classically inspired art to propel the modern age toward a goal of human fulfillment. Both were convinced that the key to genuine social advancement lay not in the violent political upheavals characteristic of the French Revolution, but rather in an aesthetic program modeled on classical antiquity that would lead to the advent of a more civilized world.[34] And though their own creative endeavors failed to bring about the kind of cultural and social reform they had envisioned, their views concerning the relative merits of the ancients and the moderns went a long way toward instilling what was essentially a Winckelmannian image of Greece into the German cultural imagination. In the words of one prominent scholar: "What the educated German of the nineteenth century knew and thought about the Greeks was the popularized product of the intensive discussion which had taken place in the so-called Age of Goethe."[35]

Humboldt and the Neo-humanist Reform

Influenced by Winckelmann, Goethe, and Schiller alike, Wilhelm von Humboldt (1767–1835) helped to establish the classical ideal as a defining element of early nineteenth-century German pedagogy during his time as head of education in the Prussian Interior Ministry. The term "neo-humanism," which is generally used to describe Humboldt's cultural philosophy, points to the importance of the classical tradition within his educational reform program and reflects his lifelong emphasis on ancient Greece as the pinnacle of human achievement. Convinced that the Greeks had attained the highest level of individual self-cultivation, or *Bildung*, Humboldt concluded that the study of Greek antiquity was key to fostering the totality of human development in the modern age.[36] Such classical *Bildung* would in turn shape the contours of modern civic and political life. It would thus pave the way for the sort of harmonious relationship between the state and the individual that had characterized ancient Greek society.

These ideas, expressed by Humboldt in the early 1790s, bear an obvious resemblance to those espoused by Goethe and Schiller and no doubt owe something to his close friendship with the latter. Yet Humboldt departed from his predecessors by more explicitly staking a claim to German ownership in the Greek legacy. This tendency reflects a growing German national identification with ancient Greece in the opening decades of the nineteenth century. In an essay from 1807 on the "History of the Rise and Fall of the Greek City-States," Humboldt maintained that "the Germans have the undisputed merit of being the first to have truly grasped and to have deeply understood Greek culture." Humboldt went on to claim that Germans possess "an incomparably stronger and tighter-knit bond with the Greeks than any other age or nation, even ones that are much temporally or geographically closer."[37] Humboldt made these remarks within the context of an emerging German national identity defined not by the existence of a unified political state but by the increasing awareness of a shared cultural heritage. Such cultural nationalism was fueled by the threat of French domination at the hands of Napoleon, and it intensified considerably in the wake of Prussia's crushing defeat at Jena in 1806. For Humboldt and for many other German intellectuals of the time, the Greek legacy was to form the centerpiece of a German *Kulturstaat* whose mission was to redeem the modern world through its own cultural achievements.

Not surprisingly, Humboldt's views shaped his brief tenure as head of the Department of Education and Ecclesiastical Affairs from February 1809 to July 1810. During this time, he established a number of secondary schools, or *Gymnasien*, in which the study of classical antiquity formed the backbone of the curriculum. These schools provided one of the few paths leading to a university education and soon became elite breeding grounds for future bureaucrats and professionals. Another one of Humboldt's significant achievements was the 1810 founding of the University of Berlin. Conceived as a model for neo-humanist pedagogy, its goal was to place the philosophical disciplines, including the burgeoning field of classical studies, on par with the more established disciplines of medicine, law, and theology.[38]

Although Humboldt's proposed reforms were never fully carried out, his efforts had a lasting impact on German pedagogy and helped to ensure the continuing importance of classical antiquity among the educated elite in nineteenth-century Prussia. A similar educational reform program was undertaken in Bavaria of the 1820s under the leadership of the classical scholar Friedrich Thiersch (1784–1860). Thiersch had boasted that his revision of the school curriculum would place an emphasis on ancient languages that far exceeded that of any other German state.[39] But even apart from the ultimate success or failure of such reformist agendas in Prussia and Bavaria, the mere willingness of the state to implement these neo-humanist reforms points ahead to the enthusiasm with which the revival of Greek tragedy would be met at the royal courts of Berlin and Munich.

Nineteenth-Century Hellenism and the Changing Greek Ideal

The importance of the Greek ideal within the broader German cultural imagination gradually waned in the decades following the turn of the nineteenth century. To begin with, the year 1805—at least in retrospect—seemed to mark the symbolic end of Weimar Classicism. That year saw both the death of Schiller and the publication of Goethe's *Winckelmann und sein Jahrhundert* (*Winckelmann and His Century*), which many commentators have viewed as the poet's farewell to German Hellenism. Although this collection of letters and essays conjures up vivid images of a Winckelmannian Greece, it also represents the end of a phase in Goethe's literary career characterized by the self-conscious emulation of classical poetry. Still, even as he turned his attention to other literary traditions, especially those of the East, he continued to hold the Greeks in high esteem and regard classicism as an antidote to the emergence of a "sickly" Romanticism.[40]

A second factor that contributed to the declining prestige of Greece was the dawn of the German Romantic movement. For the Romantics, the Christian Middle Ages generally replaced pagan antiquity as an object of longing and nostalgia. Friedrich Schlegel (1772–1829), as one of the leading theorists of early German Romanticism, is emblematic of the shift away from Greek antiquity toward the medieval world. Schlegel began his career as an enthusiastic Hellenist, asserting in his essay "Über das Studium der griechischen Poesie" ("On the Study of Greek Poetry," 1795–97) that the literature of Greece in its prime had attained the height of ideality and beauty within the natural world.[41] Like Schiller, he sought to illuminate the essential difference between ancient and modern poetry. But unlike his older contemporary, who had praised the naïve quality of Greek literature while still acknowledging the potentially redeeming elements of a modern, sentimental poetry, Schlegel came down firmly on the side of the ancients in a display of what Schiller would later deride as "Graecomania."[42] Yet soon thereafter, Schlegel reversed his stance and came increasingly to view the Greeks through a historical lens. In so doing, he helped lay the foundation of a Romantic aesthetic by positing the existence of a modern art that was characterized by reflection and artificiality but, through its constant striving after the infinite, nonetheless represented progress relative to antiquity.

By the second decade of the nineteenth century, Schlegel had lost faith in the normative value of the Greeks. In the continuing search for an absolute ideal, he began to turn his attention toward the Middle Ages and Roman Catholicism, to which he had converted in 1808. His brother, the Romantic critic August Wilhelm Schlegel (1767–1845), expressed what appears to have been an increasingly common view among German intellectuals of the time when he proclaimed in his celebrated *Lectures on Dramatic Art and Literature* (1808; published 1809–11): "However highly the Greeks may have succeeded in the beautiful, and even in the moral, we cannot concede any higher character to their civilization than that of a refined and ennobled sensuality."[43] Heinrich Heine, aligned less with Romanticism than with the liberal, politically charged movement known as Young Germany, put forth essentially the same argument but in somewhat broader terms. As he explained, it was one thing to honor the poets of antiquity and the Middle Ages, but quite another to make vain attempts at imitating the nature of their works, a practice he described as "a lie which sane eyes see through at once, and which is then held up to scorn."[44] Implicit in both of these statements is a warning against the sort of heady idealization of Greece that had typified German Hellenism from the mid-1700s onward.

Despite changing perceptions, ancient Greece continued to symbolize a glorious lost past and thus occupied a special place in German culture of the nineteenth century. We have already seen, for example, the importance of the Greeks to the educational reforms undertaken by Humboldt early in the new century. For further evidence, one can point to Wagner's elevation of Greek tragedy as a model for operatic reform or to the vital role played by Greece in the philosophy of Hegel, for whom ancient Greek society represented the irrecoverable unity of the individual self with the collective whole. In his *Lectures on Aesthetics*, delivered in Berlin between 1820 and 1829, Hegel identified a similar unity in Greek art, which he categorized as "classical" in opposition to the "symbolic" art of the pre-Hellenic age and the "romantic" art of Christian civilization from the Middle Ages to the present.[45] For Hegel, ancient Greek art (i.e., sculpture) embodied the perfect union of form and content. As a result, Hegel claims: "Classical art became a conceptually adequate representation of the Ideal, the consummation of the realm of beauty. Nothing can be or become more beautiful."[46] But as this last statement suggests, Hegel situates classical beauty within a rigidly historical framework. As such, its attainment is impossible for a modern world in which philosophy has replaced art as the conduit of absolute truth and where the content of art is overwhelmed by its form rather than being in harmony with it.

Ultimately, the early decades of the nineteenth century can be seen as a transitional phase within German Hellenism. This transition was marked above all by changing views of classical antiquity and the general shift away from a principally aesthetic interest in Greece toward a more narrowly academic one. During this period, there emerged several divergent (often mutually dependent, though at times competing) strands of Hellenism. Among these was the wave of Philhellenism that arose following the onset of the Greek War of Independence in 1821 and that was aimed at supporting modern Greece in its struggle for liberation from the Ottoman Empire.[47] This support was offered almost exclusively by members of the *Bildungsbürgertum*, or educated bourgeoisie. It came in the form of volunteer service on the battlefield, financial donations, and most commonly, literary contributions of one kind or another. The last appeared especially following the crackdown by German authorities on the so-called *Griechenveriene* that were set up to organize support efforts but that quickly came to be feared as vehicles for planting the seeds of homegrown revolution. Such Philhellenism, which ebbed and flowed until the establishment of an independent Greece in 1828, was fueled by the widely accepted notion of a uniquely German affinity with the Greeks. And insofar as it made appeals to defending Christian brethren against the "barbarism" of the Turks, this campaign points to the general desire among German Hellenists to reconcile the pagan worldview of the ancients with the religious values of the modern age.

Another strand of Hellenism that appeared around the same time manifested itself in the neoclassical architecture of Karl Friedrich Schinkel (1781–1841). Schinkel's monumental structures, including the Neue Wache (New Guardhouse, 1818) and the Altes Museum (1830), transformed the Berlin cityscape and captured the spirit of an increasingly powerful and influential Prussia. Schinkel believed firmly in the power of architecture to shape civic and moral consciousness, and he viewed ancient Greece as a model of aesthetic beauty and ethical life.[48] Rooted in the neo-humanist values of the late Enlightenment, Schinkel's classical designs reflected the ambitions of a largely conservative Prussian regime operating in the wake of Napoleon and at the same time symbolized in highly visible form the significance of ancient Greece for an emerging German cultural and national identity.

Yet by far the most influential form of Hellenism in early nineteenth-century Germany concerned the establishment of classical philology as a rigorously historical discipline. This burgeoning field of *Altertumswissenschaft*, pioneered by Friedrich August Wolf (1759–1824) in the late eighteenth century, reflected both a general rise in historical consciousness, as well as the renewed interest in antiquity fostered by, among other things, the influence of Winckelmann and the impact of recent archaeological excavations in Herculaneum (1738) and Pompeii (1749). In contrast to the earlier study of classical antiquity, this one encompassed a more comprehensive approach aimed at exploring all facets of ancient life. Moreover, it was carried out primarily by trained scholars within the confines of Germany's new research universities.[49]

Wolf outlined the discipline's main tenets in his influential *Darstellung der Altertumswissenschaft* (*Encyclopedia of Philology*) of 1807. There he defined philology's main objective as "the knowledge of human nature in antiquity, which comes from the observation of an organically developed, significant national culture, founded on study of the ancient remains."[50] For Wolf, this task began—but did not end—with a detailed analysis of classical texts. Thus he looked to fields as diverse as geography, grammar, mythology, and numismatics in the quest to locate a given text within its political, social, and economic framework. His celebrated *Prolegomena ad Homerum* (1795), which persuasively made the claim that the Homeric epics had grown out of an oral tradition and were the joint product of poets and scholars over the ages, symbolized the emergence of German philology from out of the shadow of theology and heralded the newfound status of *Altertumswissenschaft* as a historical discipline in its own right. Among the many classicists inspired by Wolf was his star pupil August Böckh (1785–1867), who for nearly six decades taught as a professor at the University of Berlin (and who would eventually serve as the scholarly advisor to the Prussian court production of *Antigone* in 1841). Even more determined to grasp the totality of ancient life, Böckh devoted much of his energy to exploring the material side of Greek culture. Such an approach is reflected in his groundbreaking study of silver mines and their effect on the Athenian economy, published in 1817 as *Die Staatshaushaltung der Athener* (*The Public Economy of Athens*).

Of course, not all classical scholars embraced this new historical philology, which acquired the name *Sachphilologie*, or "material philology," and came to be associated above all with Böckh. Opposed to this camp were those scholars who espoused what came to be known as *Wortphilologie*. Chief among them was the prominent Leipzig philologist Gottfried Hermann (1772–1848), for whom philology was defined primarily as the linguistic analysis and explication of ancient texts.[51] But despite such divisions within the field, the overall trajectory of *Altertumswissenschaft* was one of increasing professionalization and institutionalization. As Suzanne Marchand has shown, this trend contributed to the gradual undermining of Winckelmannian notions concerning the universal nature of Greek culture and society. In other words, the historicized view of antiquity fostered by the practitioners of this new science made it increasingly difficult to imagine a return to the glories of ancient Greece. This shift entailed the gradual transformation of a normative, aestheticized image of Greece into a relativist, historicized view shaped by university professors whose goal it was to shed light on the more prosaic aspects of ancient life. As Marchand has aptly noted, "To investigate the wider history of Hellenism is to describe how the triumph of historicized classical scholarship over poetry and antiquarian reverie eroded the norms and ideals that underwrote Hellenism's cultural significance."[52]

Yet even as emerging scholars swore allegiance to a thoroughly historical philology, they generally maintained faith in the moral and aesthetic superiority of Greece and thus elevated it above ancient cultures such as those of the Egyptians, the Jews, and the Persians.[53] These scholars offered a host of reasons justifying the exclusion of other cultures, including the claim that the Greeks were more humane or more original in their pursuits. Wolf, for example, concluded that only the study of Greece was essential to his vision of classical philology, for only the Greeks embodied "true humanness."[54] Even a figure as staunchly historicist as Böckh was, according to the classicist Rudolf Pfeiffer, "convinced...under Winckelmann's influence that the fundamental ideas of the creative human mind and the first patterns of the beautiful had originated in the achievements of the Greeks."[55] Moreover, scholars generally downplayed indications that the Greeks had been influenced by these more "barbaric" cultures. And to the extent that the Greeks *had* appropriated foreign elements, they had succeeded in transforming the source material into something uniquely Greek, thereby affirming their cultural autonomy and, ultimately, superiority.[56]

Such persistent views of the Greeks shaped the collective consciousness of those Germans who had been educated at the *Gymnasium*. For not only did its curriculum place a heavy emphasis on classical antiquity, many of its instructors had studied philology under scholars who were themselves reluctant to give up a belief in the cultural supremacy of ancient Greece. As Marchand has argued, the Winckelmannian image of Greece remained foremost among the *Bildungsbürgertum* during the early decades of the nineteenth century and would continue to do so long thereafter. This persistence was especially apparent in Prussia, where Humboldt's ideas on the redeeming power of Greek antiquity had left a lasting imprint on virtually all facets of German pedagogy.[57]

The Enduring Legacy of Greece

Two important points that I hope have emerged so far should remain foremost in our minds as we consider the intersection between music and Hellenism in Germany of the mid-to-late nineteenth century. The first is that, although German Hellenism reached a peak of sorts around 1800, the distinctly German reverence for—and appropriation of—Greek antiquity continued well into the new century. Second, the notion of ancient Greece as representing the apex of art and humanity was deeply ingrained in German culture by the time Hellenism began to wane in influence. Indeed, the impulse to stage Greek tragedy at the Prussian court and the Wagnerian attempt to reclaim Attic drama in the name of operatic reform are manifestations of an enduring Greek legacy. Both reflect a growing German interest in Greek literature that itself was fueled by the rediscovery of ancient Greece around the middle of the eighteenth century.

This rebirth of ancient Greek culture spawned, among the many developments already mentioned, a steady stream of new German translations that continued well into the nineteenth century.[58] Among these were groundbreaking translations by Johann Heinrich Voss of Homer's *Odyssey* (1781) and *Iliad* (1793), which reproduced the hexameters of the original poetry and were described by Friedrich Schlegel as "a shining example of how truly and successfully the language of the Greek poets can be imitated in German."[59] Voss's efforts validated the growing practice of imitating ancient meters and helped pave the way for translators such as Johann Jakob Donner, whose metrical renderings of Sophocles were generally used for the revivals of Greek tragedy that began with the 1841 *Antigone*. Such translations, which sought to convey the original prosody by mapping the qualitative syllables of the German text onto the quantitative ones of the ancient Greek, became increasingly common in the decades following the appearance of Voss's Homer translations and are clearly related to the efforts undertaken by poets such as Goethe, Schiller, Friedrich Klopstock, and Friedrich Hölderlin to adapt ancient meters in their own works.[60] Furthermore, the success of these metrical translations was thought to provide further proof of the uncanny affinity between the Greeks and the Germans—one that may have been rooted in a certain national character but that also extended to the realm of linguistics.

The image of Greece inherited by German intellectuals of the mid-nineteenth century makes it easy to see why rulers such as Friedrich Wilhelm IV would have looked to Greek tragedy to further their cultural and political aims or why Wagner would have pointed to the Greeks as models for artistic renewal. Bequeathed by a generation of late Enlightenment intellectuals and influenced by the powerful currents of Romanticism, this view of Greece shaped the consciousness of educated Germans in the early part of the nineteenth century who were faced with the task of constructing a nation on the foundations of a shared historical and cultural past. It thus forms a constant backdrop to the events discussed in the pages that follow and leaves its distinctive mark on both the words and the music written by two of the most distinguished composers of the time. One of these, Felix Mendelssohn, would help to spark a new wave of "Graecomania" that was rooted in the promise of a more meaningful engagement with ancient Greek tragedy through the power of the German Romantic musical tradition.

CHAPTER TWO | Mendelssohn's *Antigone* and the Rebirth of Greek Tragedy

ON THE EVENING of October 28, 1841, an audience of prominent Berlin intellectuals, high-ranking government and military officials, and members of the European aristocracy gathered in the intimate court theater of the Neues Palais in Potsdam to witness a production of Sophocles' *Antigone* with staging by Ludwig Tieck and music by Felix Mendelssohn. Commissioned by King Friedrich Wilhelm IV, this production aimed to re-create certain aspects of Greek tragedy as faithfully as possible. Thus it featured Johann Jakob Donner's 1839 metrical translation of the play, which sought to convey the poetic meter by substituting accented and unaccented syllables for the long and short ones of the original Greek verse.[1] For his part, Tieck oversaw an elaborate reconstruction of the palace stage in accordance with ancient theatrical conventions.[2] To aid in this process, the king appointed as scholarly advisor the Berlin philologist August Böckh, who also made minor changes to Donner's translation. And in the spirit of historical authenticity, the play's choral odes were sung by an all-male ensemble divided into two semi-choruses, the music for which was routinely thought of as one of Mendelssohn's finest works around the time of his death in 1847.

For those in attendance at the court premiere, the import of the moment was not lost. The classical archeologist E. H. Toelken described the production as a "noteworthy achievement for German theater,"[3] while the actor, singer, and theater historian Eduard Devrient—who had played the role of Haemon—recalled several decades later that, "with this performance, ancient tragedy was removed from the narrow confines of academic scholarship and placed upon the freely accessible foundation of a living art."[4] Even with the benefit of hindsight, modern scholars have tended to agree with these assessments. The philologist Hellmut Flashar has identified this production as the first modern German staging of a Greek tragedy to feature an unabridged or unaltered translation, describing it as a self-conscious effort to eliminate the concessions to modern taste that defined Goethe's 1809 production of *Antigone* at the Weimar court theater.[5] Edith Hall and Fiona Macintosh have recently pointed to the 1841 *Antigone* as a production that "secured the preeminence of this play in the nineteenth-century European repertoire."[6]

Because of its groundbreaking efforts to re-create Greek tragedy through text, staging, and music, the Mendelssohn-Tieck *Antigone* offers a compelling example of the characteristic nineteenth-century impulse aimed at recovering the past in some authentic fashion—or, to borrow the phrase of the celebrated German historian Leopold von Ranke, to show "how it really was" (*wie es eigentlich gewesen*).[7] As such, it resonates with the overall rise of historicism that occurred beginning in the late 1700s and that would later provide the conceptual framework for many of the political, social, and cultural reforms undertaken by the Prussian king in the mid-nineteenth century, of which the revival of Greek tragedy was one of the more successful examples. Indeed, the 1841 *Antigone* spawned countless productions of the play featuring Mendelssohn's score that were staged throughout Germany and in several European and American cities, including Paris, Athens, London, and New York. It thus not only marks the beginning of a trend characterized by the performance of Greek tragedy with music, but also occupies an important place in the broader European revival of ancient drama for the modern stage.

Also of significance to the 1841 *Antigone* was the role played by the newly crowned Friedrich Wilhelm IV, who had commissioned the performance. From his perspective, this event was a triumphant manifestation of an ambitious sociopolitical undertaking aimed at reshaping the Prussian capital in accordance with his own ideological beliefs. This goal was to be accomplished in part through a robust patronage of the arts and letters. Thus *Antigone*, insofar as it showcased the talents of two recent court appointees, was a potent symbol of the king's initiative to reinvigorate Berlin's cultural life by recruiting Germany's most celebrated artists and intellectuals. Moreover, by commissioning the performance of Greek tragedy, the king affirmed an image of himself as an enlightened ruler while also tapping into the widespread German belief in a unique cultural affinity with the Greeks.

The present chapter explores the various political and cultural impulses behind the king's decision to stage Greek tragedy. Its aim is to provide a broad context in which to situate the 1841 production of *Antigone* and, above all, Mendelssohn's music for it. Scholars in recent decades have shown renewed interest in trying to understand the personal and political life of a monarch once described indirectly as a "Romantic on the throne."[8] The research of historians David Barclay and John Edward Toews has been of particular importance in this regard. Both scholars have put forth a view of the king that stresses the fundamentally historical orientation of his reign and points to his keen awareness of the potential for using the monarchy as a tool to shape collective identity. Toews's recent book includes a chapter on Mendelssohn's significance to the king's overall project. It even features a brief discussion of *Antigone* but ultimately provides little insight into the nature of this production or the music written for it.

Where Mendelssohn's score is concerned, this chapter will show that, while his ultimate aim was to write music that would reconcile ancient drama with modern aesthetic sensibilities, he also adopted a number of unconventional techniques designed to create an "ancient" musical language that evoked defining elements of Greek tragedy and reflected the production's goal of re-creating the past.[9] Thus he attempted to convey the original prosody by shaping the rhythm to approximate the longs and shorts of the Greek verse. Likewise, he composed several passages of choral recitative and melodrama with the aim of highlighting important shifts in the poetic meter. And while recent scholarship on Mendelssohn's *Antigone* has acknowledged aspects of this approach, it has generally overlooked the full range and complexity of such efforts. As such, it has underestimated the degree to which this work participated in the attempt to recover Greek antiquity.

At the same time, however, Mendelssohn appears to have viewed his music as a way of expressing the different moods of Sophocles' play and filtering the themes raised by its plot through a distinctly German cultural consciousness. As we shall see, Mendelssohn used an eclectic mix of styles and musical *topoi* that not only suggest the defining sentiment of the dramatic moment at hand but also conjure up notions of German nationalism and cultural identity—evocations that in turn resonate with the overall objectives behind the Prussian court production of *Antigone*. The picture that finally emerges is of a musical work situated at the intersection of converging political, cultural, and aesthetic aims. This work contributes to the German appropriation of classical Greek antiquity and to the more historically oriented re-creation of it at the same time, mediating at nearly every turn between the past and the present, between Greek and German, and between ancient and modern.

Friedrich Wilhelm IV and the Politics of German Identity

For many Prussians, the ascension to the throne of Friedrich Wilhelm IV in June 1840 signaled the dawn of a new era. Seen as cultured and intellectual, the incoming king offered hope to reform-minded individuals for the possibility of real social and political change and the fulfillment of the broken promises for a constitution made by his father, Friedrich Wilhelm III, as early as 1815. The king himself seemed to usher in the start of a new chapter in Prussian politics when, during the first several months of his reign, he appointed a handful of moderates to his cabinet, eased censorship restrictions, and granted amnesty to political offenders in what appeared to be a turn away from the more repressive measures enacted during the previous regime.[10]

Before long, however, it became clear that Friedrich Wilhelm was opposed to the idea of genuine reform. Rather, he was broadly committed to the conservative program of restoration that emerged following the Congress of Vienna in 1815. A devout Pietist, he envisioned the rise of a Christian-German state inspired by his idealized notion of a medieval German Empire erected on the twin pillars of Christianity and the divine right of kings. Included in this vision was the establishment of a patriarchal state in which the king stood at the top of a hierarchical structure comprising various estates controlled by members of the aristocracy whose power had been preserved and handed down from previous generations. This conception of the state left no room for a constitution, which would only disturb the natural power structure leading from God to the king and from there to the people. For Friedrich Wilhelm, the implementation of such a model offered the dual benefits of ensuring monarchical sovereignty while guarding against the harmful revolutionary spirit of the time.

To his credit, however, the king appears to have realized that his belief in a God-given monarchical authority could not be taken for granted as it had been by his royal forebearers. Faced with a post-Napoleonic world defined by an increasing challenge to the tenets of absolutism, he shrewdly recognized the need for winning at least some measure of popular support for the monarchy. Identifying this outlook as a distinguishing characteristic of the age, David Barclay has argued that Friedrich Wilhelm spent much of his reign furthering what Barclay has called the king's "monarchical project." This endeavor was defined by the attempt to establish an anti-revolutionary society through the creation of a monarchy that would be "at once popular and genuinely sovereign."[11]

But, as the king himself acknowledged, a major obstacle to attaining this goal was Prussia's lack of a strong historical basis for monarchical authority.

Unlike the centuries-old Habsburg or Bourbon dynasties, the Hohenzollerns had gained royal authority over Prussia only as recently as 1701. Moreover, the kingdom itself was a geographical patchwork of territories and formerly sovereign principalities with widely varying traditions and degrees of relative autonomy, leading Friedrich Wilhelm to conclude that it was "impossible to come up with any kind of concept that could describe the political entity called Prussia."[12] Faced with this situation, Barclay argues, the king set out to invent a monarchical tradition by appealing to the religious and social values of the medieval German Empire—values that in turn would help to shape the contours of an emerging German national identity. As Friedrich Wilhelm explained: "It is not possible to speak of anything that might logically be described as 'reform,' because one can only reform—that is, improve—something which already exists. In Prussia, however, we have to create something new, because what already exists there is an absurdity."[13]

John Edward Toews has documented the historically oriented nature of the king's political agenda. He identifies a post-1840 shift in Prussian cultural policy from a more neutral attempt to maintain order and suppress revolutionary sentiment to a more partisan effort aimed at fostering a Christian-German identity by invoking the collective memory of a shared historical past.[14] Toews views this shift as rooted in a brand of historicism that is related to, but in many ways dissimilar from, what arose in the late eighteenth and early nineteenth centuries. Although both forms of historicism reflect the belief in a unique and historically determined ethno-cultural identity, the "Romantic historicism" that emerged around the turn of the century seemed to point toward the creation of a political and ethical community predicated on a German identity born of the struggle against Napoleon and French cultural dominance. In contrast, this somewhat later form of historicism was defined by the failure to establish a unified Germany and by a governmental repression of the nationalist movement in the years following the reactionary Carlsbad Decrees of 1819. Toews argues that such developments contributed to a fragmentation of the earlier turn-of-the-century paradigm of German cultural and national identity, with the result that "the transition from ethnicity to ethical life became a problem and a task that demanded specific and contingent action."[15] Thus a defining element of the cultural policy pursued by Friedrich Wilhelm was the attempt to undermine the liberal bent of German nationalist discourse by reclaiming it in the name of an anti-revolutionary, paternalistic state erected on traditional social, religious, and monarchical values.[16]

As part of his "monarchical project," the king worked to transform the intellectual and cultural landscape of the Prussian capital by enticing some of Germany's most distinguished scholars and artists to Berlin or nearby Potsdam. His aim was to win public support for the monarchy and establish Berlin as the undisputed center of a Prussian-led Germany conceived along quasi-national lines. With the help of his advisers, the king secured the temporary, permanent, or seasonal appointment of such celebrated figures as the poet Friedrich Rückert (1788–1866), the painter Peter Cornelius (1783–1867), the folklorists (and brothers) Jacob and Wilhelm Grimm (1785–1863 and 1786–1859), and the philosophers Friedrich Schelling (1775–1854) and Friedrich Julius Stahl (1802–1861)—all within the first year of his reign. Also among those who heeded the call to Berlin were Mendelssohn and Tieck, both of whom arrived in the summer of 1841.

On the one hand, this initiative is a clear reflection of the king's own personal affinity for the arts and letters. As a youth he had been an avid reader of Romantic literature and throughout his life cultivated a considerable talent for art and architecture, even drawing up his own plans for certain building projects.[17] During his adult years as crown prince, he regularly hosted evening salons attended by some of Berlin's most eminent literary, artistic, and scientific figures, including Tieck, the naturalist Alexander von Humboldt, and the architect Karl Friedrich Schinkel, who had designed many of the capital's most visible neoclassical structures.

On the other hand, these court appointments were pursued in the hope of finding individuals who could provide historical, cultural, and aesthetic legitimization of Friedrich Wilhelm's own ideological program. Thus, for example, the decision to offer Hegel's former philosophy chair at the University of Berlin to Friedrich Schelling was motivated by a desire to stem the rising tide of Hegelianism, with its dangerous secular and liberal underpinnings. As the Prussian diplomat, scholar, and influential royal advisor Karl Josias von Bunsen explained in a letter to Schelling, the king's aim was not simply "to decorate the foremost university of his kingdom with the celebrated name of the nation's foremost philosopher," but to root out "the dragon seed of Hegelian pantheism"—a phrase Bunsen ascribed to the monarch himself.[18] In short, Friedrich Wilhelm and his circle recognized the need to construct an intellectual and artistic framework within which to establish a Christian-German identity defined by the consciousness of a rich cultural heritage and its successful continuation into the present. Viewed within the context of his monarchical project, the king's patronage of the arts and sciences points to one of the more traditional representations of royal influence and authority by which he sought to gain popular support for the new monarchy. As the nineteenth-century poet Robert Prutz recalled of these efforts: "People were...pleased to see a king on the throne who, so it seemed, was determined to surround himself with not just military splendor but also with the glory of science and the gentle radiance of the arts."[19]

Mendelssohn's Call to Berlin

Mendelssohn's call to Berlin must also be understood within the broader context of the king's long-term cultural and political aims. The idea of a post for Mendelssohn evidently originated with Bunsen sometime shortly after the king's accession to the throne in 1840.[20] He had conceived of it as part of a plan to restructure the Academy of Arts in such a way that its separate branches of sculpture, painting, architecture, and music would each be appointed a permanent director to oversee the entire institution on a rotating basis.[21] Responding to this suggestion, Alexander von Humboldt—also a royal advisor—worried that Mendelssohn would have limited musical opportunities, since the directorships of both the court opera and the Singakademie were currently filled. He thus proposed the idea of a state-sponsored conservatory to be led by the illustrious composer.[22] In a letter to the king, Bunsen stressed the need to integrate music of the highest caliber into the fabric of everyday life, outlining a three-pronged approach: the creation of a musical institute; the use of suitable music for the recently reformed liturgy of the Evangelical Church; and the performance of old and new oratorios as a branch of the theater. Bunsen conceded the daunting nature of this task, but added: "Is this not enough for one man and master? I think it is rather too much for anyone other than Felix Mendelssohn."[23]

Mendelssohn had by this time gained considerable fame throughout Europe as a composer, pianist, and conductor. He was also known as the scion of a privileged and wealthy German-Jewish family in Berlin that included the composer's father, the banker Abraham, and famous grandfather, the Enlightenment philosopher Moses Mendelssohn (1729–86). Mendelssohn's compositional training, which included rigorous instruction in figured bass, counterpoint, and chorale writing under the Berlin composer (and musical confidante of Goethe) Karl Friedrich Zelter, had helped to instill in the young musician a strong veneration for the music of the past, resulting in such early works as the string symphonies, a host of sacred choral pieces, and cantatas reminiscent of Bach. In 1833, buoyed by the musical triumphs of his Grand Tour but with the wounds of his failure to win the directorship of the Berlin Singakademie still fresh, Mendelssohn accepted a position as municipal director of music in Düsseldorf. There, among other things, he conducted Beethoven's incidental music to Goethe's *Egmont* and organized a series of tableaux vivants for the visiting Friedrich Wilhelm IV, then crown prince of Prussia. Increasingly dissatisfied with his duties in Düsseldorf, however, Mendelssohn quit that post and accepted yet another job as municipal music director, this time in Leipzig, where he would serve as head of both the Thomasschule and the famed Gewandhaus. Mendelssohn officially assumed his new post in the summer of 1835, and it was nearly halfway through his twelve-year tenure in Leipzig that he was first approached about the possibility of a court position in Berlin.

Mendelssohn first learned of this post in a letter dated November 23, 1840, from Ludwig von Massow, the undersecretary of the royal household. In it, Massow mentioned only the academy position and offered little in the way of detail. He did, however, employ rhetoric that highlights the nature of such court appointments as vehicles for furthering Friedrich Wilhelm's social and political agenda. He noted, for example, the king's desire "to give [Mendelssohn] back to the Fatherland" and "to have music in its entire scope, emanating first and foremost from the capital, exercise a significant influence upon the entire nation."[24] Mendelssohn, with his widespread popularity and the success of his recent oratorio *St. Paul*, was clearly seen as a force capable of elevating the stature of sacred music and thus providing a vital aesthetic component to Friedrich Wilhelm's vision of a conservative Christian-German state.

As for his own political sympathies, Mendelssohn appears to have been something of a moderate liberal. Like many members of the *Bildungsbürgertum*, he passively supported the advent of a constitutional monarchy and looked forward to the sort of political and social reform that would follow in its wake.[25] Yet he was opposed to the tactics of more radical liberals and apprehensive about the revolutionary stirrings in the years leading up to 1848. And though his general political outlook was opposed to that of the king, he was almost certainly among those who viewed the latter's ascension to the throne as a moment of hope.

Nevertheless, Mendelssohn was reluctant to leave Leipzig for Berlin. In the course of roughly yearlong negotiations with the court, the composer pressed in vain for more details concerning the nature of his proposed duties.[26] Privately, he voiced continued reservations about the post even as he conceded his excitement at the prospect of returning to the family home.[27] In May of 1841, Mendelssohn traveled to Berlin to meet with court officials, having been guaranteed up to that point only that he would conduct several concerts each year with a focus on oratorios. It was during this visit that he was first approached about writing incidental music for a proposed production of Sophocles' *Antigone*.

It was ultimately determined that Mendelssohn would accept the court position on a one-year trial basis while plans to reform the academy and establish a conservatory moved forward. During that time, he would be at the king's disposal and would hold the title of Kapellmeister, but without the usual duties and still entitled to the handsome salary he was initially promised. If the academy reforms took place as expected, Mendelssohn could assume the directorship of the musical division and the new conservatory; if not, he was free to quit the post and return to Leipzig. Against his better judgment, Mendelssohn departed for the Prussian capital along with his wife and three young children on July 29, 1841, famously concluding that Berlin was a sour apple into which he must bite.[28]

Although it is easy to point to family as the primary factor in Mendelssohn's decision, one cannot discount what appears to have been a genuine desire to reform music in the city where he spent his formative years. Mendelssohn's correspondence from this period suggests the appeal of shaping Berlin's musical life in much the way he had that of Leipzig. There he had helped make the Gewandhaus orchestra one of Europe's leading ensembles. He had also worked tirelessly to improve the lives of orchestra members by increasing pension funds and raising salaries. Moreover, even as he was contemplating a move to Berlin, he had secured funding to establish the Leipzig Conservatory, which opened in 1843. Hinting at the significance he attached to such institutions, Mendelssohn noted in a memorandum that a conservatory in Berlin would not only enrich the city's musical life but would also "provide the musical character of the nation with a new and powerful impulse."[29] This sentiment may help explain why he ultimately accepted the post in Berlin and why, even on the verge of turning it down altogether, he stressed his willingness to offer input on the musical reforms being proposed there.

Mendelssohn's belief in music as a vital component of German identity has been well established in the secondary literature.[30] Because of travels abroad that had highlighted perceived distinctions between Germany's musical tradition and that of England, France, and Italy, Mendelssohn's own musical identity was defined strongly in terms of his German heritage. Coupled with this self-awareness was a conviction that music powerfully shaped the German collective consciousness, twin ideals that forged the composer's commitment to musical institutions such as the Gewandhaus, the Leipzig Conservatory, and the proposed conservatory in Berlin.[31] Mendelssohn articulated this view of music in a letter written to the Saxon official J. P. von Falkenstein in hopes of receiving funds to establish a conservatory in Leipzig. Noting Germany's rich musical heritage, he claimed that music had become "not simply a momentary pleasure but a more elevated, spiritual necessity" and as such had contributed significantly to the development of German *Bildung*.[32]

Another key element of Mendelssohn's musical identity concerns his affinity with the music of the past. This orientation involved not just the adaptation of older forms and styles but also a sustained effort to call attention to an Austro-Germanic musical tradition that began in earnest with Bach and Handel and was passed down to the current generation of composers. Such an outlook owes much to Mendelssohn's conservative training under Zelter and to his involvement with the Berlin Singakademie, where he sang eighteenth-century choral works by Handel, Bach, and Johann Friedrich Fasch. Mendelssohn's orientation toward the past gained widespread visibility in 1829, when he led the Singakademie in a celebrated revival of Bach's *St. Matthew Passion*. Later, as director of the Gewandhaus, Mendelssohn programmed a steady diet of Mozart and Beethoven, in addition to which he often presented—unusually for the time—works by Bach and Handel, balancing out this older repertoire with the music of more recent composers, including his own.[33] In 1838, 1841, and again in 1847, he presented a series of historical concerts that surveyed chronologically an array of works from Bach to Beethoven over the span of several evenings, each time culminating with a concert of contemporary music. Mendelssohn's programming thus contributed to the emerging sense of a European canon of art music weighted heavily toward the Austro-Germanic tradition as it was then defined.

In a broader sense, the composer's reverence for the musical past reflects the overall rise of historical consciousness characteristic of the late eighteenth and early nineteenth centuries. Mendelssohn's musical historicism—both in his own compositions and in his performance of older ones—offers a parallel of sorts to the historicist impulse to venerate works of the past with the aim of creating new aesthetic norms for the present. Yet, as James Garratt has argued, Mendelssohn's compositional historicism of the 1820s is fundamentally distinct from that of the 1830s and '40s, insofar as the earlier variety represents a relatively ahistorical assimilation of the music to which he was exposed in his youth.[34] His later historicism, however, appears rooted in an effort to establish the formal and stylistic norms of the late German Baroque and especially the Viennese classical era as enduring models—not so much to be imitated by modern composers but to be adapted in a way that emphasizes the "pastness" of the present and thus highlights the continuity of the Austro-Germanic musical tradition.[35]

It is this sort of mediation between the past and the present that characterizes much of Mendelssohn's output. It also represents his basic approach to *Antigone*, and as such offers a useful construct for considering this work. On an even more obvious level, Mendelssohn's *Antigone* resonates with his dedication to restoring past musical works and in this way also reflects his overall cultural and artistic aims. As we shall see, his settings of Sophocles' choral odes embody his view of music as an autonomous language divorced from words—a language that serves to bridge the vast historical divide between play and audience.

Greek Tragedy on the German Stage

Part of the king's plan for cultural revitalization in Berlin entailed a reform of the theater. Within weeks of assuming the throne, he took his first step toward this goal by attempting to recruit Ludwig Tieck (1773–1853). This celebrated German poet had served as director of the Dresden court theater since 1825 and had been a frequent guest at salons hosted by the king during his days as crown prince. Following an exchange of letters with Friedrich Wilhelm and his surrogates during the second half of 1840—including one in which the king expressed his desire to once again hear the poet read aloud at one of his evening teas—Tieck agreed to spend his summers in Potsdam in return for a generous 1,000-thaler annuity.[36] From the outset of negotiations, it was assumed that he would have some connection to the court theater, with the king hoping that Tieck's presence would initiate long-term theatrical reform.

In February of 1841, Tieck received a letter from the king requesting his involvement in staging a Greek tragedy at the theater of the Neues Palais in Potsdam.[37] Offering no indication of a possible date or choice of play, this letter appears to contain the earliest reference to Friedrich Wilhelm's plans for staging Greek drama at court. To judge from comments later made by the king and those around him, the impetus for this undertaking stemmed from his general discontent with the standard theatrical repertory of the day, which included regular performances of French comedies and farces by minor German playwrights.[38] Thus an official decree addressed to Tieck in 1842 reads in part: "You have long known my wish to use your talent for the benefit of the theater in order to stage the best possible performances of respectable works, the current performance of which leaves so much to be desired."[39] Clearly encouraged by the success of *Antigone*, which had premiered at court some eight months before the date of this cabinet order, the king issued a directive stating that "the performance of Greek dramas in translation and of Shakespearean plays shall constitute the objective of your artistic efforts."[40] The actor and playwright Louis Schneider, who beginning in 1849 served as official reader at the royal evening salons, confirmed the king's dissatisfaction with the standard fare of the court theater. Schneider explained that the only productions for which Friedrich Wilhelm showed any interest were "curiosities" such as Tieck's *Blaubart*, "antiquities" including Racine's *Athalia*, and "fantastical" works such as Shakespeare's *A Midsummer Night's Dream*—the latter two being collaborations between Tieck and Mendelssohn that followed in the wake of *Antigone*. Schneider added that, because the king was "too learned and too clever to find pleasure in the usual stage repertory, he sought a more elevated kind of enjoyment and believed this to be attainable through the implementation of Ludwig Tieck's ideas."[41]

Friedrich Wilhelm's desire to stage Greek tragedy can be seen in the broadest terms as a reflection of the German obsession with ancient Greece outlined in the previous chapter. The king himself had studied Greek language and literature as a youth, copying passages from Aeschylus and completing reading exercises using Voss's translations of Homer.[42] Though he would eventually come to possess a much greater affinity for medieval culture and for the Romantic literature in which it was so often glorified, he nonetheless maintained a lifelong interest in classical antiquity, including an enthusiasm for Greek tragedy and Greco-Roman architecture.

To be sure, the king's interest in having Greek tragedy staged at court was unusual for the time. Prior to the nineteenth century, productions of ancient drama had been relegated largely to school theaters, and even there performances of Roman plays were more the norm.[43] Outside of the school theaters, the first sustained effort to present ancient works on the German stage—notwithstanding the operatic adaptation of classical plots—occurred at the Weimar court theater under Goethe's direction. Between 1801 and 1803, Goethe staged four comedies by the Roman playwright Terence and, in 1806–07, two by Plautus, in each case using German adaptations of the original. He also looked to Greek tragedy around this time, staging, among other works, A. W. Schlegel's version of Euripides' *Ion* in 1802. This was followed by a production in 1809 of Sophocles' *Antigone* using an adaptation by the writer and music critic Friedrich Rochlitz, the founding editor of the Leipzig *Allgemeine musikalische Zeitung*. As was customary for the time, these adaptions were tailored to meet modern aesthetic demands and often departed from the original in significant ways. Similarly, Goethe's productions made only minimal efforts to re-create elements of ancient drama, among them the use of masks and of costumes designed in accordance with then-current research on antiquity.

Rochlitz's adaptation of *Antigone*, in particular, drew sharp criticism from a vocal faction of classical scholars who objected to the liberties he had taken.[44] One such liberty extended to the work's poetic meter. Rochlitz consistently replaced the iambic trimeter of the dialogue scenes with the more familiar iambic pentameter while transforming the complex meters of the play's lyric, or sung, parts into a regular succession of simple, repetitive rhythms. And despite Goethe's once-stated desire to stage a Greek tragedy "as close as possible to the performance practice of the Greeks," his Weimar production of *Antigone* did very little to accomplish that goal.[45] So, for example, the choruses were generally spoken by a pair of chorus leaders whose text was occasionally echoed by the entire ensemble, and there appears to have been no use of music whatsoever.[46]

Unlike the Prussian court performances of Greek tragedy, these experimental productions failed to have any significant impact on the German theatrical world. Likewise, the handful of Greek tragedies performed in Germany during the intervening decades generated at best only passing interest and were generally defined by concessions to modern taste. Thus it becomes easier to understand why the Mendelssohn-Tieck *Antigone* of 1841 was hailed by many contemporaries as the first genuine revival of Greek tragedy on the German stage.

Antigone *in the German Cultural Imagination*

Exactly how and when *Antigone* was chosen to be performed at the Prussian court theater is not entirely clear. It appears, however, that this decision was made sometime between February of 1841, when the king first mentioned to Tieck the possibility of staging a Greek tragedy, and May of the same year, when Mendelssohn was asked specifically about his willingness to provide music for this play. What is clear is that, upon arriving in Potsdam in the summer of 1841, Tieck assumed the role of reader at the king's evening salons and presented, among other works, a recitation of tragedies by Euripides and Sophocles' *Antigone*.[47] Whether or not this reading occurred in view of a future production cannot be said with certainty, though it does appear to have been distinct from readings that were performed by Tieck in September, once plans for a court production were firmly in place.[48]

The timeline sketched above refutes the claim made by some scholars that Tieck's reading of *Antigone* served as the initial inspiration for the 1841 court production.[49] Nor is there any evidence to support the position that, when Tieck first read the play as part of an evening tea, he did so using the same 1839 translation by Donner that would eventually be used for the court performance.[50] Such an assertion, moreover, ignores both Tieck's self-proclaimed preference for Karl Wilhelm Solger's translation of 1808, as well as a separate published report explaining that the decision to use Donner's translation was made by Tieck somewhat reluctantly and in consultation with a group of prominent Berlin intellectuals.[51]

According to Eduard Devrient, it was Tieck who first suggested *Antigone* in response to the king's proposal for staging a Greek tragedy. He did so, Devrient explains, because in Tieck's mind this work came closer than any other Greek drama to conveying a modern Christian sentiment.[52] Tieck was presumably thinking of Antigone's willingness to give up her own life in exchange for granting her brother a proper burial—an act sometimes thought to indicate love in a Christian, as opposed to a pagan, sense.[53] This interpretation would have appealed to Friedrich Wilhelm's vision of a Christian-German state and may help to explain why he later allowed for public performances of a play in which the king (Creon) was widely regarded as the villain.

In other respects, however, the choice of *Antigone* is entirely unsurprising. German intellectuals of the eighteenth and early nineteenth centuries had consistently lauded Sophocles as the greatest of the classical dramatists, often singling out *Antigone* as the pinnacle of his literary achievement.[54] Hegel described it in his *Lectures on Aesthetics* as "one of the most sublime and masterful artworks of all time."[55] In a book tracing the historical legacy of this play, the classicist George Steiner explains that, between roughly 1790 and the beginning of the twentieth century, "it was widely held by European poets, philosophers, and scholars that Sophocles' *Antigone* was not only the finest of Greek tragedies, but a work of art nearer to perfection than any other produced by the human spirit."[56]

Antigone also offered a timely parallel to pressing political and social concerns, including a growing debate over the increasingly visible role of the state in the lives of individuals. At the center of the play is the clash between Antigone, the daughter of Oedipus, and Creon, her uncle and the reigning king of Thebes. The latter has assumed control of the city following the deaths of Eteocles and Polynices, the two sons of Oedipus who killed one another battling for the crown. As his first official act, Creon issues a decree prohibiting the burial of the traitorous Polynices, who led the Argive invasion against his native city. Despite her knowledge of this proclamation, Antigone performs the burial rites required by divine law and remains defiant upon being brought before Creon, who condemns her to die in accordance with his edict. He does so with utter disregard for the pleas of his son (and Antigone's betrothed), Haemon, who argues that public opinion favors the young woman. Creon soon learns from the blind prophet Teiresias that his refusal to bury Polynices—whose rotting flesh now litters the city's altars—has angered the gods. Creon initially dismisses Teiresias, accusing him of taking bribes. Teiresias responds with the devastating prophecy that, because of the king's decisions to leave the dead unburied and order the premature death of Antigone, he will not only suffer the loss of family but will become the object of hatred among Thebans. Shaken, Creon turns to the chorus of Theban elders, who advise him to bury Polynices and free Antigone at once. But by now it is too late: holed up in a cave, Antigone has taken her own life, and upon finding her, Haemon does the same. The latter action in turn prompts the suicide of Eurydice, Haemon's mother and Creon's wife.

Because of its relevance to contemporary political issues, Sophocles' play was a frequent topic of discussion in academic lectures and publications during the first half of the nineteenth century. Hegel famously pointed to this tragedy as an illustration of the inherent conflict between the competing spheres of private and public. Beginning with the *Phenomenology of Spirit*, published in 1807, he repeatedly invoked this play as part of a broader attempt to highlight the historical development of self-consciousness (and self-alienation) that inevitably accompanied the realization that different aspects of "ethical life" (*Sittlichkeit*) are frequently in opposition to one another.[57] On Hegel's reading, the actions of the play's two central figures are equally justified, because both characters are ultimately motivated by an ethical power. Antigone personifies the family—the domain of woman, divine law, and private ritual. Creon, on the other hand, embodies the state (or in Greek terms, the *polis*)—the realm of man, human law, and civic ritual.

This interpretation is articulated even more clearly in Hegel's *Lectures on the Philosophy of Religion*, where he states:

> The collision between the two highest moral powers is set forth in a plastic fashion in that supreme and absolute example of tragedy, *Antigone*. In this case, family love, what is holy, what belongs to the inner life and to inner feeling, and which because of this is also called the law of the nether gods, comes into collision with the law of the state.[58]

Whereas earlier commentators such as Friedrich and A. W. Schlegel tended to view Antigone as the heroine and Creon the villain, Hegel stresses the balanced nature of this "collision." "Creon is not a tyrant," he contends, but rather an "ethical power" that seeks to uphold the law of the state and to punish those who violate it.[59] As the guardian of divine law, Antigone too is an ethical power. She is not, however, entirely blameless, as she does in fact commit a crime. And while both Antigone and Creon have legitimate claims, each character ultimately represents only one moral power, and it is precisely this "one-sidedness" that defines the tragic essence of Sophocles' drama. According to Hegel, the task of Greek tragedy is not only to reveal the potential conflict between aspects of ethical life but to offer a resolution as well, thereby pointing the way toward a kind of dialectical synthesis. Thus, as George Steiner explains, conflicts of this sort will continue to arise even after the deaths of Antigone and Creon, but they will "be enacted on a richer level of consciousness, of felt contradictions, than that which arose from the corpse of Polynices."[60]

Hegel's relatively balanced reading of *Antigone* was often mischaracterized as pro-Creon, and construed as such, it went on to dominate German views of the play in the nineteenth century.[61] With reference to the pervasiveness of Hegel's interpretation, Steiner maintains that the Mendelssohn-Tieck *Antigone* "presents Creon as a noble, tragically constrained, defender of the law."[62] Nowhere, however, does he offer any concrete evidence supporting this claim, except to imply that the impact of Hegel's analysis was such that it must inevitably have shaped the 1841 production of the play. Michael Steinberg reaches a similar conclusion. Yet he also takes into account August Böckh's essentially symmetrical reading of *Antigone*, which the latter outlined in a pair of lectures delivered to the Berlin Academy of Sciences in 1824 and 1828.[63] Echoing Steiner's assertion but with one important qualification, Steinberg concludes that "the relative conservatism of Hegel's and Böckh's 'Creonism' certainly inhabits the production of 1841, at least as far as Ludwig Tieck's participation is concerned"—a reference presumably to the poet's royalist sympathies.[64]

But in the absence of detailed firsthand accounts, it is impossible to say for certain to what extent this production was influenced by interpretations such as those of Hegel and Böckh. At the very least, it would seem that such readings underscored the play's conflict between the demands of the state and the will of the individual. As Steinberg points out, this theme would have taken on particular relevance at a time when many Germans were confronting the reality of an increasingly powerful, centralized state.[65] Throughout many parts of the German Confederation, the state had come to assume greater control over aspects of both public and private life, perhaps most conspicuously through the advent of compulsory education, taxes, and military service.[66] No longer simply an extension of the reigning monarch, the modern German state had grown ever more bureaucratic, and with this transformation had begun gradually to encroach upon the individual.

Tellingly, the overture to Mendelssohn's *Antigone*, which the composer labeled an "introduction," embodies the idea of conflict at the center of Sophocles' play. It does so by juxtaposing a solemn C-minor opening (mm. 1–30) with a somewhat longer allegro (mm. 31–101) that centers on the keys

EXAMPLE 2.1A Mendelssohn, *Antigone*, introduction, mm. 1–12.

EXAMPLE 2.1B Mendelssohn, *Antigone*, introduction, mm. 31–34.

of E-flat major and its parallel minor but ends on the dominant of the original key, resolving, as it were, into the action of the play itself (example 2.1). As R. Larry Todd has suggested, this bipartite introduction seems designed to establish the conflict between Creon and Antigone. The dotted rhythms, the imitative counterpoint, and the ceremonial character of the initial music symbolize the Theban state, while the relative harmonic instability and unpredictable melodic line of the ensuing section hint at the threat that Antigone poses to the authority of Creon's new regime.[67]

At the same time, however, these two sections suggest a contrast between old and new—or, within the context of the 1841 production, ancient and modern. With its initial evocation of the French overture and its subsequent reference to the "learned style," the first part clearly gestures toward the past, whereas the music that follows seems firmly rooted in a Romantic aesthetic. In the case of the former, the imitative passage that begins at measure nine bears a certain resemblance to the outset of Gluck's overture to *Iphigénie en Aulide*, which also features a minor-mode contrapuntal passage as part of a slow introduction that gives way to an allegro. This allusion underscores Mendelssohn's backward glance by invoking the spirit of a composer whose own legacy was inextricably linked to his engagement with the ancient Greek tradition. Indeed, the prominent nineteenth-century music theorist and historian A. B. Marx maintained that Mendelssohn clearly had the music of Gluck in mind as he composed *Antigone*.[68]

It is also worth noting that Mendelssohn had further highlighted the idea of contrast in an earlier version of the overture, which exists as an undated manuscript in full score. In this version, he repeated the slow-fast juxtaposition twice, the first time beginning in E-flat minor and moving to G minor in the manner of a development and the second time presenting both sections in the tonic C minor but ending on a dominant chord.[69] Susanne Boetius has argued convincingly that it was this version of the overture that listeners heard at the Prussian court premiere on October 28 and its November 6 encore. It was sometime after these first two performances, she claims, that Mendelssohn refashioned the piece into its current form.[70] But because both versions rely so heavily on contrasts in tempo and style, it seems a reasonable conclusion that Mendelssohn's aim was to highlight the clash between Creon and Antigone and thus to reflect the contemporary view of Sophocles' tragedy as a representation of the potentially explosive conflict between the state and the individual.

Michael Steinberg has argued with some justification that the conflict in *Antigone* between religious custom and the demands of the state recalls the Mendelssohn family's path of Jewish assimilation. Whereas Mendelssohn's grandfather Moses had achieved fame as the spokesman of an enlightened German-Jewish symbiosis, the composer's parents had their children baptized and themselves later converted to Christianity as a way of more fully integrating into early nineteenth-century German bourgeois culture. Citing evidence of Mendelssohn's continued identification with Judaism, Steinberg suggests that Antigone's stance against the state may well have resonated with his own "discomfort with the previous generation's modernizing, secularizing, state-oriented practice."[71]

Less convincing, however, is Steinberg's notion that the "rhetorically understated" nature of Mendelssohn's music to *Antigone* reflects the composer's personal ambivalence toward the patriarchal Christian-German state fostered by Friedrich Wilhelm. Steinberg views this aesthetic as both a departure from and a response to "the entirely different rhetorical, moral, and political style of the *Lobgesang*" from roughly a year earlier.[72] Although he never specifies the elements of this rhetorical understatement, he is undoubtedly referring to the work's frequently unison and predominantly homophonic choral writing and to its sparse, often chamber-like orchestration. Those traits associated with the vocal line, however, can be attributed to the composer's attempt at conveying the meter of Sophocles' play, an effort that results in an almost entirely syllabic setting of Donner's text. The nature of the work's orchestration, for its part, clearly owes something to the limited number of singers engaged for the 1841 court performance and the relatively small dimensions of the palace theater for which the production was conceived. These factors strongly suggest that the "rhetorical understatement" to which Steinberg refers stems more from the unique demands of this production than from Mendelssohn's potential ambivalence toward the Prussian court.

Re-creating Antiquity

As previously noted, the Mendelssohn-Tieck *Antigone* stood apart from earlier German productions of ancient drama through its efforts to re-create Greek tragedy. To spectators who witnessed this event, the clearest manifestation of this impulse would have been Tieck's ambitious effort to reconstruct the ancient playing space within the confines of the intimate theater of the Neues Palais. This theater was built during the reign of Frederick the Great and its semicircular, tiered seating arrangement was thought to offer a fitting parallel to the general design of the massive outdoor amphitheaters of ancient Greece.[73] Tieck relied primarily on the authoritative work *Das Theater zu Athen* (1818) by his one-time friend, the architect and archaeologist Hans Christian Genelli (1763–1823).

Figure 2.1 shows an anonymous rendering of the Prussian stage in the form of a pencil drawing that was made in advance of the Leipzig production of *Antigone* in 1842.[74] In accordance with Genelli's findings and with input from Böckh, the actors performed atop a raised platform at the rear of the stage, while toward the front, the chorus occupied a circular area modeled after the Greek *orchestra*. In the center of this space was an altar—in Greek, a *thymele*—around which the chorus (or in some cases a single character) gathered at moments of heightened drama and which also served (in a wholly inauthentic fashion) to conceal a prompter.[75] In another concession to modern convention, the orchestra under Mendelssohn's direction was seated alongside the perimeter of the circular *orchestra*, but in such a way that the musicians remained as inconspicuous as possible.[76] The actors entered through the *orchestra* and from there ascended one of two narrow, opposite staircases

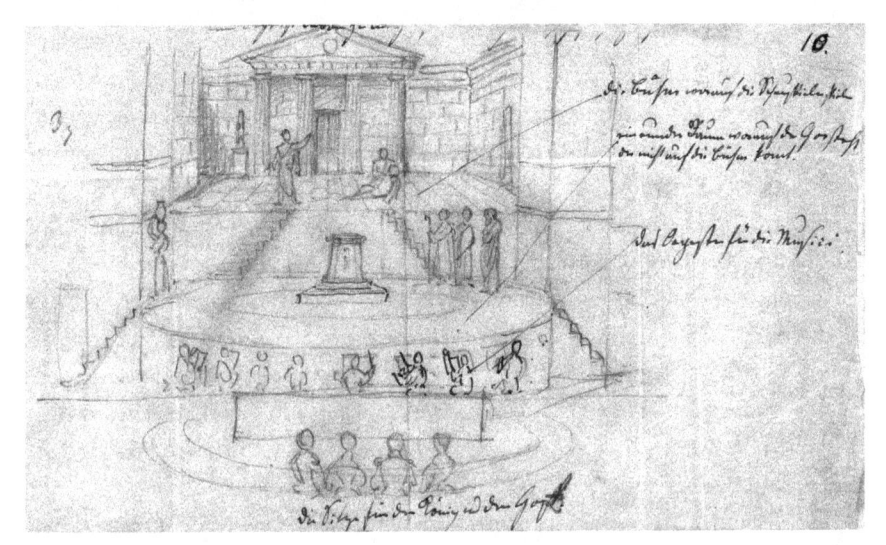

FIGURE 2.1 Anonymous pencil drawing from late 1841 or early 1842 showing the stage for the production of *Antigone* in 1841 at the Neues Theater in Potsdam. The four sentences from top to bottom read: (1) "die Bühne, worauf die Schauspieler spielen"; (2) "ein rundes Forum, worauf der Chor steht, der nicht auf die Bühne kommt"; (3) "das Orchester für die Musici"; (4) "Die Sitze für den König und den Hof."

leading to the elevated stage. This process was reversed upon exiting and reportedly posed some danger when done during moments of great intensity. As for the scenery, Tieck dispensed with a traditional approach in favor of a more architectonic one thought to be in keeping with ancient convention. Instead of movable sets, he erected a stationary rear facade depicting the Theban royal palace that included a center door used by characters entering or exiting the palace.[77] Upon opening, it offered the audience a glimpse of the palace altar; toward the end of the play, it was left open to reveal Eurydice's corpse—a sight that Böckh described as "an incomparable image."[78]

Both the size and the makeup of the chorus were dictated by ancient convention. As Mendelssohn explained in a letter to the violinist Ferdinand David, "There are sixteen men's voices, as in the chorus of ancient times, divided into two choruses that alternately sing strophe and antistrophe and that generally end together in eight parts."[79] This description conflicts with that of Böckh, who noted that, like the ancient Athenian chorus, this one used fifteen singers—a discrepancy that may stem from the exclusion or inclusion of the chorus leader in the final tally.[80] Although modern scholars agree on the existence of a fifteen-member Sophoclean chorus that included its leader, or *coryphaeus*, some nineteenth-century classicists apparently regarded the chorus leader as separate from the rest of the ensemble. The 1835 *Wörterbuch der griechischen Musik* compiled by Friedrich von Drieberg describes the function of the chorus leader as primarily that of a timekeeper. Drieberg explains that, because this individual refrained from singing and dancing, it is incorrect to translate the term *coryphaeus* as "lead-singer" or "lead-dancer."[81]

In another apparent effort to re-create Greek tragedy, the chorus of the 1841 *Antigone* occasionally performed simple choreography. Little is known about this choreography, though Mendelssohn appears to have regarded it as significant.[82] In a letter to the English composer George Macfarren, who was preparing to conduct the 1845 London premiere of *Antigone*, Mendelssohn stressed this aspect of the production: "Then there is the *acting* of the [two semi-] choruses, which remains important. They must but very seldom...be *entirely* without motion, and even then they must stand in *groups*, not the usual theatrical *rows*."[83]

Reporting on the court premiere of *Antigone*, the archaeologist E. H. Toelken seems to suggest that the desire for an "authentic" production originated with the king himself: "At the command of His Majesty the king, Greek tragedy was brought before us in its original form to the fullest extent possible."[84] Yet regardless of its source, this vision of re-creating antiquity reflects a broader nineteenth-century interest in recovering (and preserving) a genuinely historical past, as manifested in the growing number of state-sponsored museums, archaeological institutes, and excavations to unearth ancient treasures.

Similarly, the production's reliance on recent archaeological research and on Böckh's philological expertise resonates with the more narrowly academic aim of uncovering the historical reality of ancient Greece, as discussed in the preceding chapter. Nonetheless, unique challenges were posed by the lack of precise knowledge concerning aspects of Greek tragedy. Such obstacles were often overcome by concessions to modern practice, and even in certain instances where ancient convention was clear, the decision was made to set aside historical authenticity in favor of appealing to modern taste. Thus the choice to employ one actor per part and to use both male and female performers was dictated by modern conventions, as was the decision to dispense with masks.

Music occupies a dual role in the 1841 *Antigone*, insofar as it represents both an adherence to ancient practice and one of the more obvious concessions to modern taste. Most scholars of the time agreed that the choruses and other lyric parts of Greek tragedy were originally sung (though a small handful continued to insist that the entire play was rendered musically). Yet no one could say for certain what this music sounded like, except to note that its apparently homophonic, unison texture and its secondary importance relative to the text seemed utterly at odds with the essential nature of modern music.[85] It is unclear who first suggested that the choruses for the 1841 *Antigone* be set to music, though again the king emerges as a likely candidate. By early September of that year, Mendelssohn could report to Karl Klingemann: "The king would very much like to have Sophocles' *Antigone* performed at the [royal] palace, for which he said I was to compose the choruses and Tieck was to provide the staging."[86]

As many commentators have pointed out, Mendelssohn's classical education rendered him uniquely suited for this task. At the age of ten, Mendelssohn began learning Greek and Latin with the family tutor Karl Heyse. He excelled at Latin and, by his mid teens, had gained a respectable command of Greek. Mendelssohn continued his studies with the promising young ancient historian Johann Gustav Droysen, who took over as *Hauslehrer* in 1827. Droysen, who was then studying with Böckh at the University of Berlin, tutored the children in subjects including classical history, languages, and literature. In 1826, when he was just sixteen, Mendelssohn completed a metrical translation of Terence's *Andria*, which was published anonymously the following year with an introduction by Heyse, for whom the effort had been undertaken as a surprise birthday gift.[87] This remarkable achievement suggests not only Mendelssohn's mastery of Latin but also his grasp of Latin poetic meter, which shares many similarities with classical Greek prosody. As Leon Botstein has noted, Mendelssohn's translation preserves both the meter and the poetic structure of the original Latin but eschews the use of self-consciously antiquated or archaic German in favor of a modern vernacular.[88] This approach thus looks ahead in certain respects to that of *Antigone* some sixteen years later.

According to Devrient, who was a close friend of the composer, Mendelssohn had initially considered writing "ancient" music. Devrient recounts how he and Mendelssohn engaged in lengthy discussions about the latter's compositional approach:

> His first thought was to have the choruses sung—if not spoken—entirely in unison recitative and in part by solo voices to an accompaniment of only those instruments that are believed to have been in use during Sophocles' time: flutes, tubas, and harps in place of the lyre. Opposed to this initial suggestion, I noted that the vocal part would be unbearably monotonous, but without achieving an understanding of the words.... Felix nevertheless made an attempt at this manner of recitative but confessed to me after only a few days that it could not be carried out.[89]

In addition to conceding the monotony of the vocal line and the near impossibility of rendering the text fully comprehensible, Mendelssohn reportedly concluded that such a limited instrumentation posed a major expressive obstacle. He maintained that any attempt at writing ancient music would ultimately be perceived as a childish effort to re-create a phenomenon about which so little was known for certain. As Devrient explains:

> He therefore came to believe that the choruses had to be sung in the same manner that the dialogue [of the play] was to be spoken, that is, not in an attempt to imitate the delivery characteristic of Attic tragedy—something which indeed could lead us to laughter—but rather in a way that we express ourselves nowadays in speech and song.[90]

Mendelssohn thus composed "modern" music scored for a sixteen-voice double men's chorus accompanied by an orchestra consisting of paired woodwinds, horns, and trumpets, three trombones, timpani, strings, and harp—the last used only on occasion with the apparent aim of lending the music a certain air of antiquity. The result is an overture and seven relatively short choral numbers that, rather than self-consciously evoking the sound of ancient music, use a contemporary musical language to convey the dramatic mood of each choral ode or otherwise sung passage. The work thus amounts to something like a succession of highly individual character pieces, each of which exists in its own emotional and psychological world, features unique musical material, and employs a different key signature, save the C minor tonality common to both the overture and the final chorus.

Yet despite a general adherence to modern practice, Mendelssohn's approach to the score was nonetheless influenced by the production's overall aim of recovering Greek antiquity. For instance, the musical form of Mendelssohn's choruses mostly reflects the strophic nature of the Greek choral ode, which typically features one or more pairs of stanzas comprising a strophe and antistrophe that share the same poetic meter. Labeling these strophes in the score and proceeding from the standard assumption that they were identical not only metrically but musically, Mendelssohn generally sets a given strophe and its corresponding antistrophe using the same, or nearly the same, music, resulting in the form *aabb* or often *aabb'*. Moreover, his decision to divide the ensemble into two half choruses reflects a view common among nineteenth-century classical scholars.

This strategy of re-creating aspects of Greek tragedy seems to have begun with Mendelssohn's decision to write music not just for the choral odes, as was requested, but also for those remaining parts of the play thought to have been sung (or recited to music) in ancient times. This approach, however, is obscured by the composer's own rubric, the "choruses" to *Antigone*. As shown in table 2.1, Mendelssohn's music corresponds entirely to the sung lyric and chanted anapestic verse of Sophocles' play, with only two exceptions. The first of these is the overture, which clearly owes its existence to modern operatic and theatrical convention. The

TABLE 2.1 The structure of Sophocles' play and Mendelssohn's score.

Dramatic Structure	Verse Type	Plot Synopsis	Score	Key
—	—	—	Intro.	c
Prologue	Spoken iambics	Antigone tells Ismene of her plan to bury Polynices	—	—
Parodos (chorus enters)	Sung lyrics/ chanted anapests	Celebration of Thebes' victory over the Argives	No. 1	C
Chorus announces Creon	Chanted anapests	Creon enters to address the council of Theban elders		C → E♭
Episode 1	Spoken iambics	Creon learns that someone has violated his decree	—	—
Stasimon 1	Sung lyrics	Praise of man's manifold accomplishments	No. 2	A
Chorus announces Antigone	Chanted anapests	Antigone is brought in under guard		a
Episode 2	Spoken iambics	Antigone is defiant in the face of Creon	—	—
Chorus announces Ismene	Chanted anapests	Ismene is brought in under guard	No. 2a	g
Episode 2 Cont.	Spoken iambics	Creon sentences Antigone to interment	—	—
Stasimon 2	Sung lyrics	The elders point to the curse on the House of Labdacos	No. 3	F/f
Chorus announces Haemon	Chanted anapests	Haemon enters to confront Creon		F → d
Episode 3	Spoken iambics	Haemon's pleas to spare Ant. lead to a rift with Creon	—	—
Stasimon 3	Sung lyrics	The elders point to the inescapable power of love	No. 4	G
Chorus announces Antigone	Chanted anapests	Antigone is brought in under guard		
Kommos	Sung lyrics/ chanted anapests	Antigone laments her fate and the chorus responds		g

(*Continued*)

TABLE 2.1 (Continued)

Dramatic Structure	Verse Type	Plot Synopsis	Score	Key
Episode 4	Spoken iambics	Ant. delivers her final address to Cr. and the chorus	—	—
Episode 4 Cont.	Chanted anapests	Exchange btw. Antigone, Creon, and the chorus leader	No. 5	e
Stasimon 4	Sung lyrics	Comparison of Antigone's fate to that of past figures		
Episode 5	Spoken iambics	Tiresias prophecies disaster for Creon	—	—
Stasimon 5	Sung lyrics	The elders appeal to Dionysus for protection of Thebes	No. 6	D
Exodos	Spoken iambics	A messenger tells of the suicides of Antigone and Haemon	—	—
Chorus announces Creon	Chanted anapests	Creon enters bearing the corpse of Haemon	No. 7	c
Kommos	Sung lyrics/ spoken iambics	Creon laments Haemon's death; messenger tells of Eurydices' suicide; Creon laments further		
Choral summary	Chanted anapests	The chorus states the moral: never dishonor the gods		

second such passage occurs in the final scene, where Mendelssohn included music for a series of otherwise spoken lines for the chorus, presumably to heighten the dramatic impact of the choral response to Creon's outpouring of grief at the deaths of Haemon and Eurydice. Thus the individual numbers of the score should be thought of not as mapping directly onto the play's choral odes but rather as presenting several musico-dramatic complexes that together constitute the musical content of Sophocles' *Antigone*. Although this design of Mendelssohn's work obviously reflects the production's historicist aims, it also serves as a reminder of the degree to which even his assigned task of setting the choruses to music differed in nature from the traditional undertaking of writing incidental music (in German, *Bühnenmusik*, or "stage music").

The claim has been made with some justification that the history of incidental music begins with Greek tragedy.[91] The practice inherited by Mendelssohn, however, placed more emphasis on providing "external" music to be performed in between the acts of a play (i.e., entr'actes) or in conjunction with the dialogue than on writing "internal" music prompted by the script in the form of dances, songs, or choruses. In the case of *Antigone*, Mendelssohn was confronted with a historical model according to which the use of music was determined by the poetic meter, itself related to a dramatic structure marked by the alternation of spoken dialogue and choral song.

According to Aristotle, who outlined the basic design of Greek drama in the twelfth chapter of his *Poetics*, a tragedy typically opens with a spoken prologue (*prologos*) for the actors followed by the *parodos*, an ode sung by the chorus as it marches onto the stage.[92] Thereafter a series of episodes (*epeisodia*) occur, or passages of spoken dialogue in which the action of the play is advanced. These are followed in each instance by a choral ode known as a *stasimon* (plural *stasima*)—a term suggesting the "static" nature of a piece that, unlike the parodos, is performed by the chorus from within its customary place in the *orchestra*. The last stasimon is followed by the exodus. This final scene, which features dialogue and occasionally singing as well, generally concludes with the chorus reciting the moral of the play as it departs the stage. Poets, of course, were free to deviate from this model, for example, by composing a lyric monody for one of the main characters or including a (partially) sung exchange between actors or between the chorus and one or more actors (called an *amoibaion*).

As noted above, the overall structure of Greek tragedy was linked to the poetic meter, which in turn dictated the means of vocal delivery employed by the performers. The episodes comprised mostly spoken verse for the actors written in iambic trimeter but might also include occasional lines for the chorus, in all probability intended for the chorus leader. The choral odes, on the other hand, were made up of various lyric meters and thus were sung. Although lyric poetry traditionally had been accompanied by the lyre, in the case of Greek tragedy, it was performed to the accompaniment of an *aulos*, a single- or double-reed wind instrument with a shrill, penetrating tone.[93] In addition to speech and song, Greek drama featured a third type of vocal delivery referred to by some ancient commentators as *parakatologe*, which was reserved for certain kinds of anapests and tetrameters and also for iambics inserted among lyric passages.[94] The exact nature of such verse, generally called recitative by modern scholars, remains unclear. It was almost certainly accompanied by the aulos and appears to have been an intermediate mode of utterance somewhere between speaking and singing, perhaps similar to what today we would characterize as chanting.

Part of Mendelssohn's attempt to re-create elements of an "ancient" musical language entailed a reliance on contrasting vocal idioms meant to suggest these different forms of delivery and thus highlight the presence of different verse types within the play. So, for example, he reserved the use of recitative entirely for poetry that was originally meant to be chanted as opposed to spoken or sung. In the play, such verse is associated primarily with groups of anapestic lines based on the metrical pattern short-short-long, short-short long, or some variant thereof.

Sometimes called "marching anapests" by modern scholars, these lines mostly serve to announce the arrival of a character. Such is the case with the choral anapests that immediately follow the parodos and the first three stasima. Mendelssohn set the first three of these four passages using predominantly unison choral recitative (refer to table 2.1 above). For the anapestic system announcing Antigone's entrance at the conclusion of the third stasimon, however, the composer rejected the use of recitative in favor of introducing a melodic idea that returns twice over the course of the ensuing exchange between Antigone and the chorus. Thus in all but one instance, the shift in the original poetry from sung lyrics to chanted anapests that occurs after each of the first four odes is marked by a parallel change in the music from conventional singing to recitative. Moreover, this recurrence of mostly unison, choral recitative calls to mind the semi-sung mode of delivery thought to have been characteristic of such passages in Sophocles' day. It also, of course, retains vestiges of Mendelssohn's initial plan for writing "ancient" music.

Example 2.2, which shows Mendelssohn's music for the beginning of the anapestic system that immediately follows the first stasimon, illustrates the nature of such choral recitative. Here the change in vocal idiom corresponding to the onset of anapestic verse (m. 101) is further highlighted by a sudden move from A major to the parallel minor. This harmonic shift marks an abrupt end to the pastoral character of the preceding music and suggests the elders' shock at seeing Antigone led into the palace by royal guards as a suspect in the crime of burying Polynices. That Mendelssohn's rhythmic setting of this passage only occasionally reflects the characteristic short-short-long pattern of anapestic meter can be attributed to Donner's translation, which is less strict in its syllabic re-creation of the anapestic verse than of either the sung lyric verse or the iambic trimeter that makes up the spoken dialogue.

Further evidence of Mendelssohn's attempt to highlight the presence of anapestic verse is offered by his setting of the parodos, in which the council of elders celebrates Thebes' victory over the Argive invasion led by Polynices. Here Sophocles inserted anapestic stanzas between each of the ode's lyric strophes, resulting in the alternation of sung and chanted verse. Mendelssohn

EXAMPLE 2.2 Mendelssohn, *Antigone*, No. 2, mm. 101–106.

set the anapestic system occurring between the final two strophes as unison choral recitative, while for that following the first strophe and its corresponding antistrophe, he employed a recitative-like style that combines the use of repeated rhythmic and melodic patterns with regular phrasing and up to four-part harmony (example 2.3).

CHORUS I

Più lento e poi poco a poco accelerando

Der durch Po-ly - nei-kes' feind-li-chen Zwist zu dem Kam-pfe ge-führt auf un-se-re Gau'n, mit schar-fem Ge-tön, wie ein Ad - ler da - her-flog ü-ber das Land,

EXAMPLE 2.3 Mendelssohn, *Antigone*, No. 1 [parodos], mm. 22–30.

In this case, the accentuation of Donner's text more accurately reflects the anapestic meter of the original Greek. Mendelssohn further emphasized this pattern through the frequent use of two sixteenth notes followed by an eighth or a quarter note. The repeated pitches characteristic of this passage again evoke the semi-sung nature of such verse in ancient times, while the *accelerando* seems to suggest the actual approach of the enemy army toward Thebes. Moreover, the use of such recitative-like music marks a clear departure from the more tuneful style corresponding to each of the preceding lyric stanzas and thus represents a change in vocal idiom analogous to that which occurs with the onset of anapestic verse at the conclusion of the first three choral odes.

Remarks made by August Böckh indicate that Mendelssohn's choice of recitative (or something approaching it) accords with the general nineteenth-century view of how the Greeks might have uttered such anapests. The classicist lent his approval to the composer's use of this vocal idiom, but he questioned whether such passages would have been recited by the entire chorus:

> [Mendelssohn] set the anapestic systems of the parodos, as well as those attached to other choruses, mostly as recitative for the entire chorus and seldom as recitative for the chorus leader; the latter [approach] is in accordance with the views of the most respected philologists.... The use of solo recitative for all of the anapestic systems, and especially those in the parodos, in my opinion would have provided a nice contrast to the full chorus featured in the lyric strophes and antistrophes.[95]

But whether or not these anapestic lines would have been chanted by the whole chorus or by the chorus leader alone is of little concern once we have acknowledged Mendelssohn's use of choral recitative as part of an effort to evoke certain defining elements of ancient Greek tragedy.

Yet whereas each occurrence of recitative in the score corresponds with an anapestic passage in the play, the reverse is not always true. In the midst of the second episode, for example, Mendelssohn rendered an isolated group of five anapestic lines as melodrama (i.e., text spoken to the accompaniment of music) for the chorus leader. This brief passage announces the arrival of a weeping Ismene, who has been seized by royal guards as a suspected accomplice to her sister. Here Mendelssohn composed only five bars of melodrama with an accompaniment for flutes, clarinets, and bassoons. Designated "No. 2a" in the score, this music is absent from the composer's earliest complete draft of the work. It appears for the first time in a copyist's manuscript of a piano-vocal score to which Mendelssohn made some changes in the summer of 1842, among them the addition of this piece onto the blank staves between Nos. 2 and 3.[96] Susanne Boetius has cited this source as evidence that this piece was included in neither the Prussian court premiere of *Antigone* nor the two public performances that took place in Leipzig and Berlin the following year.[97] This conclusion, however, is at odds with an account of the 1841 production by the Berlin music critic Ludwig Rellstab, who, clearly not recognizing Mendelssohn's motivation for including this number, noted that music was used "as a general feeling of expression" to mark the arrival of Ismene.[98] It would seem, then, that Mendelssohn composed this music sometime between completing the initial draft of the score in late September and the time of the court premiere in late October.[99] He may have also included it in the autograph manuscript of the full score, the whereabouts of which remain unknown. Exactly why he chose to set these anapests using melodrama as opposed to recitative is a matter of speculation, though he presumably decided on the former approach as a way of maintaining greater continuity with the surrounding lines of spoken dialogue.

On at least two other occasions, Mendelssohn made no attempt to highlight the presence of anapestic verse through either recitative or melodrama. For the group of anapestic lines that announce the entrance of Creon carrying the corpse of his son Haemon, Mendelssohn composed a funeral march that features a mostly unison choral line. He thus eschewed a more "authentic" approach in favor of music that reflects the plot through its associations with death and mourning. Portions of this march are played by the orchestra at the moment Eurydice's body first becomes visible to the characters onstage, in effect affirming this music as a representation of Creon's grief and the untimely deaths brought about by his actions. Moreover, both its C-minor tonality and its ceremonial nature recall the overture and on some level represent the fulfillment of a tragic outcome foreshadowed in the somber character of the play's opening music.

This tragic mood finds a final echo in the music that Mendelssohn composed for the anapestic lines delivered by the chorus as it exits the stage and concludes the play with a warning that "great words spoken by men with too much pride are paid for with great blows."[100] Again rejecting the use of recitative, Mendelssohn responded with music for full chorus, often in four-part harmony. Written in C minor and characterized by frequent tonic pedal points, this music seems to suggest the inescapability of this key and of fate more generally. R. Larry Todd has pointed to the "sobering pedal points and inexorably descending lines" of this closing music as evidence that Mendelssohn was alluding to the final movement of Bach's *St. Matthew Passion*, which is also in C minor and opens with a pedal on C. As Todd suggests, this allusion was one way in which Mendelssohn sought to establish a link between, on the one hand, Greek tragedy, and on the other, "the German past and Christian adumbrations that Tieck detected in Sophocles."[101]

As for Mendelssohn's use of melodrama, it is generally restricted to passages of lyric verse assigned to Antigone or Creon. Such lines in the play occur as part of a *kommos*, a ritual lament involving the chorus and one or more actors. The first of these exchanges comes after the third stasimon. Here Antigone bemoans her tragic fate in a series of lyric stanzas to each of which the chorus responds, initially with chanted anapests and then with lyrics of its own. The play's other kommos takes place toward the end of the tragedy and involves Creon mourning the deaths of his wife and son as he comes to terms with his own culpability. Mendelssohn explained his strategy for setting these kommoi in a letter to Ferdinand David, noting: "All of the instances in which strophe and antistrophe are spoken by Creon or Antigone are set melodramatically, and the chorus responds singing."[102]

The question, of course, immediately arises: Why not have such passages sung, as they were in Sophocles' day? The answer to this question is not immediately clear. It may simply be that the two principal actors in the production, the famed German actress Auguste Crelinger and the Bohemian-born Karl Moritz Rott—both of whom appear to have been chosen without any input from the composer—were unable or unwilling to double as singers. What is clear, however, is that Mendelssohn intended the melodrama assigned to these actors to function as a surrogate form of song, as Böckh suggested when he remarked that the music accompanying the text in these passages "offers the listener's imagination a substitute for the missing song."[103]

EXAMPLE 2.4 Mendelssohn, *Antigone*, No 4, mm. 84–88.

On three separate occasions in his setting of Antigone's kommos, Mendelssohn highlighted this function of the melodrama by indicating in the score that brief sections of the text were to be spoken in rhythm along with the accompanying music (example 2.4). Both Devrient and the critic Rellstab suggested that this unorthodox approach was inspired by passages from the incidental music to Goethe's *Faust*, composed by Prince Anton Radziwill in 1831.[104] In the example given here, Antigone laments the prospect of sacrificing marriage for death in an obvious reference to her planned nuptials with Haemon: "No wedding hymns ring forth, no bridal song honors me with joyous sounds."[105] Understood in conjunction with this text, Antigone's unconventional "song" can be heard as an ironic rendition of the wedding music that she herself will never hear.

Creon's kommos features a series of increasingly emotional lyric stanzas separated by passages of spoken verse for the chorus and for the messenger, the latter of whom enters with news that Eurydice has taken her own life in response to Haemon's suicide. Acknowledging his own guilt and at one point even summoning death, Creon often finds himself unable to utter anything more than cries of anguish and sorrow. Unlike in Antigone's kommos, the chorus never adopts the lyric meter of its main interlocutor, thereby reinforcing a sense of Creon's isolation.[106] Curiously, however, the music that Mendelssohn provided to accompany Creon's melodrama does nothing to suggest the lament's trajectory of an ever-intensifying and overwhelming grief. Rather, it follows something of an opposing path, decreasing in prominence with the onset of Creon's penultimate stanza and, in the final strophe, ceasing altogether in what amounts to an attempt at further highlighting Creon's isolation and despair. Utterly defeated and lacking even the will to live, Creon ends the play as bankrupt musically as he is spiritually.

The few passages of melodrama that occur apart from these two kommoi generally correspond with lines of anapestic verse, as in the example of Ismene's arrival (No. 2a). Yet there too, the use of a vocal idiom other than conventional singing suggests the composer's desire to highlight significant changes in the poetic meter. The result is a score that, by encompassing song, speech, and speech-like singing, mirrors the same tripartite division between the modes of utterance characteristic of ancient Greek tragedy. As such, it clearly reflects the effort to re-create antiquity that formed such an integral component of the 1841 Prussian court production of *Antigone*.

Yet by far the most complex strategy employed by Mendelssohn to evoke elements of ancient Greek drama involves his attempt to convey the poetic meter of Sophocles' text through the medium of Donner's German translation. Even in Mendelssohn's day, a handful of commentators—most of them classical scholars—recognized this aspect of the score. In November 1841, after attending a reading of the play heard along with Mendelssohn's music at a private residence in Leipzig, the eminent philologist Gottfried Hermann reportedly approached the composer afterward and exclaimed, "You even observed the meter in the choruses!"[107] Similarly, Böckh maintained that Mendelssohn's setting of the penultimate ode in particular came closer than any other number to approaching antiquity because of its concern for emphasizing the rhythm of the original Greek verse.[108]

More recently, scholars taking into account the composer's classical education have begun to explore this relationship between music and poetry in greater detail. Hellmut Flashar, for example, has revealed correspondence between Böckh and Mendelssohn showing that the latter sought clarification on meter from the former, who was happy to oblige and even offered suggestions on how best to render certain passages rhythmically.[109] And perhaps most significantly, Douglass Seaton has shown that the work's opening chorus not only highlights the qualitative nature of Donner's translation but also accounts for the quantitative aspect of the ancient Greek poetry.[110]

As noted above, Donner's *Antigone*, which appeared in 1839 along with several other translations of Sophocles, sought to reproduce the Greek prosody by substituting accented and unaccented syllables in place of the original long and short ones. Donner drew attention to this approach by including a metrical index at the end of his translation that provides a line-by-line scansion of the play's lyric verse (see figure 2.2). Following convention, Donner used the symbols – and ◡ to indicate longs and shorts, respectively. He also employed the symbols ⏒ and ⏓ to indicate an anceps, a position in the metrical scheme that allows for either a long or a short and to which Donner responded by freely employing a stressed or unstressed syllable.

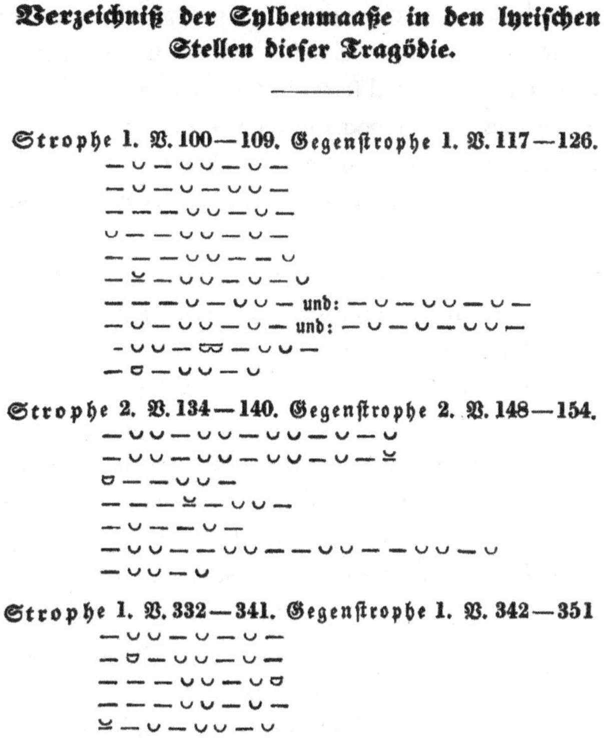

Verzeichniß der Sylbenmaaße in den lyrischen Stellen dieser Tragödie.

Strophe 1. V. 100—109. Gegenstrophe 1. V. 117—126.

— ᴗ — ᴗ ᴗ — ᴗ —
— ᴗ — ᴗ — ᴗ ᴗ —
— — — ᴗ ᴗ — ᴗ —
ᴗ — — ᴗ ᴗ — ᴗ —
— — — ᴗ ᴗ — — ᴗ
— ᵕ — ᴗ ᴗ — ᴗ — ᴗ
— — — ᴗ — ᴗ ᴗ — und: — ᴗ — ᴗ ᴗ — ᴗ —
— ᴗ — ᴗ ᴗ — ᴗ — und: — ᴗ — ᴗ — ᴗ ᴗ —
- ᴗ ᴗ — ⌒ — ᴗ ᴗ —
— ᵓ — ᴗ ᴗ — ᴗ

Strophe 2. V. 134—140. Gegenstrophe 2. V. 148—154.

— ᴗ ᴗ — ᴗ ᴗ — ᴗ ᴗ — ᴗ — ᴗ
— ᴗ ᴗ — ᴗ ᴗ — ᴗ ᴗ — ᴗ — ᵕ
ᵓ — — ᴗ ᴗ —
— — — ᵕ — ᴗ ᴗ —
— ᴗ — — ᴗ —
— ᴗ ᴗ — — ᴗ ᴗ — — ᴗ ᴗ — — ᴗ ᴗ — ᴗ
— ᴗ ᴗ — ᴗ

Strophe 1. V. 332—341. Gegenstrophe 1. V. 342—351

— ᴗ ᴗ — ᴗ — ᴗ —
— ᵓ — ᴗ ᴗ — ᴗ —
— — — ᴗ ᴗ — ᴗ ᵓ
— — — ᴗ ᴗ — ᴗ —
ᵕ — ᴗ — ᴗ ᴗ — ᴗ

FIGURE 2.2 A page from the metrical index of Donner's 1839 translation of Sophocles' *Antigone*.

To be sure, Donner's attempt at a faithful metrical translation was nothing new. By the mid-nineteenth century, numerous German translations of both Greek and Latin works had appeared along with the subtitle "im Versmasse des Originals," using essentially the same approach as the one just outlined. This practice gained widespread currency in the late 1700s, fueled by the influence of Voss's Homer translations and a growing belief that poetic meter offered unique insight into the essence of a literary work. In the widely read preface to his 1816 metrical translation of Aeschylus' *Agamemnon*, Wilhelm von Humboldt described meter as the foundation of all other forms of beauty within a particular work and claimed that no translator could go too far in the attempt to convey the original prosody of a text. "Rhythm as it occurs in Greek poetry," claimed Humboldt, "exists to a certain extent in a world unto itself, separated even from thought and from music combined with melody."[111] For Böckh, meter provided a clue as to the nature of ancient music. Envisioning future musicians tackling a project similar to Mendelssohn's *Antigone*, Böckh concluded that "if the composer subjects himself to the admittedly difficult constraint of a given rhythm, it can also steer him rather close to the ancient *melos*, since both elements must be in agreement."[112] Mendelssohn himself suggested the importance of meter when, in a much-cited letter to Droysen, he explained with regard to the play's choruses: "The mood and the verse rhythms are throughout so truly musical that one does not have to think about the individual words, but rather needs only to compose those moods and rhythms, and then the chorus is finished."[113]

Due to the nature of Donner's translation, any predominantly syllabic setting of the text can be said on some level to reproduce the play's poetic meter. Indeed, several scholars have pointed to this attribute of Mendelssohn's work as evidence of his concern for highlighting the Greek prosody.[114] Seaton, however, has gone the furthest by demonstrating that, in the initial strophe of the parodos, Mendelssohn "mostly set the choriambs [long-short-short-long] similarly, in a durational transcription treating the long syllables as quarter or half notes, and the short ones as dotted eighth and sixteenth notes on the second or fourth beat of the measure" (see example 2.7 below).[115] This consistency undoubtedly owes something to the ode's predominantly aeolic meter, in which, according to one classicist, every line contains "an essential nucleus consisting of a choriamb or an expansion of it."[116] The "durational transcription" that Seaton described in the first strophe (and, by extension, the near-identical music of the corresponding antistrophe) applies also to the composer's setting of the second strophic pair, despite the use of contrasting music and rhythms. Exactly how Mendelssohn would have understood the term "aeolic" may be up for debate, but the consistency with which he set the choriambic foot throughout the parodos strongly suggests an awareness of its importance within the ode's overall metrical scheme.

Elsewhere in *Antigone*, Mendelssohn pursued a similar strategy for suggesting the quantitative aspect of the original Greek verse. Within each chorus or in some cases a section thereof, he typically employs the use of a recurring rhythmic pattern that coincides with a particular metrical component and that somehow reflects the relative value of the original longs and shorts. This metrical component is most frequently the choriamb, which forms an integral part of the aeolic meter that dominates the play as a whole. Like the parodos, the third stasimon, in which the elders describe the effects of love on human behavior, includes a choriamb in nearly every line. Mendelssohn again set each choriambic foot in a way that approximates the quantitative nature of the poetry. The long-short-short-long pattern is represented by three distinct rhythmic configurations (allowing for the occasional longer note value on the final syllable): a half note, two quarter notes, and a half note; a quarter note, two eighth notes, and a quarter note;

and a quarter note framing a dotted eighth- and sixteenth-note pair. And while the note values corresponding to the longs and shorts may change from one measure to the next, the relationship between the two consecutive short syllables and the long one immediately preceding is always such that the former is equal in value to the latter. This principle generally applies throughout the work, suggesting that Mendelssohn was influenced in his approach to rhythm by the dominant nineteenth-century view of Greek meter, which held that a long syllable was almost invariably equal to two short ones.[117]

As Seaton explains, Mendelssohn's efforts to reconstruct classical prosody resulted in a unique musical style, insofar as "the rhythm has a distinctive repetitiveness, but the phrase lengths become somewhat irregular."[118] Strictly speaking, however, this asymmetrical phrasing stems more from the nature of Donner's metrical translation than from Mendelssohn's concern for reproducing the poetic meter. In stark contrast to most other texts that Mendelssohn set to music, Donner's translation is marked by irregular, unpredictable line lengths. It also includes the frequent use of enjambment, such that the end of a line often fails to correspond with a syntactic break in the language. As we shall see below, Mendelssohn frequently responded with equally irregular and unpredictable phrases, thus maintaining a certain textual integrity while at the same time creating a distinctive musical style.

Bridging Ancient and Modern

For all of his efforts to recover elements of Greek tragedy, Mendelssohn ultimately appears to have envisioned his music to *Antigone* as a means of bridging the vast historical divide between ancient Greece and nineteenth-century Germany. That is, by relying on a modern compositional language, he could draw on a wide range of common generic and stylistic references in hopes of reconciling audiences with what was, after all, a relatively strange and unfamiliar form of dramatic representation. As A. W. Schlegel claimed in the context of a passage discussing the puzzlement with which modern critics react to the Greek chorus: "The Greek tragedy in its pure and unaltered state will always remain for our theaters an exotic plant, which we can hardly hope to cultivate with any success, even in the hothouse of learned art and criticism." The reason for this, he explained, is that "Greek mythology, which supplies the material of ancient tragedy, is as foreign to the minds and imaginations of most spectators as is its form and manner of presentation."[119] Although Schlegel was making these claims roughly three decades before the Mendelssohn-Tieck *Antigone*, there is no reason to suspect that this state of affairs would have changed dramatically during the intervening period, especially judging from remarks made by commentators on this production who stressed the "otherness" of Greek tragedy.[120]

Mendelssohn sought to mitigate this potentially alienating effect of Greek tragedy by, in effect, translating what he perceived as the underlying sentiment of the play's lyric odes into a musical language familiar to German audiences.[121] This decision was motivated at least in part by his sense of the odes' inherent musicality. Writing to David one week before the Prussian court premiere of 1841, the composer explained:

> It was odd to me how in art there is so much that remains unchanged. The moods of all these choruses are still today so truly musical and yet so different from one another, that one could wish for nothing more beautiful to compose.[122]

Recall that, in the letter to Droysen cited above, Mendelssohn had spoken of the choruses in similar terms, noting that their "moods" were so inherently musical that he needed only to "compose" them. He went on in this letter to describe in remarkably specific terms the defining character of each ode (or kommos) that he set to music, with the exception of the fourth stasimon (No. 5), which he presumably left out inadvertently:

> Even today one cannot wish for a more fulfilling task than that of [setting] these varied choral moods: victory and daybreak [No. 1], quiet reflection [No. 2], melancholy [No. 3], love [the stasimon of No. 4], a death lament [the kommos of No. 4], a song for Bacchus [No. 6], and a serious warning at the end [No. 7].[123]

The notion of expressing a prevailing mood in favor of depicting various elements of the text is consistent with the composer's overall song aesthetic, which in recent years has received increasing attention, particularly in discussions of his Lieder.[124] Convinced of music's ability to communicate more effectively than language, Mendelssohn believed that the role of the former was to reflect not the individual words of a text but rather its defining sentiment. Such thinking must have factored into his decision against writing "ancient" music. To do so would have undermined his effort to express the various moods of Sophocles' tragedy by relying on a set of culturally determined codes of meaning rooted in the conventions of a modern musical language. Thus while the pervasive use of unison choral recitative may have somehow seemed more "authentic," it clearly would have failed to offer Mendelssohn the sonic resources necessary to meet his larger aesthetic goals.

To this end, the composer drew upon an array of choral idioms common to the Austro-Germanic tradition, ranging from secular types such as the march and the unaccompanied part-song to quasi-sacred ones that evoke the more elevated style characteristic of an oratorio or cantata. These various idioms were obviously meant to correspond to the specific "mood" that the composer identified with each ode, or kommos, and thus they represent the essence of his attempt to reconcile contemporary audiences with Sophocles' ancient drama. In the play's second stasimon (No. 3), sung after Creon has pronounced death sentences on Antigone and, for the time being, Ismene, the chorus initially points to the generational curse on the house of Oedipus that threatens to destroy the family's two remaining members. It then invokes the all-powerful Zeus as the guarantor of justice, stressing the point that mortals are rarely free from misery during their short time on earth.

Summarizing the character of this ode as "melancholy," Mendelssohn responded with an elevated style of composition, the overall texture and sonority of which often recall portions of his earlier secular cantata *Die erste Walpurgisnacht* and the oratorio *St. Paul*—albeit without the echoes of a Baroque musical language sometimes characteristic of the latter. His setting of the initial strophic pair, which uses essentially the same music for strophe and antistrophe, features a cantabile bass solo with occasional choral passages that constitutes the work's only extended vocal solo and that suggests a kinship with similar movements from the two works just mentioned. Although each stanza begins and ends in F major, the frequent minor-mode inflections hint at the unending sorrows that have befallen the Oedipal clan, while the many fleeting tonicizations offer a parallel to the instability of a house plagued by the gods.

For the ode's second strophic pair, Mendelssohn composed highly contrasting music. These two stanzas feature a frequently unison choral texture as part of a driving *allegro con fuoco* in F minor that is clearly motivated by the thematic shift that occurs as the elders turn their attention from the Oedipal curse to the unassailable power of Zeus and the concept of justice that it symbolizes.[125] Though vastly different in content and character, the two halves of this piece are both rooted in a serious, relatively highbrow musical aesthetic whose association with quasi-sacred genres such as the oratorio and the cantata provides a suitable vehicle for expressing the "melancholy" that Mendelssohn identified as the ode's underlying sentiment.

By contrast, Mendelssohn's setting of the third stasimon (No. 4) reveals the influence of a more secular idiom rooted in the popular tradition. The pervasive four-part harmony and the scoring of this piece, sung by a largely unaccompanied quartet of tenors and basses, calls to mind the then-flourishing practice of amateur choral singing, in this case suggesting a link specifically to the all-male *Liedertafel* or *Männergesangverein*. These mostly amateur organizations, whose membership often cut across several social strata, were widely thought to embody republican ideals manifested in the fellowship and camaraderie of communal music-making.[126] As a result, such amateur choral societies frequently assumed a political cast and performed music that was overtly nationalist.

Although such connotations may have resonated with the notion of a Greek chorus that is in some way representative of the larger polis, Mendelssohn appears to have used this stylistic reference simply as a way of drawing a distinction between the more elevated, sacred-oriented tone of settings such as the previous one and the more secular-inspired *Klang* of a piece such as this one. Here the secular associations suggest the earthly love between Antigone and Haemon that Mendelssohn clearly had in mind when he used the term "Liebe" to describe the essential character of this ode. In it, the elders blame eros for the rift between Creon and Haemon, implying that the latter's love for Antigone has infected him with the "madness" that comes from being seized by the grips of passion. For his part, Mendelssohn enriched the four-part choral texture through unexpected chromatic harmonies that seem to offer a parallel to this madness brought on by love. And perhaps as a way of hinting at the tragic events precipitated by Haemon's love for Antigone, the popular orientation of this piece—the *Volkstümlichkeit* that characterizes so much of the repertoire for unaccompanied men's chorus—is somewhat mitigated by the slow tempo and the solemn music played by a brass choir with bassoons that precedes each strophe and lends the piece an air of sobriety.

Concerning the basic division between sacred- and secular-oriented idioms within Mendelssohn's *Antigone*, the work's first two choruses fit comfortably within the framework of the latter. In both of these pieces, however, Mendelssohn's music not only translates the ode's essential character but also engages with contemporary social and political concerns. In the case of the second ode (i.e., the first stasima), Mendelssohn relies on surface musical detail to reflect its content, and in one instance appears to highlight the importance of a secure state. In the entrance ode, or parodos, the composer employed a stylistic allusion whose broader musical and cultural associations help to convey the underlying dramatic mood and also trigger thoughts of German cultural nationalism. In each case, the effect is one of appropriating the classical Greek past by translating its ancient civic and cultural ideals into wholly modern Germanic terms. In this way, Mendelssohn's music can be said to intersect with Friedrich Wilhelm's own political project involving the attempt to weave a uniquely German national identity out of the fabric of a rich cultural heritage defined in part by the legacy of ancient Greece.

Often called the "Ode to Man," the first stasimon has the chorus responding indirectly to the news that someone has violated Creon's decree against burying Polynices. The elders suggest the daring and skill involved in this shocking act of defiance with their famous opening line: "There are many wonders in this world—and none is greater than man."[127] They go on to chronicle some of mankind's most significant achievements, beginning with those essential to survival, such as farming and hunting, and progressing to highly sophisticated ones including the advent of language and the establishment of societies governed by civic and religious law. Mendelssohn's setting of this ode evokes a distinctly pastoral character through its use of a lilting melody in 6/8 time sung largely in unison over a modest accompaniment dominated by woodwinds and strings (example 2.5). These elements lend the music a folk-like naïveté that on the surface seems incompatible with the extraordinary power of the human mind that is being celebrated by the chorus. Yet Mendelssohn appears to have intended the pastoral associations to resonate with the ode's bucolic images of man plowing the earth and domesticating wild animals. This link would explain the move from A major to F-sharp minor and, with it, the shift away from a quasi-folk idiom that coincides with the description of higher-level human skills beginning at the start of the second strophe.

EXAMPLE 2.5 Mendelssohn, *Antigone*, No. 2, mm. 3–13.

Mendelssohn's use of the phrase "quiet reflection" to describe the character of this ode may suggest an additional reason for his setting's pastoral overtones. Insofar as it constitutes a rejection of the serious, elevated style that characterizes much of the work, this piece represents a self-conscious distancing from the play's tragic plot. Thus Mendelssohn may have relied on the pastoral nature of this music to create a sense of momentarily stepping outside of the ongoing dramatic action in order to indicate the reflective stance assumed by the elders as they ruminate on the scope of human accomplishment. This approach calls to mind Schiller's argument that the ancient chorus "purifies" the tragic play through such moments of reflection. It also suggests that, at least in the case of this ode, Mendelssohn subscribed to Schiller's view of the chorus as a character existing somewhat apart from the action of the play.[128]

Whatever the motivations behind Mendelssohn's use of a pastoral reference, it seems clear that the general trajectory of this piece mirrors the pattern of increasing complexity established by the ode's content. Thus the second stanza features the addition of continuous flute and clarinet arpeggios to the otherwise identical restatement of the music heard in the first stanza. This decorative passagework at once depicts the "fleeting birds" mentioned by the chorus, reinforces the music's pastoral character, and highlights the shift in focus that occurs between the strophe and antistrophe from man's control over elements of the inanimate world to his dominion over animate life. The third stanza adds harmony to the previously unison choral line in what serves as a kind of musical metaphor for man's development of language. And the final stanza introduces vocal polyphony—rarely encountered in *Antigone*—in line with the notion of increasingly sophisticated modes of human thought and ingenuity.

Mendelssohn further highlights this culminating effect by recomposing a passage toward the middle of the final stanza to provide the piece with a sense of climax. He expands what in the preceding strophe was a four-bar unison phrase ending with a falling gesture into a five-bar phrase that includes four overlapping statements of the same text and does away with the final melodic descent as it blossoms into four-part harmony (examples 2.6a and 2.6b). This phrase immediately stands out insofar as Mendelssohn generally avoids such repetition of the text owing to his concern for the poetic meter. Taken altogether, the text repetition, the expansion of the phrase, and the sudden onset of harmony—not to mention the fact that this passage ends on the dominant with a fermata and a hairpin crescendo—suggest that Mendelssohn's aim was to call attention to the words "Segen der Stadt." These words allude to the blessings bestowed on a city whose inhabitants respect both earthly and divine law. It is worth noting, moreover, that this text replaced Donner's

EXAMPLE 2.6A Mendelssohn, *Antigone*, No. 2, mm. 61–64.

EXAMPLE 2.6B Mendelssohn, *Antigone*, No. 2, mm. 83–87.

original "Hebend die Stadt," a change that appears to have been made by the composer himself. Whereas Donner's use of the verb "heben" (to raise or lift) suggests the idea of a city that rises to prominence when its citizens choose right over wrong, Mendelssohn's more religiously charged "Segen" implies the divine "blessings" from which such a morally sound community benefits. Mendelssohn may have altered this text as a way of highlighting the "justice of the gods" described in the previous line or underscoring the notion that any successful city (or state) must rest on a solid religious foundation. Whatever the reason, this change suggests a subtle connection to the ideals of Friedrich Wilhelm's emerging Christian-German state.

These words ultimately hint at what appears to be the elders' main point in this ode: Whatever remarkable things man may accomplish, he must adhere to the principles of law and justice in order to create stable communities in which to live—principles that the as-yet-unknown culprit responsible for burying Polynices has failed to uphold.[129] Within the context of Sophocles' play, the city referenced by the elders suggests Thebes, the seat of power for Creon's fledgling regime. But within the more immediate context of the Prussian court production of *Antigone*, it invokes Berlin, the public center of Friedrich Wilhelm's own relatively young monarchy. On the one hand, Mendelssohn's emphasis on this text simply underscores the elders' argument concerning the importance of a secure state and resonates with the larger conflict between the state and the individual that plays out over the course of the drama. On the other hand, this passage in the score can be seen as a sort of blessing conferred on the Prussian state by the composer himself. This "blessing" is bestowed not as a means of sanctioning the monarch's political views but rather as expressing the hope that Berlin will become the thriving German center of art and learning envisioned by the king and his most influential advisors (i.e., precisely the kind of intellectual and artistic center that Mendelssohn believed his presence in the city could help bring about).

Of the seven choruses that Mendelssohn composed for *Antigone*, this one received perhaps the most attention from commentators of the day, who frequently praised its simplicity and economy of means. One anonymous reviewer extolled its "unique charm," while the music critic August Schmidt described it as "one of the [work's] most charming numbers."[130] Schmidt added, "The melodic expression is highly original and full of emotion, while the utter simplicity of the instrumentation...is a thing of great beauty." Böckh went so far as to defend this number from its detractors: "The second chorus...has been much disputed. Yet, for me, precisely the witty cheerfulness [*die geistreiche Heiterkeit*] that animates it is the source of its delightful appeal. This music appears to perfectly express the grace and sweetness of the Sophoclean muse."[131]

Common to all three of these assessments is a favorable emphasis on the naïve, pastoral tone of the music that, on the surface, seems unsuitable to both the content of the ode and the character of Greek tragedy more generally. Yet this outlook perhaps reflects the belief expressed by Böckh that this piece had captured the essence of what was widely perceived to be the graceful quality of Sophocles' literary style. It also points to the likelihood that Mendelssohn's music was received—and perhaps even conceived—in accordance with a Winckelmannian view of the Greeks that stressed their "noble simplicity and tranquil grandeur." As noted in the preceding chapter, Winckelmann's idealized image of ancient Greece left a lasting impact on German culture well into the nineteenth century, even among scholars like Böckh who had assumed the task of painting a more realistic portrait of antiquity.

By contrast, the mood expressed in the parodos, or entrance ode, is one of pure elation. In it, the elders—unaware of Creon's decree and Antigone's plotting—celebrate the previous night's victory over Argos and make an appeal to forget the war and shake the city of Thebes in Dionysian revelry. Mendelssohn described this ode with the epithet "victory and daybreak" and responded with a musical style that, both in his own output and in German music of the time more generally, had come to assume extramusical significance. In this case, the extramusical association not only reflects the ode's celebratory mood but also suggests notions of German cultural nationalism in response to the Theban civic and cultural pride displayed by the city elders.

The composer's setting of the first strophe makes use of ceremonial, march-like music that represents one of only a few passages in *Antigone* accompanied solely by woodwind and brass instruments (see example 2.7 below). As such, this music calls to mind the distinctive sound of a men's chorus accompanied by a wind band. In Germany of the nineteenth century, wind bands—often together with male-voice choirs—were frequently heard at large public festivals and outdoor communal gatherings of a more daily sort, in addition to sometimes performing in traditional concert venues.[132] Such ensembles could be either military or civilian, and they typically comprised a mixture of woodwinds, brass, and percussion, of which the brass band was a common subspecies.

Beginning especially in the decades following the Napoleonic Wars, wind bands performing *Militärmusik*, as well as arrangements of traditional concert pieces, became an increasingly important facet of German musical life. The following report from 1830, which appeared in the *Allgemeine musikalische Zeitung*, describes an open-air concert in Berlin and offers some idea of how frequently such events occurred at the time:

> Wind music alternated with four-part songs and choruses (of male voices)....Most suitable for the time and place was the battle music played by the military band out of doors....Such an entertainment is to be held once a month during the summer at the Tivoli, which is now the favorite pleasure garden of the people of Berlin. Every Sunday, music for wind band and fireworks are included in the admission price....The usual kind of military concerts also take place in other pleasure gardens near the city.[133]

Especially in combination with men's choruses, wind ensembles also played a significant role in the many public festivals that formed such an important aspect of nineteenth-century German communal life. Describing the September 1840 *Volksfest* celebrating the return of Friedrich Wilhelm IV and Queen Elizabeth to Berlin following their coronation ceremony in Königsberg, a correspondent for the *Allgemeine musikalische Zeitung* noted the presence of over 10,000 guildsmen and trade union members. In addition, each union had its own wind band [Musikkorps], which in turn joined with the (all-male) military choruses to perform marches.[134] Only a few days later, a celebration in Berlin marking the 400th anniversary of Gutenberg's printing press included a performance of "Ein' feste Burg ist unser Gott" by the chorus of the Second Guards' Regiment accompanied by trombones, thus in keeping with the spirit of an instrumental ensemble excluding strings.

Mendelssohn himself completed a *Festgesang* for men's chorus, double brass band, and timpani that was performed at the opening ceremony of the Leipzig Gutenberg festival, held in June of the same year. Peter Mercer-Taylor has argued that the final epilogue of the "Scottish" Symphony invokes the *topos* of an accompanied men's chorus and may even allude to the second of four numbers that make up the *Festgesang*—the one featuring the tune of what would eventually be known as "Hark! The Herald Angels Sing."[135] Mercer-Taylor calls attention to the composer's rather limited output for accompanied men's chorus and points out the special role that such an ensemble seems to have played for him.

Most of Mendelssohn's works scored for an accompanied men's chorus were written in connection with some sort of festival or celebratory event. Of these, only the so-called Humboldt cantata of 1828, composed for the welcoming ceremony of an international science convention in Berlin organized by Alexander von Humboldt, included an accompaniment not restricted to wind (and percussion) instruments. Three years after the Gutenberg *Festgesang*, Mendelssohn completed an arrangement of the Saxon national anthem with brass-band accompaniment, written for the 1843 unveiling of a statue of Saxony's Friedrich August I. Then, for the 1846 German-Flemish Singing Festival in Cologne, he composed *An die Künstler*, set to a text by Schiller and scored for double men's chorus with brass accompaniment.

Mendelssohn's use of a wind-band accompaniment at the outset of the parodos is clearly meant to draw a connection between the celebration depicted in the play and the festive occasions of his own time that so often included the presence of a men's chorus along with a wind band of some kind. He clearly sensed a parallel between the mood, or *Stimmung*, of *Antigone*'s opening chorus and that of large, public festivals like the one commemorating

Gutenberg for which he had composed music roughly a year earlier. That Mendelssohn would have arrived at such a conclusion is not altogether surprising given some of the underlying similarities that exist between the two celebrations—the one imagined and the other real. Both are communal gatherings that celebrate a significant event and are rooted in a sense of shared civic, cultural, and to some extent religious values.

The Leipzig Gutenberg celebration of 1840 was simply one of many large, secular festivals that occurred in Germany in the decades following the Napoleonic Wars.[136] These festivals typically commemorated important cultural events and figures of the German past or celebrated pivotal military victories. Still others took on a more overtly political cast, such as the massive Hambach festival of 1832 that was organized as a peaceful protest against German absolutism. Sometimes conceived as "national" events—the 1840 Gutenberg celebration was held simultaneously in several German cities—such gatherings served as vehicles for expressing a burgeoning nationalism and, in some cases, aspirations for German unity. As such, they represent clear manifestations of the growing consciousness among nineteenth-century Germans of a national identity defined in terms of a shared cultural heritage rather than a unified political state.

A report by G. W. Fink on the performance of Mendelssohn's *Festgesang* at the opening ceremony of the Leipzig Gutenberg festival attests to the communal nature of such events and also suggests the important role that music played on these occasions:

> The ceremonial processions of the various guilds, with their flags and other emblems, came to an end at the center of the town square. They were then surrounded by a row of municipal guardsman, behind which a throng of eager spectators, packed shoulder to shoulder, calmly and peacefully filled up the remaining space, as onlookers peered out from nearby windows and surrounding rooftops. Meanwhile, more than 300 talented singers and all of the good brass players of our musical city...encircled the composer and conductor of the *Festgesang*, who was standing on a sturdy and beautifully decorated podium.[137]

Interestingly enough, Fink pointed out that the amphitheatric arrangement of the seats occupied by the spectators recalled the ancient Greek Olympic Games, remarking that "it was as if the joy of a long lost world had come alive once again."[138]

The chorus's victory celebration in *Antigone* is obviously on a much smaller scale, as the general public is not actually present. Nevertheless, the council of city elders can be thought of as an embodiment of the Theban polis, as the early nineteenth-century German philosopher Friedrich Förster suggested when he referred to this group as a representative of "das Volk."[139] And although national sentiment may be absent from their rhetoric, the elders clearly articulate a measure of civic pride through their repeated allusions to the city of Thebes—its seven gates, the Dirce River that flows through it, and its renown for producing chariots. Yet, with its references (in Donner's translation) to Ares, Zeus, Nike, and Bacchus (i.e., Dionysus), the chorus

Line 100   Strahl des Helios, schönstes Licht,
           Das der siebenthorigen Stadt
           Thebe's nimmer zuvor erschien!
           Du strahlst endlich, des goldnen Tags
           Aufblick, herrlich herauf, über
     105   Dirke's strömende Fluten wandelnd:
           Und Ihn, der mit leuchtendem Schild
           Kam von Argos in voller Wehr,
           Triebest du flüchtig in eilendem Lauf
           Fort mit hastigem Zügel:

EXAMPLE 2.7 Mendelssohn, *Antigone*, No. 1 [parodos], mm. 1–13.

leaves little doubt as to the ultimate source of Thebes' military triumph. The invocation of such deities points to the religious beliefs that lie at the core of the Theban polis and suggests the significance of religion within Greek culture as a whole. Along similar lines, Christian roots are not hard to discern beneath the surface of the ostensibly secular festivals that took place in Germany during the nineteenth century. Thus the opening ceremonies of Leipzig's 1840 Gutenberg celebration included both a performance of Mendelssohn's *Festgesang* (which itself featured settings of two Lutheran chorales) and an actual church service. Moreover, one of the festival's culminating events was the premiere of the composer's unabashedly Protestant *Lobgesang* in the Thomaskirche on the final day of commemorations.

Tellingly, something of the same kinship detected by Mercer-Taylor between the final coda of the "Scottish" Symphony and the second number of the *Festgesang* also exists between the latter and Mendelssohn's music for the parodos. Arguing that the symphony's epilogue shares a certain melodic and even harmonic affinity with the earlier Gutenberg chorus, Mercer-Taylor claims that Mendelssohn was invoking "a particular *Klang* that was expressed through not only parameters of orchestration, range, and general melodic style, but also a recognizable pool of melodic gestures."[140] Likewise, Mendelssohn's setting of the parodos shares several traits in common with this same number from the *Festgesang*, aside from utilizing the same basic *Klang* (examples 2.7 and 2.8). For example, both pieces open with an ascending melodic gesture that emphasizes the tonic triad and is supported by a triadic figure in the bass. Both also begin with a four-measure antecedent phrase that sets two lines of text followed by a modulating parallel consequent, which is slightly extended in the case of the parodos. These similarities most likely stem from Mendelssohn's self-conscious use in both instances of a straightforward choral style rooted in a popular aesthetic and thus aimed at appealing to the broadest possible audience.

But, as is frequently the case in *Antigone*, the otherwise conventional stylistic orientation is undermined by the presence of conspicuously asymmetrical phrasing that can be attributed directly to the nature of Donner's metrical translation. As example 2.7 reveals, all but three of the ten lines that comprise the first strophe of the parodos consist of eight syllables. Given such a poetic structure—a structure not unlike that of the Gutenberg *Festgesang*—one might have expected Mendelssohn to adopt the usual practice of composing four-measure phrases using two lines of text, as he did with lines 100–101 (mm. 1–5) and 106–109 (mm. 14–21). Doing so meant bringing the initial four-bar antecedent phrase to a close on the word "Stadt," effectively ignoring the enjambment of lines 101 and 102. He was apparently

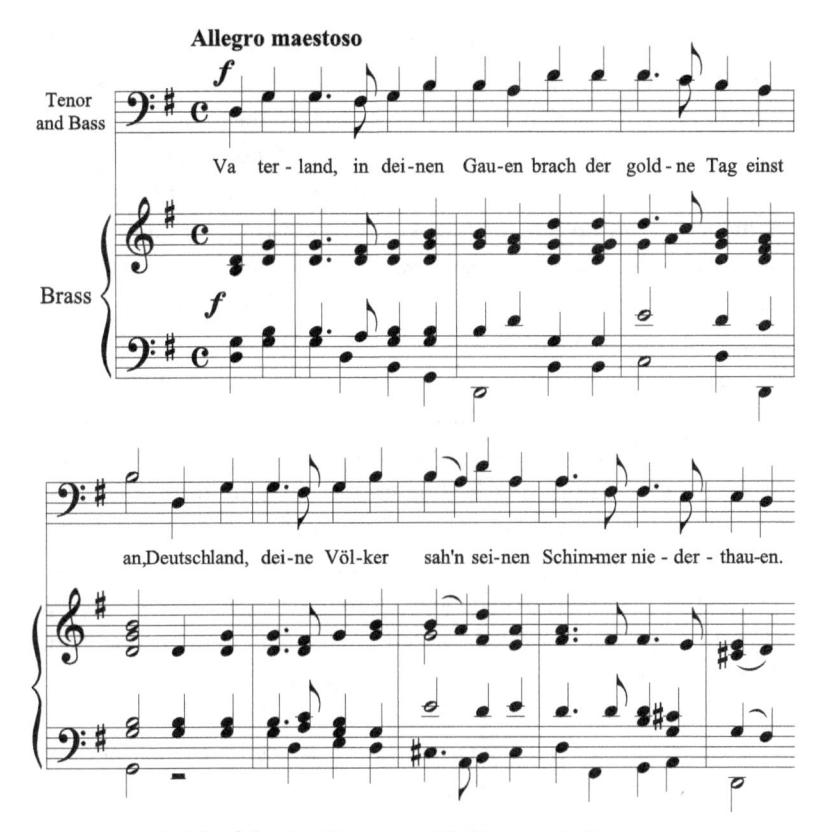

EXAMPLE 2.8 Mendelssohn, *Festgesang*, No. 2, mm. 1–8.

unwilling, however, to do the same for lines 103 and 104, both of which also extend into the following line. The result is an expanded six-bar consequent phrase (mm. 6–11) that includes not only the third and fourth lines of text but also the first three words of line 104. This phrase is then followed by a two-and-a-half measure module that sets the remaining text up through line 105 and is tacked on to the end of the consequent almost in the manner of an afterthought (mm. 11–13). Such asymmetrical phrasing, both here and elsewhere in *Antigone*, serves to defamiliarize the otherwise straightforward choral style being invoked and lends the music a sense of otherness that reflects the nature of Sophocles' original poetry while underscoring the historical remoteness of ancient Greek tragedy.

Mendelssohn's setting of the parodos limits the use of a wind-band accompaniment to the initial lyric stanza and the subsequent group of anapestic lines. He thus relies on this stylistic allusion more as a means of establishing the mood of the opening chorus rather than sustaining it. Nevertheless, key elements of this reference persist throughout the remainder of the chorus. Most obviously, the second lyric stanza is set to the same music as the first. But in order to distinguish strophe from antistrophe, Mendelssohn orchestrates the latter using precisely those instruments not heard in the former: strings, flutes, and harp (with the timpani omitted altogether). Mendelssohn also recalls the main theme of the first two stanzas at the beginning of the final antistrophe, which marks a return to C major following a contrasting section in the parallel minor. Constituting one of the few passages in the work scored for full orchestra, this final stanza goes on to present new musical material that culminates in a powerful conclusion as the elders call upon Dionysus to lead the victory celebration in song and dance. The resulting *aaba'* structure is unique among Mendelssohn's *Antigone* choruses, which generally correspond to the *aabb* form characteristic of the choral odes themselves. The use of a more conventional song form in this case further highlights the relationship of Mendelssohn's opening chorus to the Gutenberg number previously discussed, which employs the same structure and also includes a contrasting section in a minor key.

By featuring the distinctive sound of a wind-accompanied *Männerchor* at the outset of the parodos, Mendelssohn subtly evoked notions of German nationalism and cultural identity that were inextricably linked to the kinds of communal events that so often featured such ensembles—and for which he himself had composed music. Such sentiments would have resonated with some of the king's broader objectives behind the staging of *Antigone*, in particular his efforts to establish Berlin as the cultural and political epicenter of a Prussian-dominated German *Kulturstaat*. Mendelssohn's setting of this chorus offers perhaps the most compelling evidence of the role that his music for *Antigone* played in not only connecting contemporary listeners with Sophocles' tragedy but also in fusing the ancient Greek cultural and religious values embodied in the play with the Christian-Teutonic ones of modern-day Germany. Thus his score performed a function that reflected one of the main tasks involved in the German appropriation of Greek antiquity, and in so doing, it contributed at least in part to shaping the foundation upon which Friedrich Wilhelm hoped to realize his vision of an ideal Prussian state. As we shall see in the following chapter, Mendelssohn's score garnered praise from critics and musicians across Europe, and served as a model for those composers who took on the task of reconciling ancient Greek tragedy with modern German music in the manner established by the Prussian court revival of Sophocles' *Antigone*.

CHAPTER THREE | The Reception of *Antigone* and the Aesthetics of Appropriation

BY ALL ACCOUNTS, the 1841 Prussian court production of *Antigone* was a resounding success. Those fortunate enough to have witnessed it responded in mostly favorable terms to the elaborately reconstructed stage, the novel use of music, and the overall performance of the actors and musicians. And although many commentators on the production chose to focus on one or more of these elements for extended discussion, they all seemed to agree that the effect of the whole was greater than the sum total of its parts. One anonymous reviewer proclaimed that "seldom, or perhaps never, has a dramatic representation touched our hearts so deeply and powerfully," while the Berlin music critic Ludwig Rellstab concluded that "the impression of the whole was thoroughly dignified and uplifting."[1]

The sheer novelty of staging Greek tragedy—and no doubt also the stature of those involved—had been enough to generate considerable excitement in and around Berlin in the weeks leading up to the October 28 premiere. As Rellstab noted, "Already for months now the attention of all cultured people in Prussia's two royal cities [Potsdam and Berlin] has been focused on this artistic event."[2] This excitement only intensified in the wake of the premiere, and for many of those observers who doubted the effectiveness of Greek tragedy on the modern stage, this production came as a particularly welcome surprise. According to a critic who reviewed the encore performance of November 6:

> As great as the expectations of those in attendance may have been on the basis of published reports and friendly exchanges concerning the

first performance, they were nonetheless exceeded by reality. So many of the spectators believed that their contemporaries had been caught off guard and bedazzled by the novelty and splendor of the production together with its elite audience, and that they had mistaken as the impact of the play what was actually just the impact of the circumstances [surrounding its performance]. It seemed impossible that an ancient tragedy, without adaptation to our modern views and feelings, could have an effect on the heart and mind.[3]

But as the author went on to note, Sophocles' play had indeed spoken powerfully to the modern age through its "eternal, ethical truth." Other commentators pointed to the groundbreaking nature of this production and expressed the hope that similar efforts would soon follow. As it turned out, the Mendelssohn-Tieck *Antigone* not only served as a model for numerous performances of Sophocles' play in Germany and elsewhere during the 1840s and '50s, but it also inspired similar productions of other Greek dramas and was ultimately a major catalyst for the revival of ancient Greek tragedy on the European stage.

News of the 1841 *Antigone* spread rapidly throughout Germany and abroad, making it a topic of intense discussion and sometimes heated debate. The weeks and months following the premiere witnessed a steady stream of publications ranging from reviews of the performance (and its encore) to essays on the merits of reviving classical Greek tragedy. By November 15, slightly more than two weeks after the court premiere, Rellstab could write in a short piece appropriately titled "Yet Another Word on *Antigone*":

> One reads articles on Sophocles in general, as well as on his *Antigone* and on Greek drama as a whole, in the most diverse publications— South German, Rhenish, and so on. The pens of all educated and cultured writers are occupied with this task, and even in France, this artistic achievement has found such resonance that [French author and literary critic] Jules Janin referred to it in one of his *feuilletons*.[4]

Not surprisingly, Berlin quickly emerged as the center of this journalistic storm. Together the *Vossische Zeitung* and the *Allgemeine preussische Staats-Zeitung*, two of the city's largest newspapers, featured a total of eight separate articles devoted to *Antigone* during the roughly one-month period following its premiere. This number is especially remarkable when one considers that the production could not possibly have been seen by more than a few hundred people. As one reviewer explained in the November 5 issue of the *Allgemeine preussische Staats-Zeitung*:

> Up until now we have refrained from reporting on the 28 October performance of *Antigone* in Potsdam, because this was not a public performance and because the audience comprised only invited guests. But since neither local nor outside publications have been hindered by these circumstances, we no longer wish to deprive our readers of an account of this extraordinary evening.[5]

Although many of these early pieces on *Antigone* were written by anonymous correspondents, the three lengthiest and most detailed essays on the subject were authored by two venerated Berlin scholars working independently of one another.

The archaeologist E. H. Toelken wrote an article challenging key elements of the production's "authentic" staging and, in a separate essay, reflected on the potential artistic significance of reviving Greek tragedy.[6] In the latter, he identifies the Mendelssohn-Tieck *Antigone* as a pivotal moment for the modern stage, comparing it to the late fifteenth-century, semi-sung production of *Orfeo* in a version by Angelo Poliziano. Although, as Toelken explains, this earlier production had failed to inspire a large-scale revival of ancient drama, it nonetheless assumed broader significance by helping to pave the way for the advent of opera. Drawing a loose analogy between Friedrich Wilhelm IV, who had commissioned the 1841 production, and Lorenzo de' Medici, whom the author claims was a driving force behind Poliziano's effort, Toelken detects an important parallel between the two productions, claiming: "A similar enterprise is presently underway, brought about through cultured, intellectual, and expressive means and inspired by a royal love of art."[7] To what precisely Toelken believed the Mendelssohn-Tieck production might serve as a prelude is not entirely clear, though elsewhere in the essay he suggests that the revival of Greek tragedy could lead to greater integration of the various arts that make up such a theatrical enterprise.

Echoing views characteristic of German idealist thought, Toelken describes Attic tragedy as the perfect union of its constituent parts—poetry, music, dance, speech, costume, and mimesis—and he identifies such artistic unity as a timeless model for the creation and performance of dramatic works. Yet he also warns of the potential "embarrassment" resulting from an attempt at re-creating ancient drama down to the last known detail. With this danger in mind, he praises the Mendelssohn-Tieck *Antigone* for making certain concessions to modern practice, including the use of unmasked performers and a chorus that, with the exception of some simple choreography here and there, refrained from dancing. Toelken also lauds Mendelssohn's approach, concluding that, in the absence of masked performers and a dancing chorus, the composer was "fully justified in not searching for his model in Aristoxenus and Aristides Quintilianus."[8]

Another prominent intellectual to weigh in on the 1841 *Antigone* was Böckh, the classicist and University of Berlin professor who had also served as the production's scholarly advisor. Böckh's essay on the production, which first appeared in the November 15 issue of the *Allgemeine preussische Staats-Zeitung* and was reprinted roughly a week later in the *Allgemeine musikalische Zeitung*, explored aspects of its staging and performance in light of ancient theatrical practice.[9] Böckh praises above all the manner in which *Antigone* had captured the spirit of Greek tragedy by re-creating key elements of this form without blindly imitating the ancients. As he explains, "When our exalted and artistic-minded king decided to revive a Sophoclean tragedy, the aim could in no way have been a slavish or pedantic imitation of antiquity, but rather the evocation of the work's total impression [*Gesamt-Eindruck*] through the various means at our disposal."[10]

Thus while he agrees with Toelken that the production had failed to conform in significant ways to ancient staging conventions, he argues that, in many cases, such departures from Greek practice were justified by the smaller physical dimensions of the court theater. Böckh also applauds Mendelssohn's decision to write in a contemporary idiom, reasoning that, if the composer's aim was to create music that would have the same extraordinary effect on modern listeners that Greek music was thought to have had on ancient ones, then it was necessary to communicate using a conventional musical language. What's more, he adds, it would have been impossible to devise something more authentic, given the incomplete form in which Greek music has survived.

Ultimately, Böckh and Toelken agree that the success of the 1841 *Antigone* resulted largely from its ability to tastefully combine elements of ancient and modern practice while nonetheless maintaining a general aura of historical authenticity. In the eyes of both men—and in those of several other contemporaries—Mendelssohn's music, which itself melded aspects of the ancient and the modern, constituted a key ingredient of this potent mixture. As we shall see, Mendelssohn's score would go on to assume a life of its own. It would be heard throughout Europe and in the United States along with countless public or semi-public readings of Sophocles' play; in productions similar to that of the 1841 *Antigone*; and in concert settings where the work's most popular choruses were performed (to say nothing of its presence in the drawing room following the publication in 1843 of the piano-vocal score). Mendelssohn's work also served as a model for a string of compositions written to accompany productions of ancient Greek tragedy in the decade or so following *Antigone* and, in the minds of some contemporary observers, marked the advent of a new musical genre. In the end, though, it would seem that the success of this music is impossible to separate from that of the Prussian court production, which not only inspired a flurry of similar productions but also gave rise to a fresh wave of German "Graecomania."

The immediate impact of the Mendelssohn-Tieck *Antigone* is hard to overestimate. The unusually pervasive interest that it spawned is reflected in the fact that both Böckh's essay and Toelken's article on the staging reappeared in early 1842 in a publication titled *Über die Antigone des Sophokles und ihre Darstellung auf dem königlichen Schloßtheater im Neuen Palais bei Sanssouci.* Also part of this compilation was an earlier essay by the Hegelian philosopher Friedrich Förster discussing the plot of *Antigone*. At the outset of a lengthy preface to the collection, Förster explains of this joint effort: "The performance of *Antigone*... has become a subject of such widespread discussion and concern that it seems to us to have entered into the realm of being a major event [*Ereigniss*]."[11] Förster goes on to discuss, among other things, the staging, the translation, the music, and the audience, as well as the general role of theater in society, and we shall consider some of his remarks in the pages that follow.

Worth recalling at this juncture, however, are Förster's prophetic words concerning the broader cultural significance of the 1841 *Antigone*: "The impact of [this production] will not be limited merely to the stage but rather will make itself felt in much wider circles of society."[12] Indeed, the Mendelssohn-Tieck *Antigone* came to be seen as a powerful example of what could be accomplished when the spheres of art, scholarship, and politics were united under the banner of ancient Greece. The success of this production was all the more meaningful within a culture whose identity was defined in no small part by the precarious relationship between its appropriation of a distant classical past, the stark realities of a politically unstable and in many ways unsatisfying present, and the ever-invigorating promise of a glorious utopian future.

From Court Splendor to Public Spectacle

When Mendelssohn noted two months before the premiere of *Antigone* that "the entire court has all of the sudden become immensely classical," he could hardly have envisioned just how far-reaching this classicism would prove to be.[13] Not only did the Prussian court production of Sophocles' play constitute a tremendous success in its own right, but it also marked the start of a new chapter in Germany's longstanding obsession with Greece. Successful productions of *Antigone* soon followed in Leipzig and Berlin, in both cases featuring Mendelssohn's music. The performances that occurred on March 5, 6, and 8, 1842, at the Leipzig Stadttheater also made an attempt at re-creating the ancient stage, as did those at the Berlin Schauspielhaus that took place roughly a month later on March 13–15 and again on April 28–30.

The Leipzig production utilized an altered version of Donner's translation that, as Susanne Boetius has shown, included revisions to the choral texts made by Mendelssohn with input from Böckh and from the Berlin scholar and musician Johann Friedrich Bellermann (1795–1874).[14] Boetius has dubbed this version the "Leipzig libretto" as an indication of the fact that it was used solely for this production, after which point the composer restored Donner's original text to all but one of his musical settings. Leipzig had also been the site of a private performance of Mendelssohn's music along with a reading of the play that occurred on November 28, 1841, before a select audience at the home of Johann Paul von Falkenstein, a high-ranking Saxon official.[15] Mendelssohn himself accompanied the choruses on the piano, leading an ensemble that included Richard Wagner's older sister, Luise Brockhaus-Wagner, reading the part of Antigone.

Response to the public performances of *Antigone* in both Leipzig and Berlin was generally favorable. A correspondent for the *Allgemeine musikalische Zeitung* proclaimed of the Leipzig production that, "No stage work has made such a gripping, jarring, and powerful impression...as that of *Antigone*."[16] Similarly, the sold-out performances in Berlin appear to have caused quite a stir. As J. G. Droysen reported, "The city is full of talk about the play, the music, [and] the production."[17]

Such was the attention garnered by these productions that they quickly became the object of satire and ridicule. The humorist Adolf Glasbrenner, using the pseudonym Adolf Brennglas, published "Antigone in Berlin" as the twenty-third volume of his satirical series on life in the Prussian capital titled *Berlin wie es ist und—trinkt*.[18] Published in 1842 and reissued in subsequent editions, this parody of Sophocles' play features a performance of *Antigone* (without music) that includes lengthy passages of stilted German adapted from Donner's translation and is frequently interrupted by comically ill-informed spectators speaking in a distinctive Berlin dialect.

The year 1842 also saw the premiere of the comic opera *Der Wildschütz* by the Leipzig composer Albert Lortzing, who had sung in the chorus for the production of *Antigone* at the Stadttheater earlier that year. With a libretto by the composer, this opera features a Countess Eberbach, who at one point is shown reciting passages of *Antigone* (in Donner's translation) before a gathering of bemused servants. The servants respond in song, explaining that, although the Countess reads beautifully, they have no idea what she is saying. The obliviousness of the Countess and the inability of characters from the lower ranks to comprehend Sophocles seem to constitute a subtle jibe at those mostly cultural elites who were swept up in the current wave of "Graecomania."

The successful productions of *Antigone* in Potsdam, Leipzig, and Berlin inspired a host of similar ones in Germany and abroad. Among these were performances of Sophocles' play together with Mendelssohn's music in, among other places, Paris (1844), Dresden (1844), Hamburg (1844), London (1845), New York (1845), and Edinburgh (1846). Like the 1841 *Antigone*, these productions generally used unabridged translations (often in the local language) and undertook some efforts at replicating the ancient playing space.[19] At least two productions from this time sought even greater "authenticity" by combining Mendelssohn's music with the original Greek poetry: an 1844 Stettin production directed by the German composer Carl Loewe, and a performance that same year at the Friedrich-Wilhelm Gymnasium in Berlin.

Also among the many performances of *Antigone* that took place in the wake of 1841 were those that occurred in a concert setting and featured a small number of readers delivering portions of Sophocles' text in conjunction with Mendelssohn's music. One such performance, led by the German composer and violinist Louis Spohr, occurred in Kassel as part of the 1843 Conference of Philologists and Educators. Such concert productions helped to popularize Mendelssohn's music and ensure its success apart from the groundbreaking and highly visible production for which it was originally conceived.

Productions of *Antigone* in the early-to-mid-1840s were generally well received by critics and the public alike. In New York, the production of *Antigone* at the newly opened Palmo's Opera House on Broadway was attended by Edgar Allan Poe, who wrote in a favorable review for the *Broadway Journal* that Mendelssohn's music represented "Greek thought adapted into German."[20] The London production at Covent Garden got off to a somewhat rocky start, prompting mixed reviews and criticism of the under-rehearsed musicians. As a critic for the *Times* remarked one day after the January 2, 1845, premiere:

> Up to 7 o'clock last night the general belief was that the tragedy would be a failure, unless indeed it was saved by Mendelssohn's music. How have the wise been deceived. The music, as executed last night, proved detrimental, whilst the tragedy itself has been most triumphantly

successful. Far from the chorus saving the tragedy, the tragedy has saved itself, in spite of the chorus.[21]

Mendelssohn's music nonetheless went on to great acclaim in England, and the production at Covent Garden ran for forty-five nights to frequently "overflowing houses."[22] The composer George Macfarren directed the music and, with Mendelssohn's blessing, took the liberty of employing some sixty singers for the chorus.[23] And while the size of the chorus was "inauthentic"—as was the use of "ballet girls" for the Bacchus chorus—other aspects of the production were aimed at evoking antiquity, including the staging and the costumes. The satirical magazine *Punch* poked fun at this classicizing tendency in a self-described "analysis" of the production written in doggerel, reading in part:

> A feeling of classical rapture comes o'er us,
> Which is smash'd when there enters a queer-looking Chorus,
> With sheets on their shoulders and rouge on their cheeks;
> Their fleshings, which ought to fit close to their shapes,
> Are clumsily fasten'd with ill-conceal'd tapes;
> And if the theatrical text be relied on,
> The skins of the Greeks were most carelessly tied on.[24]

Mendelssohn himself was reportedly amused by the accompanying depiction of the chorus with plaid trousers shown peeking from beneath their "Greek" robes (figure 3.1).[25]

Although performances of Mendelssohn's *Antigone*, both on and off the stage, appear to have peaked in the years around 1845, the work continued to be heard with some frequency through at least the 1870s, mostly in Germany

FIGURE 3.1 A caricature depicting the chorus in the 1845 production of *Antigone* at London's Covent Garden (*Punch, or the London Charivari*, Jan 18, 1845).

and England. Undoubtedly the most important German staging to occur beyond the initial wave of post-1841 productions was the one in Munich, which occurred in 1851 and which, as we shall see in chapter 6, helped to spark the revival of Greek tragedy with music at the Bavarian court.

The Ancients and the Moderns

In addition to the overall excitement that they generated, the productions of *Antigone* in Potsdam, Leipzig, and Berlin also sparked several controversies, including debates over the relative merits of reviving Greek tragedy for the modern stage and the suitability of Mendelssohn's music for this task. Among those who questioned the value of staging ancient drama was the celebrated German playwright, novelist, and theater director Heinrich Laube (1806–84). Shortly after the Leipzig premiere of *Antigone* in the spring of 1842, Laube published two essays in the literary journal *Der Komet* that were highly critical of the production and the larger impulse toward re-creating Greek tragedy. Although these articles appeared in one of the many lost volumes of this periodical, we nonetheless possess some idea of their content from a counterattack that took the form of a sixty-three-page pamphlet from the same year titled *Über Sophokles* Antigone *und ihre Darstellung auf dem deutschen Theater*. Its author, identified only as "a friend of dramatic poetry," is now generally assumed to have been Gottfried Hermann, the venerated Leipzig philologist.[26]

Hermann takes aim at Laube, claiming that his goal is to demonstrate the enduring value of Greek tragedy in the face of recent publications such as Laube's two essays on *Antigone*. Laube had criticized, among other things, the overly operatic nature of Mendelssohn's score, which he claims results in an expressive imbalance between music and spoken dialogue. For Laube, Mendelssohn's music is so prominent that it renders *Antigone* "a veritable new opera."[27] In a later work, Laube goes further by dismissing the revival of Greek tragedy as elitist in nature. Here he describes the Mendelssohn-Tieck *Antigone* as a "hybrid genre" combining theater and opera in a way that is "strangely entertaining for the connoisseur."[28] Moreover, he regards such productions as having a harmful effect on both the general public and on contemporary playwrights:

> The public saw all of its attention directed toward alien values and alien forms, and it became entangled in these norms. The German playwright saw himself pushed aside because these galvanizing efforts

claimed everyone's time and energy. In a word, artistic experiments such as these that constitute mere reproductions are justified only in narrow circles [of society]. They may have their place in schools and in [learned] societies, but not in the public artistic arena, upon whose lively activity an entire nation is dependent.[29]

To others, however, the performance of ancient drama promised to revitalize German theater while helping to redefine modern aesthetic values. Thus the historian Johann Gustav Droysen, in an essay review penned following the Berlin production of *Antigone*, identifies classical tragedy as an antidote to the unhealthy inclination of present-day drama toward realism.[30] Lauding Greek tragedy's elevation of the ideal over the real, Droysen maintains that its presence on the German stage will have a positive influence on contemporary drama by revealing "the simplest and truest elements of artistic effect."[31] He further argues that, insofar as the purpose of Attic drama is to wrest the spectator from out of a state of conscious subjectivity to one of self-abnegation, a production such as the Mendelssohn-Tieck *Antigone* puts on display a model for attaining this lofty aesthetic goal.[32] As proof of this claim, Droysen points to the audience's response to the production of *Antigone* that he witnessed. Noting the quasi-religious atmosphere that the performance engendered, he describes a mood of "solemnity, self-forgetfulness, and devotion," concluding that it is precisely this sense of collective reverence and awe that is too often lacking from the modern experience of art.[33]

Droysen's essay carried the weight of its author's authority as a translator of Aeschylus and a venerated historian of antiquity. By this point in his career, Droysen had already completed his two-volume translation and commentary *Des Aischylos Werke* (1832), a groundbreaking study of Alexander the Great (1833), and the first of his two-volume *Geschichte des Hellenismus* (1836).[34] He had also served as a tutor for the Mendelssohn children in the late 1820s and been a student of Böckh at the University of Berlin, where he came under the influence of Hegelian thought. Inspired by Hegel's linear view of world history, Droysen believed that the idea of freedom that was born in Athens and disappeared with its downfall would reemerge in its genuine and lasting form with the advent of a unified Prussian-led Germany.[35] Thus for Droysen, who once claimed that "nothing is more wholesome...for the German spirit than fertilization with the Hellenic," the 1841 production of *Antigone* must have seemed like another step, however small, toward the fulfillment of Germany's historically determined role as a beacon of freedom and humanity for the rest of the world.[36]

Droysen and others who looked favorably upon the revival of Greek tragedy often felt compelled to defend Mendelssohn's music against critics who claimed it was somehow not "ancient" enough. To such critics, the rich choral and orchestral textures of Mendelssohn's "modern," overly operatic music seemed to overwhelm Sophocles' graceful poetry. Thus the anonymous author who reviewed the 1851 Munich production of *Antigone* praised Mendelssohn's work but claimed that its individual numbers were ultimately "opera choruses" that obscured the text. As he explains:

> The text must be understandable, word for word, if the handling of the choruses is to be even halfway in accordance with the spirit of the ancients. A simpler use of instruments and their selective use (harps in place of the ancient lyre, joined by perhaps flutes, tubas and trumpets, at most timpani and basses) along with a melody that reflects the rhythmic meter of the dialogue and that alternates with harmonized ritornello passages and, finally, the use of a syllabic text as opposed to one that is obscured by the music—this, it seems, was the task of the composer charged with the revival of ancient choruses.[37]

Not only does this passage offer some idea of what such critics must have expected from Mendelssohn, but it also suggests that their critiques were rooted in a belief that, whatever the precise nature of ancient Greek music, it was necessarily subservient to the accompanying text. This view of Greek music was widespread at the time and perhaps best reflected in the entry on "tragedy" that appears in the *Wörterbuch der griechischen Musik (Dictionary of Greek Music)* compiled by Friedrich von Dreiberg and published in 1835. In it, the author draws a comparison between Greek tragedy and modern, serious opera, concluding: "In Greek tragedy the poem was the main element and was served by the music as simply an adornment of the former, whereas in modern opera the music is the main element and the poem is used by the composer as a mere canvas."[38]

The notion that Mendelssohn's music had somehow encroached upon Sophocles' poetry seems also to be implicit in the assessment of his score by two notable figures of the time. Robert Schumann, who had witnessed the Leipzig production of *Antigone*, wrote to his wife Clara soon thereafter:

> I heard *Antigone*, and I can say that it was very edifying. The actual tragedy, though, was rendered completely unrecognizable. Much too much music and yet not deep and significant enough. Of course, the task was difficult, but I think that, say, Beethoven would have gone about it in a completely different manner.[39]

Yet perhaps the most colorful and frequently quoted expression of disapproval concerning the relationship between music and text came from the celebrated German writer Friedrich Hebbel, who noted in a diary entry shortly after attending a performance of *Antigone* that the music suits the tragedy about as well as a waltz does a sermon.[40]

For those commentators who defended Mendelssohn, however, it was precisely his choice of a contemporary musical idiom that allowed him to communicate so effectively with listeners and thereby help to bridge the divide between ancient and modern. For this reason, any effort aimed at writing "ancient" music was bound to fail. As Droysen explains:

> Any sort of attempt at composing Greek music would not have worked. Who could have done so? Neither the composer nor anyone else knows what it sounded like, except those certain critics who thought [Mendelssohn's] music was not Greek enough. His task was rather more ideal, namely to revive this ancient work long fallen silent and make it speak again by using all of the artistic means that so abundantly stand at his disposal.[41]

Böckh makes essentially the same argument when he praises Mendelssohn's score for conveying elements of the unfolding drama. He maintains that the composer employed modern musical means in a way that was "appropriate to the character of the choral odes and the ideas contained therein, reflecting the noble and the sublime, the contemplative and the elegiac, the melancholy and the more cheerful and hopeful mood of the chorus."[42] And reflecting back on the 1841 *Antigone* in his memoirs, Eduard Devrient recalled that Mendelssohn's music "undoubtedly rendered Sophocles' tragedy accessible to, and popular with, the general theater public in such a way that ... resulted in a greater understanding and a greater impression of [the play]."[43]

Such comments highlight the mediating role played by Mendelssohn's music, which served in part to counteract the potentially alienating effect of ancient drama. Although the tragedies of Aeschylus, Sophocles, and Euripides were generally familiar through published translations, they were rarely staged without adaptation. Moreover, most aspects of ancient Greek culture remained shrouded in mystery to all but those trained in the burgeoning academic field of classical studies. As A. W. Schlegel explained in his celebrated *Lectures on Dramatic Art and Literature* (1808; published 1809–11), modern readers of Greek tragedy were sure to be confronted with numerous obstacles thwarting a complete and thorough understanding of the work before them:

But even supposing a translation as perfect as possible and deviating only slightly from the original, the reader who is unacquainted with the other works of the Greeks will be perpetually disturbed by the foreign nature of the subject, by national peculiarities, and by numerous allusions (which cannot be understood without the help of scholarship). Thus unable to comprehend the particulars of the work, he will be prevented from forming a clear idea of the whole.[44]

Indeed, it was partly the role of Mendelssohn's music to mitigate such challenges.

Droysen vividly articulated this function of the score when he described how, with each subsequent chorus, the music seemed to draw the spectator further into the world of classical Greek tragedy:

The first scene between Antigone and her sister [Ismene]—with such an unusual setting and such strange-sounding verses, with its harsh subject matter and rock-hard determination [on the part of Antigone]—leaves us feeling rather cold. We see this opening scene without really feeling ourselves drawn into it; [yet] we find it really interesting to be seeing a classical play. Then comes the singing chorus, and immediately with the sound of the music we become more at home and we find ourselves in our own territory, in our own sensibility, and we grow warmer and warmer. Already the next scene finds us more prepared, more receptive than before, and the following chorus renders us fully at home in this new, ideal world.[45]

Some commentators, including Droysen, went so far as to suggest that Mendelssohn's music had served as a translation of sorts. Friedrich Förster, in his foreword to the previously mentioned compilation of essays on the 1841 *Antigone*, made the following claim:

Just as those who are unfamiliar with the Greek language can gain some understanding of, and enjoyment from, the original [literary work] only by means of a translation, we must agree that the composer was completely justified in finding a musical language of our time for the choruses of Greek tragedy.[46]

According to Förster, Mendelssohn's achievement had actually surpassed that of a literary translator because he possessed no original upon which to base his "translation." For his part, Droysen argued that Mendelssohn's subjective experience of reading Sophocles was itself translated into modern terms through the medium of music: "With his ear[s] he heard the sounds of those rhythms, as well as the tones and timbres of those great events, and this aural experience itself instantly amounted to a new and vivid understanding—a translation into our own sensibility."[47] He went on to explain that, just as Donner's translation had rendered the original Greek comprehensible to nineteenth-century Germans, so Mendelssohn's music had effectively translated the ancient feelings once engendered by this masterful work into a language that listeners could easily grasp.

Dionysian Music

Contrary to the claims of an overly rich orchestration made by many nineteenth-century commentators, Mendelssohn's *Antigone* makes pervasive use of what can only be described as a pared-down musical texture—or what Michael P. Steinberg has called the work's "rhetorical understatement."[48] Aside from its frequently unison vocal line, the work features an orchestral accompaniment limited to some combination of woodwinds, horns, and strings—thus forgoing trombones, trumpets, and timpani altogether—in three of its eight numbers (Nos. 2, 3, and 5), while employing a limited instrumentation of some other kind in two additional ones (Nos. 2a and 4). Moreover, even those numbers that do make use of the full orchestra rarely feature *tutti* passages. On only two occasions in the entire score does the composer have recourse to the full ensemble at his disposal (including harp): once in the final stanza of the parodos (No. 1), discussed in the preceding chapter, and again in the last stasimon (No. 6), to be discussed presently. In some cases, the limited instrumentation seems calculated to establish a specific mood or evoke certain associations in the minds of listeners, as with the wind-band accompaniment heard at the outset of the victory ode sung by the chorus as it marches onto the stage. In other cases, it seems to constitute part of a general attempt by the composer to create a score that reflected at least the spirit of ancient Greek music, with its purported subservience to the text.

In at least one instance, however, Mendelssohn appears to have been little, if at all, concerned with such allegiance to an "ancient" aesthetic. His setting of the play's final stasimon (No. 6), in which the chorus pleads with the god Dionysus to spare Thebes from imminent disaster, not only makes frequent use of the full orchestra but also includes passages of melismatic and harmonically dense vocal writing that are uncharacteristic of the work as a whole. This chorus also includes a line of text that—again, unusually for this work—is repeated several times during the course of the piece. Together these elements result in a general rhetorical posture that is anything but understated.

In the episode preceding this chorus, the prophet Teiresias informs Creon of the dire circumstances that have arisen from the literal and spiritual pollution of Thebes and advises him to bury Polynices, whose rotting flesh has littered the city and defiled its altars. Creon is initially unshaken, suspecting that Teiresias has been bribed. He begins to waver, however, when the seer prophesizes the king's own ruin along with the death of his only living child, and he is eventually persuaded by the town elders to free Antigone and bury Polynices. Upon his departure, the chorus sings an ode invoking Dionysus (or, in Donner's translation, Bacchus) as the resident deity and protector of Thebes, calling on his healing presence in hopes that it will spare the city from devastating sickness and disease. The mood of this ode is thus jointly characterized by a dire sense of urgency and sheer excitement at the prospect of divine intervention.[49]

Like most of the choral odes in *Antigone*, this one consists of two strophic pairs, each of whose two stanzas share the same poetic meter and are set by Mendelssohn to essentially the same music. But unlike in most of his other settings, this chorus features music in the second strophe-antistrophe pair that is vastly different in mood and character from the first. This contrast between the two halves of the piece roughly correlates to the two differing stances assumed by the elders in their prayer to Dionysus: the one tantamount to a celebration of Dionysian might and power and the other marked by a sense of fear and desperation in the face of looming disaster.

Following an eight-bar introduction for woodwinds and strings, Mendelssohn's setting of the initial strophe opens with a march-like theme in D major scored for full chorus and brass (example 3.1). Notwithstanding the introduction, this opening recalls that of the parodos, in which the composer appeared to be evoking the distinctive sound of a men's chorus accompanied by wind band to suggest a parallel between the triumphant victory celebration led by the city elders and the large German festivals at which these ensembles were frequently heard, often performing *Militärmusik*. In this case, the sonic reference, which also includes the presence of dotted rhythms and predictable four-bar phrases whose endings are punctuated with timpani rolls, clearly underscores the elders' portrayal of Dionysus as a powerful defender of Thebes and other Greek regions.

Perhaps even more notable, however, is the conspicuous change in scoring that occurs roughly halfway through the first stanza with the onset of new musical material featuring longer and more unpredictable rhythms in the voices along with a sudden flurry of accompanying sixteenth notes in

EXAMPLE 3.1 Mendelssohn, *Antigone*, No. 6, mm. 9–16.

the strings and harp. Indeed, the music for full orchestra that replaces the brass-band accompaniment at this juncture marks only the second such *tutti* passage to be heard thus far in the work. This change, which happens in conjunction with the words "Hör uns, Baccheus!" ("Hear us, Bacchus!"), reflects the elders' shift from a more general invocation of the god to a direct appeal, while the ensuing four-bar crescendo over a dominant pedal suggests the fervent nature of this plea.

The music that follows continues in the same vein but with an accompaniment limited to woodwinds and strings, and the strophe ends by recalling a portion of the march-like music from the outset, again accompanied by brass instruments. Mendelssohn's setting of this initial strophe thus alternates between two contrasting accompanimental textures: a brass band on the one hand, and woodwinds and strings (along with an isolated *tutti*) on the other. These same shifts in scoring occur in the corresponding antistrophe, except that the march-like music at the outset is sung by a quartet of soloists to a sparse accompaniment consisting of pizzicato strings, unison horns and trumpets, and a single appearance of the timpani. Insofar as this basic contrast represents the elders' praise of and pleading with Bacchus, respectively, the music for this stanza can be said to mirror on a smaller scale the difference in tone between the first half of this piece and the second.

The composer's setting of the second strophic pair clearly highlights the pleading, desperate nature of this ode. Heard in between the two strophic pairs is an orchestral restatement of the introductory theme that initiates a move from D major to B minor and, upon arriving on the dominant of the new key, gives way to a change in tempo from *allegro maestoso* to *allegro assai vivace*. But instead of commencing with the second strophe immediately thereafter, Mendelssohn introduces what amounts to an interpolation of sorts: four bars sung by the chorus—or, in this case, chorus 1—to the phrase "Hör' uns, Baccheus!" using dramatic octave leaps in the tenor supported by alternating stepwise motion in the bass (example 3.2). By repeating text heard earlier in the piece, Mendelssohn departs from his general approach to *Antigone*, and by echoing specifically the pivotal line with which the elders made their first direct appeal to Bacchus, he is clearly drawing attention to the sense of fear and anxiety behind their plea for divine assistance.

Indeed, he reintroduces this four-bar interpolation (or some variation thereupon) no less than seven times during the remainder of the piece, both in between phrases and integrated into the main thematic material, yet always marked with a loud dynamic. Mendelssohn thus succeeds in highlighting this outcry as the central message of the ode and lending his setting of this chorus an unmistakable feeling of urgency, in some ways foreshadowing the similarly fervent chorus to Baal in *Elijah*, "Baal, erhöre uns!" Accordingly, the music for the second strophic pair is characterized by an increasingly raucous energy, resulting in a rhetorical posture that seems at odds with the otherwise "understated" nature of the score.

EXAMPLE 3.2 Mendelssohn, *Antigone*, No. 6, mm. 93–97.

The concluding antistrophe in particular charts a course of steadily building momentum, beginning with an unexpected move back to the tonic D major a mere six bars into what begins as if it will be a restatement of the music from the preceding stanza. This harmonic shift leads to brief tonicizations of E minor and G major amid the onset of new melodic material as the chorus makes its final, climactic plea to Bacchus to appear before them accompanied by the bacchantes, his frenzied female followers. Mendelssohn's setting of the ode's last two lines, in which the elders refer to the celebratory nocturnal dance performed by these women in honor of Bacchus, seems musically to evoke a festive orgy of Dionysian worship and revelry. This music includes a three-bar melisma on the word "Nächte" ("nights")—by far the longest in the entire work—and a flurry of constant triplets in the violins. It then culminates in a seven-bar cadential passage combining the full orchestra (except harp) with a sustained outcry to Bacchus in chorus 2 and a semi-chromatic descending gesture in chorus 1 that leaps to a high A in the tenor before concluding the stanza with a cadence in the tonic. Thereafter follows a brief coda during which the chorus intones multiple iterations of its plea to be heard by Bacchus, leaving no doubt as to the centrality of this message where Mendelssohn's conception of the ode is concerned.

Tellingly, Mendelssohn offered no description of this ode apart from its function as a song of invocation. When, in a letter to Droysen, the composer provided descriptive words or phrases meant to reflect the various moods of the play's choruses, he simply used the term "Bacchuslied" to refer to this one, suggesting that for him the character of this ode was inextricably linked to the rapturous worship associated with the ancient cult of Dionysus.[50] Further supporting this idea is a letter of 1844 that the composer wrote to George Macfarren as the latter was preparing to conduct the Covent Garden premiere of *Antigone*:

> The acting of the Chorus to Bacchus in D must be very lively toward the end, when those who sing "Hear us, Bacchus" should always wave their canes and even ascend the steps of the altar on the last one, while those who sing the other words can stand in a row toward the back until it is their turn to sing "Hear us, Bacchus"... until finally [the chorus] ends with an animated group gathered around the altar.[51]

These remarks strongly suggest that Mendelssohn intended this number to represent the emotional and musical climax of the entire work.

Curiously enough, it was this very chorus that, despite its conspicuously "modern" orientation, seems to have been best received by audiences and also to have generated much discussion among nineteenth-century commentators.

This number was so enthusiastically applauded at the Potsdam premiere that it was immediately given an encore, and nearly every reviewer of the early productions of *Antigone* that occurred in Potsdam, Leipzig, and Berlin commented on the effectiveness of this piece. Heinrich Schmidt, a correspondent for the *Neue Zeitschrift für Musik*, praised its "dithyrambic drive" and, along with the ode to Eros (No. 4), called it one of the most effective numbers of the score.[52] Another critic, noting the prudent manner with which Mendelssohn had utilized modern musical resources in *Antigone*, seemed to be alluding to this chorus as a representative example when, in the very next sentence, he described its "splendid effect" [*vorzügliche Wirkung*] and its "rich orchestral accompaniment."[53] Along similar lines, a reviewer for the *Vossische Zeitung* praised the chorus as "brilliant and highly effective," but conceded that it was written in more of a "modern, operatic style."[54]

Other commentators acknowledged the success of the Bacchus chorus but were less forgiving of its "Dionysian" qualities. Gottfried Hermann, for example, claimed that its "noisy" music was ill-suited to the content of the ode, which he argued was not intended to whip the spectator into some sort of Dionysian frenzy but rather to celebrate in more circumspect fashion the power and splendor of Dionysus. Hermann was especially disturbed by the repeated cries of "Hör' uns, Baccheus," maintaining that they undermined the overall unity of the ode.[55] The writer and composer Julius Becker expressed a similar dissatisfaction in an essay on the revival of Greek tragedy that appeared in the *Neue Zeitschrift für Musik* in 1844. In it, Becker maintained that modern music in its customary guise was incompatible with ancient drama. He pointed in particular to the Bacchus chorus as an example of the fundamental opposition between the two, claiming that its elaborate four-part writing was wholly misguided.[56] Becker went on to say that the music written to accompany staged revivals of Greek tragedy should, as in ancient times, serve as a handmaiden of the poetry and thus be as "discreet" as possible, perhaps even rendered entirely as melodrama.

These diverging views on the Bacchus chorus represent a microcosm of the central aesthetic debate surrounding Mendelssohn's *Antigone*. For those commentators who responded favorably, this chorus reflected the overall effectiveness with which Mendelssohn's "modern" musical language had captured the essence of Sophocles' ancient poetry. Those who viewed the piece unfavorably, on the other hand, regarded it as the most extreme example of the composer's flagrant violation of a fundamental aesthetic tenet governing the relationship between music and poetry in classical Greek drama.

Ultimately, however, this chorus demonstrates not so much the manner in which Mendelssohn adopted one approach over the other, but rather his willingness to embrace competing aesthetic ideals. This willingness becomes especially apparent when one compares the musical rhetoric of the Bacchus chorus to that of the relatively austere "Ode to Man," discussed in the previous chapter. If Mendelssohn's "Ode to Man" presents a reflective, self-assured chorus that stands at a comfortable distance from the ongoing plot, his Bacchus chorus displays the elders in the throes of passion and desperately wedded to the tragic events of the play.

Considered together, these two choruses underscore the diversity of stylistic impulses upon which Mendelssohn drew in his effort to convey the various moods of Sophocles' tragedy. As we have seen, this aspect of Mendelssohn's score was to a large degree responsible for its success—and, by extension, the success of productions in major artistic centers such as Berlin, Paris, and London. These productions in turn provided impetus for the revival of other Greek dramas while at the same time ensuring the continued preeminence of Sophocles' *Antigone* within the broader European imagination. Likewise, Mendelssohn's groundbreaking score offered a compelling model for the union of modern music with ancient drama and, as such, seemed to many contemporary observers to mark the birth of an entirely new genre.

CHAPTER FOUR | **The Growth of a Genre**
Taubert's Medea *and the Greek Stage Revival in Berlin*

To MANY OBSERVERS, the success of the Mendelssohn-Tieck *Antigone* seemed to indicate that the time was ripe for a revival of Greek tragedy on the German stage. Even more significantly, this production had demonstrated the crucial role that music could play in bringing about this resuscitation of ancient drama. After witnessing the Prussian court production of Euripides' *Medea* with music by Wilhelm Taubert, an anonymous critic for the *Vossische Zeitung* expressed what must have been—allowing for minor variations—a common sentiment among German theatergoers of the time:

> Ever since the first step toward the reintroduction of ancient Greek drama on the contemporary stage was taken with Sophocles' *Antigone*, and because the tremendous effect brought about by this masterwork exceeded nearly all expectations, it was natural...to wonder what impression a work by his younger contemporary [Euripides] would make when performed in the same manner.[1]

As it turns out, *Medea* was one of several productions of Greek drama, both at the Prussian court and beyond, that followed in the wake of *Antigone* and used music in a similar fashion.

The music written for such productions was increasingly regarded as constituting an independent genre with its own distinctive traits. Mendelssohn's *Antigone* was thought to have marked the advent of this genre by exploring an entirely new avenue in contemporary stage music. Writing in the aftermath of the 1841 production, the philosopher Friedrich Förster boldly proclaimed that "German music has been enriched by a new genre: the choruses of Greek tragedy have found their composer in Mendelssohn, just as the Psalms once did in Marcello."[2] This remark attests to the sheer novelty of setting Greek tragedy to music and suggests how, in the absence of an established tradition within modern composition, Mendelssohn was forced to invent one himself. As Förster explained: "Neither the choruses of opera nor those of oratorio, neither sacred music nor secular could offer [Mendelssohn] a starting point."[3]

Even for a critic like Heinrich Laube, who stressed the conventional aspect of Mendelssohn's *Antigone* by highlighting its roots in traditional opera and stage music, there is nonetheless an implicit acknowledgment of the work's originality in his description of it as a "hybrid-genre."[4] And to the extent that the music discussed in this book seems more aligned with incidental music than with opera, it is perhaps best regarded as a constituent genre of the former, in much the same way that a nocturne might be considered an independent genre within the larger category of the lyrical piano piece. Along these lines, it is worth noting that neither Mendelssohn nor any of the other composers discussed here ever used the terms "Schauspielmusik" or "Bühnenmusik," the traditional designations for works of incidental music. Instead they used descriptions like "the choruses to" or "music to" followed by the name of the play, and in some cases, they simply used the play's title.

This chapter and the two subsequent ones focus on the three most prominent examples of this emerging genre to appear in the wake of the Mendelssohn-Tieck *Antigone*. This discussion highlights the extent to which Mendelssohn's score served as a compositional model—a sort of "ideal type" to which future composers, including Mendelssohn himself, looked for guidance and inspiration. It will also take into account the ways in which these works by Taubert, Franz Lachner, and Mendelssohn differ from the *Antigone* model, revealing the manner in which these composers responded to the distinctive elements of the individual tragedies they set. In this way, their works both conformed to and challenged what quickly came to be seen as a set of generic norms surrounding the use of music in the service of reviving ancient Greek tragedy.

Echoes of Antigone

At this juncture, it may be helpful to summarize the German development of Greek tragedy with music from the 1840s through roughly the end of the nineteenth century. The first new production to follow in the footsteps of *Antigone* occurred away from the spotlight of the Prussian royal stage. What is more, it was not a tragedy at all but rather one of the most celebrated comedies of the ancient Greek world. Aristophanes' *The Frogs* was performed sometime in late 1842, roughly a year after the Mendelssohn-Tieck *Antigone*, at the Friedrich-Wilhelm Gymnasium in Berlin with a score by the German composer and music historian Franz Commer (1813–87). Scant evidence exists documenting this production that occurred publicly but within the confines of the school theater, raising more questions than answers concerning its precise nature. We do know that, despite the longstanding tradition in the school theater of presenting ancient works in their original languages, *The Frogs* was performed using a German translation and adaptation of the play by Gymnasium professor Johann Franz.

Commer's music differs from Mendelssohn's *Antigone* in a few key respects. Most notably, Commer makes a more self-conscious attempt to compose "ancient" music. Despite the use of a conventional harmonic language, he nevertheless utilizes a sparse texture throughout, restricting the orchestra to flutes, oboes, clarinets, horns, trombones, and two harps in what appears to have been an effort at evoking the sound of various ancient Greek instruments. Like Mendelssohn, Commer employs a chorus limited to tenors and basses but allows for one exception by scoring the play's initial chorus for sopranos and orchestra. Moreover, he refrains from the use of either melodrama or choral recitative, thus eschewing two of the most distinctive features of what would eventually become a quasi-independent genre.

Commer also wrote music to Sophocles' *Elektra*, which was performed in 1843 and again in 1845 at the Friedrich-Wilhelm Gymnasium in Berlin. In this case, however, both the score and the production utilized the original Greek text of the play. The work's sole surviving manuscript source is a piano-vocal arrangement that includes a Greek transliteration of the text along with a German translation by Franz Fritze.[5] Although this source tells us nothing about the work's orchestration, it does reveal that, as with *The Frogs*, Commer set the choral odes for men's chorus and at no point called for the use of melodrama.[6]

School theaters, including those of Jesuit institutions, had long played an important role in the European theatrical tradition.[7] Yet ancient works were rarely performed on the school stage and were more often Roman, with the comedies of Terence and Plautus being particular favorites. And on those occasions when Greek dramas were staged, it was not uncommon for the plot to be heavily altered. Thus to learn that unabridged works by both Aristophanes and Sophocles had been performed at a single Gymnasium in Berlin within the span of two years is to develop a clearer picture of the wide-ranging influence wielded by the groundbreaking Mendelssohn-Tieck

Antigone. Also unusual was the fact that these productions used music, which appears not to have been a common feature of school productions in general.

Ultimately, it was the Prussian royal court that played the most important role in reviving Greek tragedy on the German stage. Besides *Antigone*, King Friedrich Wilhelm IV commissioned productions of Euripides' *Medea* and Sophocles' *Oedipus at Colonus*, the former with music by Taubert and the latter featuring a score by Mendelssohn. Premiered at the court theater in 1843 and 1845, respectively, these performances were followed in each instance by a public staging in Berlin that helped to stimulate interest across Germany and elsewhere in Europe.

The king also called for a performance of Aeschylus' *Eumenides*, but it was not meant to be. Having been approached in 1844 about providing the music, Mendelssohn responded by saying that the task of setting these choruses would present insurmountable challenges.[8] The Prussian official Karl Josias von Bunsen attempted to change the composer's mind, reasoning that "your *Antigone* choruses are making the rounds of Europe, and those of Aeschylus would do [the same]."[9] When talk later turned to performing a telescoped three-act version of Aeschylus' *Oresteia* trilogy, Mendelssohn once and for all declared the task an impossibility, though he was hardly alone in his concerns in light of Meyerbeer's refusal to take on this project.[10]

The next performance of a Greek tragedy in Berlin—again, at the king's behest—would have to wait until 1851. On April 26 of that year, Euripides' *Hippolytus* was performed at the Schauspielhaus with music by the Prussian court composer Adolf Schulz.[11] The critic Ludwig Rellstab praised the music, saying that anyone familiar with the general form and content of similar works by Mendelssohn and Taubert would have a good idea of this one. He went on to make the following assessment of Schulz's music:

> The overall character of the work, even if it fails to attain the heights of inspiration first revealed by this genre, can only be described as dignified [and] elevated, arousing artistic feeling in the most noble manner possible.[12]

Rellstab's use of the word "genre" [Gattung] is telling insofar as it suggests the degree to which works such as this had come to be thought of as part of a unique genre whose lineage could be traced back to Mendelssohn's *Antigone*.

The year 1851 also saw the premiere of *Antigone* at the Bavarian court theater in Munich. Mendelssohn's music was conducted by Franz Lachner, who the following year would himself compose music to Sophocles' *Oedipus the King* in what marked a temporary shift from Berlin to Munich as the geographical center of reviving Greek tragedy for the German stage.

Although many of these later productions were received with critical and public acclaim, none was able to duplicate the remarkable success of the Mendelssohn-Tieck *Antigone*, and already by the 1850s, public interest in such productions had begun to wane.

From its beginnings, this trend was aimed at a relatively small group of highly cultivated individuals for whom ancient Greek artistic and cultural traditions would not have seemed so alien. This "ideal" audience included classicists such as August Böckh and Gottfried Hermann, ancient historians such as Johann Gustav Droysen, and learned artists like Mendelssohn himself (i.e., precisely the sorts of figures who, along with European royalty, attended the private premieres of these Greek tragedies at the Prussian court).

Perhaps not surprisingly, the school theater eventually became the preferred venue for such performances. Thus the small handful of new productions that occurred in Germany in the decades following 1852 all occurred on the Gymnasium stage. Moreover, the music was written by a single composer. Heinrich Bellermann (1832–1903) provided the score for productions of Sophocles' *Ajax*, *Oedipus the King*, and *Oedipus at Colonus*, all in the original language. These performances occurred in 1856, 1858, and 1874, respectively, at the Berlinisches Gymnasium zum grauen Kloster, where Bellermann was a singing teacher.[13] Bellermann generally adopted the model established by Mendelssohn's *Antigone*, as he himself acknowledged in a preface to the piano-vocal edition of *Oedipus the King*, published in 1882. The publication of *Ajax* and *Oedipus at Colonus* followed shortly thereafter, in each case with a German translation given beneath the Greek text. But despite his overall adherence to Mendelssohn's approach, Bellermann departed from his predecessor in at least one significant way (i.e., aside from setting the original language). In both *Ajax* and *Oedipus at Colonus*, he composed actual songs in place of what, for Mendelssohn, would have been melodrama corresponding to the actors' lyric verse. Bellermann thus moved one step closer to the practice of conventional opera by implementing a change that, ironically enough, he viewed as being a more genuine reflection of ancient Greek practice.[14]

By the time Bellermann's works were published in the 1880s, the practice of staging Greek tragedy with music had already become something of a fringe genre with limited appeal. The production of such works was generally restricted to school theaters and the occasional public performance, most often of Mendelssohn's *Antigone*. And while the latter would continue to be heard with some regularity through the first two decades of the twentieth century, it failed to generate much enthusiasm and gradually receded from public view. The many factors behind the work's eventual slide into obscurity, to be explored in the final chapter and the epilogue, include not only the relatively esoteric nature of Greek tragedy but also changing aesthetic tastes, as well as the rise of Wagnerism and, with it, a fresh alternative model for reconciling modern music with ancient drama.

Staging Medea

Not surprisingly, Mendelssohn was initially asked to supply the music for a proposed production of Euripides' *Medea* at the Prussian court. He was first approached in the fall of 1842 and appears to have been skeptical from the outset.[15] In a letter to Tieck, he explained his reasons for refusing this project: "The difficulties related to a performance of this play appear to be so great (particularly with regard to the choruses) that I do not believe I will find a satisfactory solution for this problem, and therefore I cannot undertake the task of composition."[16]

Ultimately, the task of writing incidental music for *Medea* fell to Wilhelm Taubert (1811–91), a Prussian court composer who at the time was conducting the royal orchestra's weekly soirees and would later serve as the ensemble's principal director. A native of Berlin, Taubert, like Mendelssohn, had studied piano with Ludwig Berger, and by the mid-1830s, had secured a reputation as a respected composer of piano music and one of the city's finest virtuosos.[17] He was appointed Kapellmeister to the Prussian court in 1842 and, from 1845 to 1848, also held the title of Generalmusikdirektor. In his role at court, Taubert not only directed the royal orchestra—something he would continue to do until 1883—but also provided music for a handful of productions directed by Ludwig Tieck, including *Der gestiefelte Kater* (1844) and *Blaubart* (1846), in addition to the much anticipated *Medea*. Highly cultivated though he was, it is to be doubted whether Taubert possessed the same knowledge of Greek tragedy (and above all Greek meter) that Mendelssohn brought to bear on the composition of *Antigone*. Taubert's more modest family background would presumably not have afforded him the educational opportunities available to Mendelssohn, and while he studied for some five years at the University of Berlin, his focus there was on philosophy and aesthetics. Nevertheless, like most educated Germans of the time, Taubert would have at least been exposed to the ancient Greek language and Greek tragedy during his student days at the Gymnasium.

Medea premiered on August 7, 1843, before a private audience at the Neues Palais in Potsdam. It was staged again on October 15 in a public performance given at the Berlin Schauspielhaus in honor of the king's birthday. Two additional performances at the Schauspielhaus occurred on October

16 and November 27 of that year. Given the enormous success of *Antigone* roughly two years earlier, it comes as no surprise to find that this undertaking was modeled on its groundbreaking predecessor. Thus Tieck again oversaw the production and led an effort to replicate the ancient stage. Likewise, the translation used was that of J. J. Donner, albeit with some modifications.[18] As Susanne Boetius has recently demonstrated, parts of the text were replaced by, or in some cases combined with, passages from the 1824 translation by classicist Friedrich Heinrich Bothe (1771–1855).[19] Known as both an editor and a translator of ancient Greek and Roman literary works, Bothe had previously published a five-volume translation of Euripides between 1800 and 1803. His rendering of *Medea* appears to have been the preferred translation of Auguste Crelinger, the actress who had played Antigone in the 1841 court production and who starred in the title role of the Taubert-Tieck production of Euripides' play.[20] Perhaps for this reason, most of the changes made to Donner's translation involved Medea's spoken dialogue. Few alterations were made to those parts of the play set to music, suggesting that Taubert was reluctant to make changes to a work that, as the autograph manuscript of the full score reveals, was initially composed using Donner's translation.[21] It is worth noting, however, that most of the textual changes Taubert did incorporate were subsequently retained for the piano-vocal score published in 1843.

To depict the play's chorus of Corinthian women, Taubert used a female ensemble divided into two half choruses, each one consisting of three soprano parts. This decision represented an obvious break with ancient convention, which was widely known to have excluded the use of female performers. It remains unclear, however, whether Taubert employed an ensemble of sixteen singers, as Mendelssohn had done, or whether, as a note by Taubert connected to an 1849 production of *Medea* suggests, he used an augmented ensemble of twenty singers.[22]

Between Witchcraft and Motherhood: Medea *on the European Stage*

The choice of *Medea* as a sequel to the Mendelssohn-Tieck *Antigone* can be said to reflect a German fascination with the figure of Medea and her shocking infanticide that dates back at least to the end of the eighteenth century.[23] This appeal found expression in several German operatic works of the time and in the popular theatrical work *Der goldene Vließ*, a trilogy completed in 1821 by the Austrian playwright Franz Grillparzer. Euripides' play centers on the figures of Jason and Medea, who fall in love when the latter assists the former in his quest for the Golden Fleece. Jason is successful partly because of Medea's willingness to kill her own brother so that the couple can flee the city of Colchis. Abandoning both her homeland and her father (the king), Medea sails with Jason aboard the Argo to his native city of Iolkus in Thessaly, where he hopes to assume the throne once held by his father. Soon, however, the pair is accused of killing the reigning King Pelias and, along with their two sons, must flee to Corinth, where Euripides' tragedy is set.

By the start of the play, Jason has taken a new wife, the daughter of King Creon (not to be confused with Creon of the Oedipus legends). Medea is distraught and bent on revenge. With the sting of betrayal compounded by her status as a foreigner in Greece—literally, a barbarian—she easily wins the support of the Corinthian women who comprise the chorus, obtaining their promise of silence as she plots her revenge. Further adding to her misery, Creon banishes her from Corinth for making threats against the royal family, though Medea cunningly persuades him to grant her an additional day to make arrangements for her and her sons. Medea then reveals her plan to the chorus: Utilizing her legendary skill with potions, she will poison Jason, his new bride, and her father. The problem of where to seek refuge is solved when Aegeus, the king of Athens, fortuitously passes through Corinth and agrees to harbor Medea in exchange for help with a cure for his childlessness. Again Medea confides in the chorus, this time laying bare her true intentions. In order to strike at the depth of Jason's heart, she will murder their two sons along with his new bride. Despite their horror, the chorus maintains its silence, and in a ruse designed to fool Jason into believing that she has accepted his new marriage, Medea sends her children into the royal household bearing precious gifts laced with a vicious poison. Upon accepting the gifts, Creon's daughter dies a horrible death, whereupon Creon, who throws himself upon her disfigured remains, suffers the same fate. Meanwhile Medea, who earlier in the play had agonized over her decision to kill her sons, realizes that she must go through with her plans lest the children die at the hands of her enemies, and the brutal act itself is heard offstage as the chorus sings its final ode. Just as Jason learns what has happened, Medea appears atop the roof of the palace in a serpent-drawn chariot carrying the children's lifeless bodies. Jason and Medea exchange final barbs before the latter makes her escape to Athens, denying Jason's request to bury his sons, and the play ends leaving Jason a broken, devastated man.

Most scholars believe that Euripides was the first to introduce infanticide into the Medea story, though other ancient versions include the children's death through other means.[24] In part because of this action, Euripides' Medea appropriates the role of a male hero in ancient Greek literature. As Michael Ewans has pointed out, the play makes repeated references to Medea's dishonor in light of Jason's betrayal. Yet this notion of honor—and by implication, status—is one that in the ancient Greek world was traditionally bound up with male identity.[25] Medea herself implicitly challenges conventional gender roles when she delivers her famous line refuting the widespread belief among the ancients that women, confined to the domestic sphere, lead easier lives than men: "I would rather stand three times with a shield in battle than give birth once."[26] On several other occasions in the play, Medea expresses her refusal—again in typically male fashion—to be shamed or mocked by her enemies. She thus determines that her only true recourse is revenge of the most punishing kind, even if it means she must kill her children and become, in her words, "a miserable woman."

Despite her actions, however, Medea is portrayed by Euripides as a largely sympathetic figure. Indeed, she wins the support of other characters in the play, most notably the chorus. For not only is she a scorned wife with whom the Corinthian women can easily identify; she is also a foreigner whose past transgressions—committed to benefit Jason—make it impossible for her to return home, as most women in her situation would have done. As we shall see, the chorus initially sings what might be characterized as odes of solidarity, offered in support of Medea and yet also presented in the name of women more generally.

As shocking and challenging as Euripides' play must have been for its Greek audience, it eventually became one of the poet's best-known and most influential tragedies, resulting in a popular image of Medea that to this day remains inextricably linked to her brutal infanticide. Yet it was the adaptation of the Medea myth by the ancient Roman poet Seneca that, even more than Euripides', left its imprint on modern retellings of the story.[27] In contrast to Euripides' sympathetic portrayal of Medea, Seneca emphasizes the character's supernatural powers, highlighting her role as a sorceress who is also the semi-divine granddaughter of the sun god Helios. Depicting Medea as a witch consumed with rage and murderous vengeance, Seneca opens his play with the title character invoking the power of Hecate, the goddess of witchcraft, and summoning the dark forces of Hades. At the end, Medea is shown holding the corpse of one son before brutally slaying the other in full view of Jason, after which she tosses their bodies aside and ascends, godlike, into the heavens on her grandfather's sun chariot.[28] Seneca's relatively unsympathetic portrayal of Medea is further highlighted by his more favorable depiction of Jason. Thus Seneca's Jason is still in love with Medea and is forced by the tyrant Creon (Creo) to choose between death and marriage to his daughter, at one point even begging Creo to spare Medea's life.

Among the modern playwrights influenced by Seneca's *Medea* was Pierre Corneille, whose successful *Médée* of 1635 helped to establish the popularity of this ancient myth in seventeenth- and eighteenth-century France, on both the theatrical and operatic stage. Corneille's *Médée*, for example, influenced aspects of the adaptation by his brother Thomas, which in turn served as the libretto for Marc-Antoine Charpentier's opera of 1693. Both of these versions drew attention to Medea's witchcraft and included complicated subplots that introduced a new character and expanded the roles of Creon and his daughter. Most German adaptations of the Medea legend that appeared in the seventeenth and eighteenth centuries took their cue from Seneca—or at least the post-Senecan tradition represented by Corneille.[29] Two of these assumed the form of courtly singspiels that included music, though the scores did not survive. Friedrich Christian Bressand's *Jason* of 1692 was premiered in Braunschweig and featured music by the court composer Johann Sigismund Kusser (1660–1727), while Johann Gottlieb Klest's 1752 *Medea* was set to music by Georg Gebel (1709–53).[30]

The predominant influence of the Senecan tradition was challenged by the 1775 premiere of Friedrich Wilhelm Gotter's *Medea* with music by the Bohemian-born Georg Benda (1722–95). Eliminating extraneous subplots, Gotter placed the focus squarely on Medea. Moreover, he emphasized her maternal side by highlighting the agony of her decision to kill the children. This emphasis was apparently intended to appeal to the humanist values of the emerging *Bildungsbürgertum*. It may also help explain the success of Gotter's *Medea*, which continued to be performed along with Benda's music for some three decades following its premiere.[31] For its part, Benda's music mostly comprises brief orchestral passages that feature motives associated with specific themes or characters and that generally alternate with lines of spoken text. Because it relies more on the alternation of music and text rather than its combination, Benda's approach is fundamentally distinct from that of Mendelssohn and appears not to have served the latter as a model.

In France, a similar challenge to the Senecan legacy came with the 1779 publication of *Médée* by Jean-Marie Clément (1742–1812). In his preface to the work, Clément argued for a return to the "Greek simplicity" of Euripides' tragedy. He claimed that the material was most effective when Medea was portrayed not as a witch or a sorceress but as a more sympathetic figure whose sufferings and emotional turmoil form the centerpiece of the drama.[32] Although Clément's play proved to be unsuccessful on the French stage, its general move away from the Senecan model served as inspiration for Benoît Hoffman (1760–1828), whose version of the myth furnished the libretto for Luigi Cherubini's opera *Médée* of 1797.

In line with Euripides, Hoffman and Cherubini placed the principal focus on Medea and her extraordinary psychological journey. Thus they eschewed virtually all elements of courtly intrigue and the Senecan emphasis on Medea's supernatural abilities. As the opera opens, the wedding between Jason and Dirce (the name given to Creon's traditionally unnamed daughter) is imminent, and Medea, who still hopes to reconcile with Jason, sings an aria explaining that she has sacrificed everything for her husband and wants him back. Once she is certain of Jason's intention to marry Dirce, Medea is driven by "blind fury" and chillingly informs him that he has cemented his own demise. Nevertheless, she is later shown wrestling with the decision to kill her children—a moment poignantly captured by the Act III aria in which she explains that, despite her intense love for her sons, seeing them only reawakens her fury.

Although Cherubini's *Médée* received only some twenty performances in Paris following its premiere there in 1797, the work was a huge success in Germany and became a regular fixture on the German operatic stage. This success reflects a growing obsession with the figure of Medea in Germany of the late eighteenth century. The prior decades had witnessed several new German adaptations of the myth, including (and in addition to those already mentioned) at least four stage plays, two ballets, an opera by J. G. Naumann, and a melodrama with music by Peter Winter.[33]

But perhaps the most celebrated German adaptation came in 1821 with the premiere of Grillparzer's *Daß goldene Vließ* at the Vienna Burgtheater. *Medea*, the second play in the trilogy, depicts the title character as an outsider struggling in vain to give up sorcery and fully assimilate into Greek culture. Thus even as Grillparzer offers a generally sympathetic portrayal of Medea in the spirit of Euripides, he nonetheless draws attention to her supernatural abilities and in this way recalls the Senecan tradition. Yet ultimately, these late eighteenth- and early nineteenth-century versions of the myth can be seen as part of a gradual shift away from the prevailing Senecan image of Medea toward a more sympathetic portrayal of the character in line with the ancient Greek literary model. From this standpoint, the Taubert-Tieck *Medea* of 1843 represents a culmination of this trend, relying as it does on the original, unaltered version of Euripides' tragedy.

Reaction to the 1843 *Medea* was muted compared to the excitement generated by *Antigone* two years earlier. This difference can be explained partly by the fact that *Antigone* benefited from the element of novelty and the involvement of a famous composer, whereas Euripides' play seems to have suffered due to its relatively gruesome content. Thus Mendelssohn—admittedly not the most impartial observer—described the court audience as "disgusted and [bored],"[34] and even Tieck conceded that *Medea*'s reception was nothing like that of *Antigone*, concluding that Medea's nature was "too harsh and too bold for our prudish age."[35]

But if its overall reception fell far short of *Antigone*, the Taubert-Tieck *Medea* nonetheless elicited a generally favorable response from commentators of the day, who mostly welcomed the performance of another Greek tragedy on the Prussian stage.[36] Response to Taubert's music is perhaps best summarized by the anonymous author of a short feuilleton that appeared in the *Allgemeine musikalische Zeitung* shortly after the court premiere: "Opinions of the score vary considerably, and yet all agree that the task of completing it was an extremely difficult one."[37] Most critics agreed that setting Greek odes for a women's chorus was inherently more challenging than writing for a men's ensemble. One reviewer cited the greater risk of monotony, while another claimed that it was more difficult to impart to a women's chorus a "classical, antique character." Still others attributed the difficulty of Taubert's undertaking to the nature of the choral odes themselves, which many observers felt were less intrinsically lyrical than those of *Antigone*. In the words of one critic:

> Aside from the difficulty presented by a chorus made up solely of *women's* voices, there was also an anti-musical obstacle presented, insofar as it is not the language of feeling that dominates [the *Medea* choruses] but rather that of reflection. Thus the only path that remained open to the composer was one of generally lending his music the suitably tragic character that this play demands.[38]

So daunting were such challenges thought to have been that critical praise for Taubert's music tended to highlight the degree to which it had succeeded in spite of the obstacles posed by the nature of Euripides' play.

An Emerging Genre

Whatever the differences between the music to *Antigone* and *Medea*, there can be no doubt that Taubert fashioned his score after Mendelssohn's highly successful work. Taubert's *Medea* thus stands as a testament to the lasting impact of Mendelssohn's music and suggests the degree to which the latter had come to be seen as a model for works of its kind. As one commentator explained: "Mendelssohn's approach to this essentially new musical genre was of great benefit to [Taubert]."[39] Taubert's score combines solo singing, melodrama, and choral writing for up to six parts—though not choral recitative—to create a work that, like Mendelssohn's, extends beyond a setting of the lyric odes to include other parts of the play thought to have been rendered musically by the ancients. But as we shall presently see, Taubert's *Medea* is generally less far-reaching in its attempt to evoke the norms and structures of ancient Greek tragedy as they were understood at the time.

Like Mendelssohn, Taubert scored his work for a conventional Romantic orchestra plus the occasional use of harp, to which he also added piccolo in the final two numbers. He also appears to have embraced Mendelssohn's goal of composing in a rhetorically understated manner so as not to overwhelm the text and appear too "modern." Thus, in addition to a frequently unison vocal line, one often encounters pared-down orchestral textures consisting of limited woodwind groupings combined with strings and horns. To give just one of several possible examples, Taubert's pastorally inflected setting of the second stasimon (No. 3), in which the chorus reflects on the dangers of excess love, features an accompaniment of flutes, clarinets, bassoons, horns, strings, and harp.

No doubt because of these simple textures, critics of the day generally praised the work's orchestration for what they perceived as its unobtrusiveness relative to the text. The Berlin correspondent for the *Allgemeine musikalische Zeitung* commended Taubert for having "restrained and simplified the modern instrumentation as much as possible, in order that it not stand in too glaring a contrast with the ancient drama."[40] Discussing a Berlin production of 1844, a critic for the *Berliner musikalische Zeitung* made essentially the same point by drawing a comparison between Taubert's *Medea* and Mendelssohn's *Antigone*. While the latter had left an imprint on Sophocles' play that was both "brilliant and utterly individual," its composer had failed to sufficiently distance the work from a conventional Romantic aesthetic. Taubert's music, on the other hand, was not nearly as original but was nonetheless more satisfying because it refrained from dominating the spectator's experience of the play.[41] Such commentators were clearly judging Taubert's work in light of the widely accepted belief that music in ancient tragedy had consistently played a subordinate role to that of poetry.

Taubert's *Medea* comprises an overture, labeled an "introduzione," and nine numbered pieces that correspond to the play's six choral odes and to the other sung or chanted portions of Euripides' tragedy (see table 4.1). Like Mendelssohn, Taubert generally conceived of individual numbers as extended musico-dramatic complexes that encompass not only the play's lyric (i.e., sung) verse but also its anapestic (chanted) and occasionally iambic (spoken) verse. In certain cases, the composer designated those settings that correspond to the anapestic and/or iambic lines as sub-pieces (e.g., 1a or 1b),

TABLE 4.1 The structure of Euripides' play and Taubert's score.

Dramatic Structure	Verse Type	Plot Synopsis	Score	Key
—	—	—	Intro.	f
Prologue	Spoken iambics	The nurse highlights Medea's devastation; the tutor reveals Creon's plans to banish Medea and her sons	—	—
	Chanted/sung anapests	Medea laments her suffering and the nurse responds	No. 1 (melodrama)	f
Parodos (chorus enters)	Sung lyrics /chanted anapests	The chorus sympathizes with Medea as she expresses suicidal and vengeful thoughts	Nos. 1a–d	f/A♭
Episode 1	Spoken iambics	Medea laments her statelessness and wins the support of the chorus	—	—
Ch. leader announces Creon	Spoken iambics	Creon enters	No. 1e (melodrama)	D♭
Continued dialogue	Spoken iambics	Creon banishes Medea and her sons	—	—
Episode 1 Cont.	Chanted anapests	The chorus asks Medea where she will go	No. 2	b♭
	Spoken iambics	Medea plots revenge on Creon, Jason, and his bride	—	—
Stasimon 1	Sung lyrics	The chorus empathizes with Medea	No. 2a	B♭

(*Continued*)

112 | THE POLITICS OF APPROPRIATION

TABLE 4.1 (Continued)

Dramatic Structure	Verse Type	Plot Synopsis	Score	Key
Episode 2	Spoken iambics	Medea berates Jason, and he counters in defense	—	—
Stasimon 2	Sung lyrics	The chorus prays never to suffer a fate like Jason or Medea	No. 3	E
Episode 3	Spoken iambics	Aegeus promises Medea refuge in Athens	—	—
Ch. addresses Aegues	Chanted anapests	Aegeus departs Corinth	No. 4	C
Episode 3 Cont.	Spoken iambics	As Medea plots revenge, the ch. begs her to spare her sons	—	—
Stasimon 3	Sung lyrics	The chorus wonders how Athens could possibly welcome a child killer into its midst	No. 5	g
Episode 4	Spoken iambics	Medea tricks Jason into giving poison-laced gifts to his new wife	—	—
Stasimon 4	Sung lyrics	The chorus gives up any hope that the children will live	No. 6	f♯
Episode 5	Spoken iambics	Medea wavers but determines to carry out her plan	—	—

(Continued)

TABLE 4.1 (Continued)

Dramatic Structure	Verse Type	Plot Synopsis	Score	Key
Anapestic Interlude	Chanted anapests	The chorus points to the benefits of being childless	No. 7	D → d
Episode 6	Spoken iambics	Learning of the deaths of Creon and his daughter, Medea resolves to kill her children	No. 7a (melodrama for ch. leader)	f
Stasimon 5	Sung lyrics /spoken iambics	As the chorus prays for Medea to stay her hand, she is heard attacking the children	No. 8	f
Exodos	Spoken iambics	The chorus informs Jason of his children's fate	No. 8a	d/f
Medea appears	—	Medea appears in her chariot with the bodies of the children	Orchestral	F
Continued dialogue	Spoken iambics	Jason and Medea trade insults; she denies him burial rights	—	—
	Chanted anapests	After further insults, Medea departs and Jason laments	No. 8b (melodrama)	f
Choral summary	Chanted anapests	The chorus states the moral: The gods will always impose their will, even when unexpected or unimaginable	No. 9	F

resulting in a total of nineteen individual vocal numbers. Taubert was generally less concerned than his predecessor with consistently providing music for those sung or chanted portions of the play apart from the choral odes. Thus whereas Mendelssohn set all of the anapestic lines, Taubert set only about half of them, mostly as melodrama. Those he did not set were delivered as spoken text, meaning that they were indistinguishable from the lines of spoken iambic trimeter that make up the play's episodes.

Consider, for example, the anapestic passage shared between Medea and her nurse that occurs in the prologue. A distraught Medea, heard from within the palace, cries out in agony, expressing her longing for death and cursing the house of her unfaithful husband Jason. The nurse responds by wondering aloud what will come of this storm brewing in her mistress's soul. The onset of anapestic verse, which begins with Medea's initial outcry and marks her first lines of the play, corresponds with the beginning of a melodramatic setting in Taubert's score (No. 1). The presence of music here highlights the metrical shift from the preceding iambic verse to anapestic verse and at least hints at what was believed to have been the corresponding change in the original performance of Greek tragedy from a spoken to a chanted or, in some cases, sung delivery. And there is virtually no doubt that Taubert recognized these (and other) lines as anapestic, since they were labeled as such in the metrical index of the translation by Donner that he is known to have used.

Taubert places the text of these lines above a succession of quiet, mostly sustained chords in the strings that are initially augmented by clarinets. Using the same F-minor tonality as the overture, he employs several diminished sonorities that underscore the pathos of the dramatic situation. Thus both stylistically and in terms of his decision to set this passage in the first place, Taubert's approach is fully in line with that of his more illustrious contemporary. But whereas Mendelssohn would have set this entire passage as melodrama, Taubert sets only about half of the lines as such and provides no music at all for the rest.

In what may offer an important clue to understanding the uniqueness of Taubert's approach, he sets all of Medea's lines to music but less than half of those spoken by the nurse. Taubert's aim appears to have been that of lending greater weight to Medea's lines by contrasting them with the nurse's frequently unaccompanied ones. This rationale might help to explain the change in orchestration that occurs with the onset of Medea's second outburst, at which point the accompaniment's string texture is replaced by a distinctive combination of horns and bassoons. This darker-hued scoring, along with the diminished-seventh chords that punctuate Medea's cries of woe ("Ach, ach!"), not only suggest the growing intensity of Medea's lament but also render the contrast between this passage of melodrama and the lines of purely spoken text that precede it all the more jarring.

It is also possible that, by setting all of Medea's lines to music, Taubert was responding to the difference between her anapests and those of the nurse. Whereas the nurse's lines constitute what are known as "marching anapests" and thus would have been chanted in some fashion, Medea's lines offer an example of so-called sung or "lyric anapests," which were typically used for moments of heightened emotion and which, as the term suggests, would have been sung.[42] But whether or not Taubert knew enough about Greek meter to recognize this distinction must remain a matter of speculation. Donner's metrical index indicates no difference between Medea's anapestic lines and those of the nurse, labeling them all simply "Anapäste." Moreover, one has to wonder why, if this was Taubert's intention, he would have bothered setting any of the nurse's lines at all. Ultimately, it appears as though Taubert's use of music in this passage—and elsewhere in *Medea*—was motivated more by a desire to heighten the unfolding dramatic action than to evoke the norms of Greek tragedy in an "authentic" fashion.

This strategy would account for why, in contrast to the preceding example, Taubert's setting of the anapestic exchange between Jason and Medea that occurs toward the end of the play calls for nearly all of the lines to be delivered as melodrama (No. 8b). These lines form part of a lengthy dialogue in which the two characters trade insults and assign blame to one another. Lines of spoken text give way to chanted anapests, which culminate in Medea's triumphant escape bearing the bodies of her slain children. This passage thus constitutes a pivotal moment, not only because it represents a final, highly emotional exchange between the two principal characters but also because it provides the dramatic momentum that propels the tragedy toward its conclusion, in which the chorus proclaims the moral of the play in one last anapestic stanza.

The emotional intensity of these anapestic lines may explain why Taubert chose to render all of them musically. Jason begins this passage by cursing Medea, who has refused his request to bury the children. In response, Medea hurls multiple insults and mockingly tells Jason to bury his bride instead. Taubert's music is cast in the F-minor tonality that by now has come to be associated with the tragic nature of the play as a whole. The first half of the piece features the repeated use of a half-step, mostly ascending appoggiatura figure that consistently falls on the downbeat of the measure and serves as a clear symbol of the collective grief experienced by Jason and Medea. A fleeting change in the character of the music, marked by a feint first toward G-flat major and then A-flat major, occurs toward the middle of the piece as Jason moves from insulting Medea to reflecting on his desire to hold and kiss his children. But as Medea coolly points out, his wish is made in vain, and just as Jason is forced to return to the harsh reality of his situation, so the music returns inexorably to the F-minor tonality with which it began.

The conversation ends abruptly with Medea's departure, after which Taubert inserts a brief orchestral interlude that recalls a motivic idea heard when Medea first appeared on the palace rooftop in her serpent-drawn chariot. The lines uttered by Jason in the wake of Medea's exit mark the only ones in this anapestic exchange for which Taubert does not supply a continuous stream of music. He mostly provides no accompaniment, but on two occasions inserts three repeated chords in between pairs of lines. Followed as they are by a group of choral anapests that Taubert sets to music (No. 9, "Schlusschor"), Jason's final lines stand out as two isolated passages of purely spoken text amid a sea of otherwise musically rendered lines that extend from the onset of the anapestic exchange between Jason and Medea to the end of the play.

The absence of music at a point when Jason has no other recourse against Medea but to call upon the gods as witnesses to her actions can be seen as a reflection of his sheer impotence. As one scholar has explained the relationship between the two characters at this point in the play:

> The contrast between Jason and Medea could not be greater. Medea is now fully in command, literally on high, in control of the children, and about to depart for Athens. She has exacted her vengeance, and Jason is reduced to idle words and feeble threats.[43]

Helpless and alone in the face of unimaginable loss, Jason, it would seem, is as depleted musically as he is emotionally and psychologically.

Further evidence of Taubert's relatively free approach to setting Greek tragedy involves the composer's decision to provide music for several iambic lines that would have otherwise been spoken. He does so only in connection with choral iambics, which Euripides most likely intended for the chorus leader. In this way, his approach is once again aligned with that of Mendelssohn, who occasionally set choral iambics to music but never those of the actors. Yet what differentiates Taubert's *Medea* from Mendelssohn's *Antigone* is that, while the latter includes only a small handful of such instances, the former contains several that often encompass four or five lines in succession.

One example of this "extraneous" music occurs toward the end of the play when the chorus informs Jason that his children are dead. Jason has come rushing onto the scene to interrogate the Corinthian women as to Medea's whereabouts, aware only that she is responsible for the deaths of Creon's daughter and, indirectly, Creon himself. He explains that it will be near impossible for Medea to escape the wrathful vengeance of the ruling house, and he expresses his concern for the children, naturally believing that they too will be targets of the royal family's revenge. The chorus pities Jason's ignorance and delivers the sobering news about his children:

		CHOR:	In welches Leid du hingerathen, weisst du nicht;
1280			Sonst, armer Jason, sprächst du diese Worte nie.
		JASON:	Was ist's? Beschlossen sie wohl auch meinen Tod?
		CHOR:	Die Hand der Mutter hat entseelt die Söhne dir.
		JASON:	Was sagst du? Wehe! Du vernichtest mich, o Frau.
		CHOR:	Du weisst es, Jason, deine Kinder sind nicht mehr.
1285		JASON:	Wo ward der Mord vollendet, innen oder hier?
		CHOR:	Thu' auf die Pforten, und du siehst der Söhne Blut!

	CHORUS:	Poor Jason, if you realized how bad it was,
1280		you wouldn't have said that.
	JASON:	What is it? Does she want to kill me now?
	CHORUS:	Your sons are dead, killed by their mother's hand.
	JASON:	What are you saying? Ah! You have destroyed me, women.
	CHORUS:	Know this, Jason: your children no longer exist.
1285	JASON:	Where did the murder take place? Inside the house, or here outside?
	CHORUS:	Open the gates, and you'll see your children's blood.

Although Euripides' poetry (and Donner's metrical index) indicates that these lines would have been spoken, Taubert takes the liberty of setting the choral part to music (No. 8a; see example 4.1). The chorus's first two lines are set as melodrama for the chorus leader using a motivic gesture in the strings that features a prominent tritone leap. Its next line (l. 1282) is also set as melodrama for the group leader, this time with an accompaniment that adds clarinets and bassoons and that wrenches up the tonality a half-step from D-flat minor to D minor. By contrast, the last two lines for chorus (ll. 1284 and 1286) are sung in unison by the entire ensemble and feature a chant-like idiom characterized by several repeated notes intoned over a quiet chordal accompaniment (now with the inclusion of bass trombone).

The use of music for this passage lends even further gravity to the tragic news delivered by the chorus. The perfect authentic cadences in D minor that occur at the end of lines 1282 and 1284 underscore the stark reality exposed

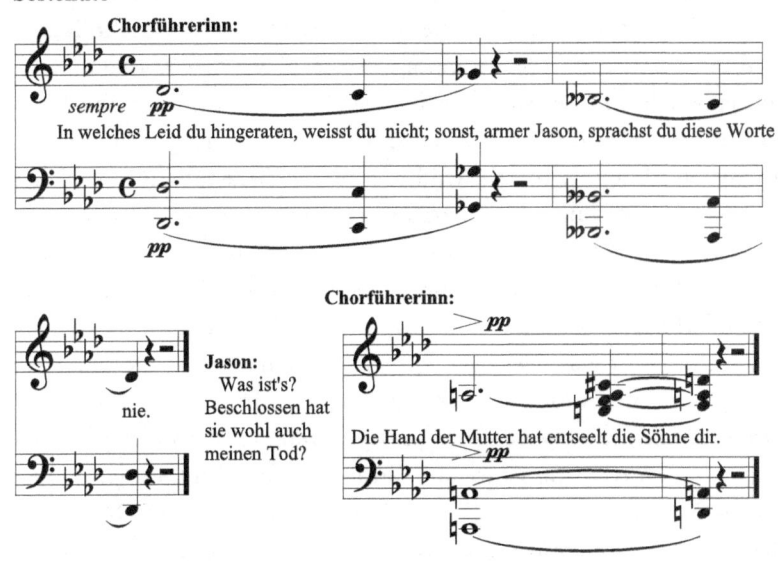

EXAMPLE 4.1 Taubert, *Medea*, No. 8a, mm. 1–6.

by the chorus and suggest the finality of Medea's actions. Furthermore, the quasi-chant idiom used for lines 1284 and 1286 assumes a dirge-like quality and gives the children's death a sonic dimension by evoking the funereal. Yet this form of vocal delivery also ensures maximal understanding of the text and may have been intended to conjure up the sound of "ancient" music, with its purportedly unison line and inconspicuous instrumental accompaniment.

The contrast here between the musically accompanied lines of the chorus (leader) and Jason's purely spoken ones serves to highlight the latter's isolation and helplessness at this point in the tragedy. He is excluded from the musical realm not only on the basis of his ignorance of Medea's actions but also as an indication of his sheer inability to exact revenge upon the murderer of his children. Jason's threats directed at Medea—both before and after he learns the fate of his sons—are seen as empty by a chorus (and audience) aware that Medea has already planned her escape and secured refuge in Athens. This power differential between Jason and Medea is further emphasized in Taubert's score by the inclusion of a raucous orchestral number in F major that comes almost immediately on the heels of No. 8a and seems to virtually celebrate Medea's act of vengeance. Heard as Medea appears in her chariot on the palace rooftop bearing the bodies of her children, this music makes conspicuous use of a triumphant ascending fourth gesture (first played by the brass) and marks one of the few instances in which Taubert employs the full orchestral resources at his disposal (though not including harp).

In still another example of his more liberal approach relative to Mendelssohn, Taubert adds music in between lines of spoken verse to highlight Creon's arrival toward the beginning of the play's first episode (No. 1e). Creon enters to inform Medea of his decision to banish her and her sons from Corinth, rightfully taking her to be a potential danger to himself, his daughter, and Jason. Using the iambic trimeter characteristic of spoken dialogue, the chorus announces Creon's arrival, noting that he has something important to say. Taubert frames this statement—here assigned to the chorus leader—with two short unison gestures played by woodwinds and brass, the second of which is expanded into a harmonized cadential figure. His use of music at this point may have been inspired by Mendelssohn's *Antigone*, which also employed music for those passages announcing a character's arrival. In the case of *Antigone*, however, such passages were written in anapestic meter and thus warranted being set to music in accordance with the approach established by Mendelssohn. It is also worth noting that Taubert's No. 1e seems to have been a late addition, appearing as it does along with three other addenda on the last folio of the autograph manuscript full score and raising the possibility that it was added by the composer after seeing a rehearsal (or performance) of the play.

Another indication of Taubert's willingness to depart from Mendelssohn's established model is the fact that he was generally less consistent in his use of contrasting vocal idioms as a way of suggesting the different types of delivery employed in the performance of ancient drama. Thus whereas Mendelssohn unfailingly set the play's choral anapests using recitative or a recitative-like idiom, Taubert typically rendered the choral anapests as conventional song, thereby drawing no distinction between the anapestic and lyric verse intended for the chorus. And whereas Mendelssohn reserved the use of melodrama almost exclusively for the actors' lyric verse, Taubert, as we have seen, more freely uses it for both anapests and spoken iambics.

To be sure, Taubert employs several strategies designed to evoke the presumed characteristics of ancient Greek music. He makes even more frequent use of a unison vocal line than Mendelssohn, thereby conjuring up the unison singing of the Greeks. Also like Mendelssohn, Taubert occasionally utilizes a largely monotone declamatory vocal idiom meant to suggest the chant-like mode of delivery thought to have existed in classical tragedy. In some cases, he employs this approach even for passages of lyric verse where one might have expected a more tuneful style.

At the outset of the first stasimon (No. 2a), in which the Corinthian women express sympathy for the plight of Medea and women more generally, the chorus intones nearly all of the first two lines of text on a repeated

CHORUS I
[Andante con moto]

Soprano: Die Quel-len der hei-li-gen Strö-me flies-sen rück-wärt's,
Recht und Al-les hat sich auf Er-den ver-kehrt:

EXAMPLE 4.2 Taubert, *Medea*, No. 2a, mm. 3–6.

F-natural (example 4.2). What little melodic element exists is concentrated entirely in the orchestra, where a repeated descending gesture played by flutes and clarinets is heard above a string accompaniment that suggests the "streams of the holy rivers" referred to in the text. Even with the shift to D minor initiated by the subsequent phrase, this chant-like idiom continues, now with a repeated A-natural. Not until the second half of this phrase does a more tuneful melodic style emerge, leading up to the antistrophe and, along with it, a repeat of the music heard in the initial strophe.

Perhaps the most striking usage of this declamatory style comes at the conclusion of a brief number corresponding to an isolated passage of anapests delivered by the chorus in response to Creon's announcement of exile for Medea and her sons (No. 2). Bemoaning Medea's fate and anxiously inquiring about her plans for exile, the chorus ends this group of lines by noting that some god has clearly engulfed her in a sea of misfortune. This final statement is met in Taubert's score with a change from a tuneful melodic style in

CHORUS I & II

EXAMPLE 4.3 Taubert, *Medea*, No. 2, mm. 22–28.

mostly three-part harmony to a unison chant-like idiom (example 4.3). The one measure of rest preceding this passage further highlights this change in texture, while the shifting harmonies beneath lend it a quality of incantation that, in this case, embodies the very spirit of the curse under which the chorus believes Medea to be suffering. And while it would seem that such declamatory singing is ideally suited to reflect the poetic meter as conveyed by the German translation, neither of the examples provided here corresponds rhythmically in any meaningful way to the pattern of longs and shorts found in Donner's metrical index. Indeed, Taubert was generally unconcerned with trying to emulate classical prosody in a manner similar to what Mendelssohn did in *Antigone*.

To what extent the kinds of liberties discussed here reflect Taubert's lack of knowledge about Greek tragedy cannot be determined with any certainty. Yet the degree to which his music did conform to the approach established by Mendelssohn points not only to his general aim of creating a score with an aura of historical authenticity, but also to his awareness of at least some of the basic elements that characterize ancient drama and its original performance (even if such an awareness was gleaned mostly from Donner's translation). Ultimately, the similarities between the incidental music to *Medea* and that of *Antigone* far outweigh the differences, which in terms of the overall compositional approach would have seemed negligible to observers of the time. To its contemporaries, Taubert's *Medea* offered proof of an emerging musical genre associated with the revival of Greek tragedy and characterized by its own unique stylistic markers.

A Divided Medea

True to the model established by Mendelssohn's *Antigone* (and notwithstanding some of its "ancient" evocations), Taubert's *Medea* employs a "modern" compositional language. Mendelssohn, it will be recalled, had quickly set aside the notion of writing "ancient" music in favor of "composing the mood" associated with each choral ode or other extended portion of the play that he set to music. Likewise, Taubert appears to have envisioned his musical numbers as reflecting, if not the underlying mood of the text, then at least the nature of the dramatic action at any given moment in the play. Taubert, however, was generally not as successful as Mendelssohn in this endeavor, resulting in a score that lacks the rich stylistic diversity of *Antigone* and comes across as somewhat monochromatic.

Along these lines, several numbers in Taubert's score reveal a folklike, even pastoral, character. Taubert's inclusion of these settings, with their simple melodies and relatively modest orchestration, may have formed part of his attempt to compose music that, in accordance with prevailing ideas about the Greeks, was meant to avoid overshadowing the text. Yet when one considers that these predominantly major-mode, pastorally inflected numbers all occur toward the beginning of the work, and that they stand in stark contrast to a succession of mostly minor-mode, emotionally fraught numbers that occur toward the end of the play, it seems rather that Taubert was responding to a certain dichotomy inherent in Medea's character and, by extension, the tragedy as a whole.

Over the course of the play, Euripides presents Medea from two highly contrasting perspectives. On the one hand, she is shown—despite her non-Greek status—to be a normal "Greek" female who, as such, elicits the sympathy of the Corinthian women. Thus early on, the nurse makes reference to Medea's welcome presence in the city and alludes to her pale skin, a typical feature of high-born Greek women, who were taught to avoid exposure to the sun.[44] Similarly, Medea's invocations of Themis, Zeus, and other gods are fully in keeping with the theology of the play's other characters (one notable exception being her invocation of Hecate).[45] On the other hand, Medea is shown to possess attributes that are in stark opposition to the Greek ideal of womanhood and are more characteristic of a Greek man of noble birth. As Michael Ewans points out, "Images of Medea as like a wild beast, coupled with the nurse's fears for the children, have already hinted that Medea is more than the weeping 'female-as-victim' that she at first appears to be."[46] The vengeance that she exacts on Jason, Creon, and Creon's daughter is rooted in a typically male concern with avoiding being dishonored and laughed at by one's enemies.

These two sides of Medea's character—her more traditional, quintessentially feminine nature and her more male-oriented pride and desire for revenge—give rise to the conflict at the heart of the tragedy between her "passionate anger and womanly need to let the children live."[47] The Corinthian women who make up the chorus seem to be keenly aware of and sensitive to this dual aspect of her nature, insofar as they initially sympathize with her as women and mothers but ultimately reject the part of her that is bent on vengeance at any cost. Taubert seems to have responded to this aspect of the play by dividing his score more or less in two: a first part consisting of gentle, pastorally inflected settings that evoke the feminine side of Medea's character and suggest the chorus's sympathy toward her; and a second part made up of darker, more turbulent pieces that reflect the fear and concern on the part of the Corinthian women and hint at their change in outlook toward Medea. In other words, the score appears to chart the gradual reversal of the sympathetic feelings that the chorus initially displays, with the turning point coming at the moment when it is finally revealed that Medea's plans for revenge also include the murder of her own children.

The work's overture itself encapsulates this basic opposition inherent in the figure of Medea. It immediately recalls the overture to Cherubini's *Medée* through its F-minor tonality and the severe character of the opening thematic material. But whereas Cherubini's overture is a fully worked-out sonata form, Taubert's is a more compact sonata without development in which only the secondary theme is heard in the recapitulation. In Taubert's piece, the initial F-minor material quickly gives way to a contrasting lyrical idea in A-flat major (m. 9) that is unable to sustain its new tonality and within just three measures initiates a move to B-flat minor on its way to a prolonged dominant of C minor.

What emerges, though, is yet another lyrical theme in A-flat major, the relative stability of which seems to affirm its role as the secondary theme. Yet it too soon gives way to the minor mode, in this case F minor and, with it, a recapitulatory statement of the secondary theme that leads to a fourteen-bar coda during which the curtain rises. Thus, insofar as the two lyrical themes in A-flat major can be seen as evocations of Medea's more tender, feminine nature, the fact that this music is unable to sustain itself for more than a handful of measures before succumbing to the forceful musical rhetoric and minor-mode tonality of the opening suggests a parallel with Medea's own inability to curb her passionate desire for revenge. Taubert later returns to A-flat major as the key of one of the early pastoral numbers, while F minor is associated throughout the work with the general pathos that characterizes the tragedy as a whole.

The first such pastoral evocation occurs in the midst of the parodos, the ode sung by the chorus as it files onto the stage. Here the parodos includes four lyric stanzas for the chorus, in between which are placed lines of anapestic verse for Medea and the nurse.[48] Having heard the cries coming from Medea's house, the chorus of Corinthian women rushes onto the scene to ask the nurse about Medea's state of mind. As Medea continues to be heard from within, the chorus remarks disapprovingly of her calls for death, instructing the nurse to bring her outside so that she might benefit from their friendly words of advice and encouragement. Of the four lyric stanzas assigned to the chorus, the first and last each possess its own unique poetic meter while the two middle ones form a metrically identical strophe-antistrophe pair. Taubert's setting of the first stanza, during which the chorus enters to inquire about Medea, features a unison choral line that approximates recitative and is dominated by a running eighth-note accompaniment. Beginning in Db major and moving to Bb minor before finally ending on the dominant of F minor, these 24 bars of music suggest the overall sense of urgency and alarm on the part of the Corinthian women.

Following an exchange between Medea and the nurse, the chorus resumes this stance at the outset of the second lyric stanza (No. 1b) by crying out to Zeus, now in four-part harmony. This outcry gives way to the sudden onset of A-flat major and, with it, a complete change in mood, constituting the first of the work's several pastorally inflected passages. It begins with a lyrical melody sung by a soprano soloist over a static five-bar tonic pedal (example 4.4) and continues with a second solo that makes its way back to F minor, followed this time by a short unison choral interjection in C minor that undermines the pastoral nature of the preceding music. The remainder of the strophe alternates between passages for soloist and chorus, bringing about a return of both A-flat major and the pastoral character associated with it. The chorus expresses a sense of solidarity with Medea by explaining that,

EXAMPLE 4.4 Taubert, *Medea*, No. 1b [parodos], mm. 5–9.

rather than descend into emotional turmoil, a jilted wife should simply trust in Zeus, the guardian of oaths, to exact vengeance on an unfaithful husband. The women echo this general sentiment in the corresponding antistrophe (i.e., the third stanza), which Taubert sets using essentially the same music (No. 1c). The chorus again articulates its desire to speak with Medea, imploring the nurse to convince her to come outside and reasoning that, if only Medea will do so, then she will be comforted by their friendship and support.[49]

Viewed from the perspective of the chorus, the parodos represents an ode of female solidarity intended to console Medea (albeit in absentia) by sympathizing with her plight and by assuring her that, left in the hands of Zeus, Jason will one day suffer the consequences for his infidelity. The shift from the frantic, predominantly minor-mode music in No. 1a to the simple pastoral music in A-flat major that governs much of the next two stanzas seems designed to portray the chorus as a comforting and sympathetic voice of reason, whose aim is to appeal to the softer, more rational, and, from the standpoint of both ancient Greek and nineteenth-century German culture, more feminine side of Medea's character.[50] Accordingly, Taubert's setting of the concluding epode (No. 1d), during which the chorus comments on the anguished cries coming from within the house, marks a return to F minor and, more importantly, to the dark character of the music heard at the outset of the parodos.

The music for the first stasimon (No. 2a) displays a similarly bucolic spirit. The chorus again expresses notions of female solidarity in what constitutes perhaps the most celebrated ode of the play. Reacting in part to Creon's announcement of exile for Medea, the Corinthian women turn the tables on conventional wisdom and suggest that it is in reality men who are the deceitful sex and who thus should be immortalized in poetry and song. By now the chorus has already promised not to reveal Medea's revenge plot (which as yet excludes the children), and they attempt to further console her by saying that the time is ripe for women to shed the mantle of inconstancy and restore to the world a sense of justice and fidelity to one's sworn oaths. Medea herself had already opened the door to this line of thinking when, in the preceding episode, she delivered a stirring speech concerning the plight of women.

The chorus's song is made up of two strophic pairs (*aabb*) set by Taubert as a rounded-binary structure (*aaba'*). The music corresponding to the three *a* sections recalls the simple pastorally inflected music of the preceding chorus. Like that one, this chorus includes a tonic pedal at the outset (see previous example 4.2), but here the sense of stasis extends beyond the accompaniment to the mostly unison vocal line. Marked by the repetition of a single pitch over multiple bars of music, this idiom was presumably meant to evoke the unison chanting of the Greeks. Again as in the case of the preceding ode, this music can be understood in opposition to the more anguished tone of the music connected with Medea's rage and, later, with her bloody acts of vengeance.

This pastoral tone is retained in the next stasimon (No. 3). In it, the Corinthian women implicitly reiterate their support for Medea by singing of the dangers of excess love and the devastation of being stateless (as Medea presently is). The chorus has just witnessed an angry exchange between Medea and Jason with each expressing moral outrage toward the other: Medea because Jason has abandoned her for another woman, leaving her without a home, family, or friends; and Jason because Medea, so consumed with thoughts of her own marriage bed, has failed to see the benefits that marrying into the royal family will bring to their children and even to her. The Corinthian women side with Medea by telling Jason that he has unjustly betrayed his wife, and their choral ode gives lyric expression to this belief.

Taubert's setting in many ways recalls that of the "Ode to Man" from Mendelssohn's *Antigone*, a piece that itself evinces a distinctly pastoral character. Both numbers make use of a simple, predominantly unison melody in 6/8 time and feature an accompaniment limited to flutes, clarinets, bassoons, horns, and strings (plus harp in the case of *Medea*). Moreover, both choruses share a similar melodic and rhythmic profile, and both also introduce new musical material with the onset of the second strophe (i.e., the third of four stanzas). There are, however, some notable differences between the two. While Mendelssohn employs no solo voices, Taubert scores the entire first half of his chorus for two soprano soloists, and whereas Mendelssohn adheres to a strophic setting for each pair of matching verses, Taubert employs different music for the first two stanzas.

Taken as a whole, however, the many parallels suggest that Taubert looked to Mendelssohn's highly praised and much discussed chorus as a model for his own. Indeed, Taubert may have detected a certain parallel between the content of the two odes, insofar as both allude to the importance of belonging to a city-state, or polis, and both end with the chorus rejecting the thought of keeping company with dishonorable individuals. But whereas the pastoral character of Mendelssohn's chorus appears to have stemmed primarily from the nature imagery in Sophocles' poetry, the pastoral character of Taubert's setting seems calculated to express a conciliatory tone in keeping with the music of the two previous odes.

The next piece in Taubert's score (No. 4) corresponds to a group of anapests delivered by the chorus as a farewell to Aegeus, whose fortuitous visit to Corinth allows Medea to secure refuge in Athens and thus move ahead with her plans for revenge. As befitting an Athenian king, this brief number features fanfare-like music in C major with prominent trumpets and drums.

It is with the subsequent chorus (No. 5), however, that we reach a turning point in Taubert's *Medea*. From here onward, the composer rejects the predominantly major-mode, pastorally inflected music of the first three choruses in favor of music that is written overwhelmingly in minor keys and is on the whole darker and more agitated. This change appears to come about as a result of Medea's revelation that her plans for revenge also include killing her children. In a reversal of its previous attitude, the chorus responds disapprovingly. It pleads with Medea to reconsider and tells her that, if she goes through with her plan, she will become "the most miserable of women." When she dismisses their objections, the Corinthian women launch into a choral ode in which they begin by wondering how a city like Athens could possibly welcome a child-murderer and conclude by predicting that Medea will surely be prevented by her maternal love from committing the ghastly deed she has in mind.

Taubert's setting of this ode, by omitting the first two strophes, shifts the focus away from the women's praise of Athens and places it squarely on their appeal to Medea. In contrast to the sense of stasis that characterized the work's first three choruses, this one is marked by a strong rhythmic and harmonic drive and is further distinguished through its use of a

EXAMPLE 4.5 Taubert, *Medea*, No. 5, mm. 1–12.

EXAMPLE 4.5 (Continued)

minor key and fast tempo (example 4.5). It also reflects the chorus's state of mind by making prominent use of two familiar symbols of dread in nineteenth-century music: the diminished-seventh chord, which the accompaniment repeatedly outlines in broken-chord figuration; and the tritone, an interval heard several times in the bass as the chorus begs Medea not to murder the children. Although both stanzas employ the same music, the second is extended to include multiple repetitions of key portions of the last three-and-a-half lines of text. Using a series of alternating, sometimes overlapping chromatic ascending gestures, Taubert has the chorus repeatedly tell Medea that she will surely be unable to carry out this bloody act. The result is a rousing, breathless conclusion to the piece, leaving the listener with the sense that perhaps the multiple iterations of this statement are made less to convince Medea of its truth than to convince the chorus itself.

The next choral setting (No. 6), though much slower in tempo, possesses the same dark character. Here the funereal quality of the music, centered on F-sharp minor, reflects the sorrow of the Corinthian women as they sing an ode lamenting the inevitable deaths of the princess and the children (now that Medea has successfully initiated her revenge plot). Feigning support for Jason's marriage, Medea convinces him to keep the children and to have them offer expensive gifts to his new bride in hopes that they will be spared from exile. The chorus is painfully aware that these gifts have been laced with a deadly poison, and their ode expresses pity for all involved. Notably, however, Taubert's setting omits the pair of strophes that express pity for Jason and Medea, instead maintaining the focus on the innocent victims of this imminent tragedy. Taubert, it seems, is subtly suggesting that Jason and Medea, because of their culpability in these events, are less deserving of our sympathy than either the princess or the children.

The next choral utterance constitutes a long series of anapestic lines with which the chorus reflects on the anguish and sorrow that often comes with having children. These anapests occur after it has been revealed that the princess has accepted the children's gifts and after Medea's famous soliloquy during which she momentarily wavers but ultimately resolves to kill her children. Taubert's setting of this verse (No. 7) includes melodrama for the chorus leader, brief solo passages for members of the chorus, and a concluding passage for unison chorus. The hymn-like nature of this music, which is scored entirely for muted strings, marks a noticeable retreat from the two preceding choruses. Yet its harmonic trajectory, which moves from D major to the parallel minor and includes an extended passage in F-sharp minor, underscores the theme of sorrow at the heart of the chorus's message and thus establishes a connection to events in the play both past and future.

The subsequent number (No. 7a) corresponds to five lines of spoken text for the chorus, which the composer took the liberty of setting as melodrama for the chorus leader. Delivered after hearing details of the gruesome deaths of Creon and his daughter, these lines once again express pity for the princess and, for that reason, feature the return of music first heard in No. 6 as the chorus lamented these impending murders. This number was evidently a late addition to the score, since it appears at the end of the autograph manuscript along with other addenda. The fact that Taubert ultimately chose to set this passage seems to lend further credence to the idea that his score charts the gradual reversal of the chorus's initially sympathetic response to Medea, in this case by using music to highlight the pathos of the princess's tragic fate.

It is Taubert's setting of the final stasimon (No. 8), however, that represents the culmination of the dark, agonizing music that dominates the second half of the score. In this ode, the chorus prays in vain for the gods to stop Medea from carrying out her grisly task. But Medea has already entered the house, and the cries of the children heard in the middle of the ode confirm the chorus's worst fears. In the first strophe, the Corinthian women implore the gods of earth and sun—the latter Medea's grandfather—to intervene, while in the corresponding antistrophe, they turn their thoughts toward Medea, wondering how she could possibly kill children that she not only birthed but also reared. Taubert's music for these two stanzas recalls his setting of the third stasimon (No. 5), in which the chorus first predicted that Medea would be unable to murder her own offspring. This, of course, was also the chorus that marked a conspicuous shift in Taubert's score away from a prevailingly tranquil and bucolic character toward one that was altogether more urgent and fearful—and ultimately more disdainful of Medea. Like the music of the third stasimon, the music of the final one features a minor-mode tonality,

EXAMPLE 4.6 Taubert, *Medea*, No. 8, mm. 1–9.

EXAMPLE 4.6 (Continued)

driving rhythms, a fast tempo, and stark dissonances, including a plethora of diminished-seventh sonorities intended to underscore the sense of horror and dread felt by the chorus (example 4.6).

What most distinguishes the final stasimon, however, is the inclusion of a pivotal dramatic event: the actual murder of the children, indicated by their offstage cries. At this point, Euripides includes two lines of spoken text for the children, followed by the resumption of choral lyrics interspersed with spoken iambics for Medea's two sons and for the chorus itself. In Taubert's setting, the onset of the iambic verse, during which one child is overheard asking the other how they can escape their mother's hand, brings about a shift to melodrama along with the introduction of highly contrasting musical material. The F-minor tonality of the first two stanzas is replaced first by F-sharp minor and then G minor before ending on the dominant of F minor. This harmonic motion by ascending semitones suggests a general heightening of tension as the action moves inexorably toward the dramatic climax of the play. The Corinthian women even consider entering the house to intervene, but just as soon as they contemplate this action, the children reveal that they have been cornered by a sword-wielding Medea. Not surprisingly, this passage features several diminished sonorities, while the children's final cries bring about two biting dissonances in the form of first-inversion major seventh chords. That the murder has indeed been carried out is signaled by a *morendo* that unfolds over several measures on the dominant of F minor and seems to depict the life ebbing away from Medea's slain children.

The start of a subsequent lyric stanza for the chorus is marked by a return to F minor, but now with new music meant to express the shock and horror that the Corinthian women feel upon realizing that Medea has carried out her plan. This music echoes melodic and harmonic elements from the first two stanzas, thus further contributing to a sense that the passage corresponding to the murder itself is something of an interpolation set between two outer sections that share a certain musical affinity. But even more important than the internal organization of this number is its significance within the broader narrative scheme of Taubert's work. As the culmination of a succession of choruses that share a similar character and contrast starkly with the work's three initial choruses, this piece seems to represent the clearest manifestation of the chorus's rejection of its previously sympathetic stance toward Medea. As one classical scholar recently described this pivotal juncture in Euripides' play: "At the crucial moment of the infanticide, the female solidarity which Medea established in the beginning dissolves; the chorus can no longer empathize with Medea, but only pity her."[51]

Also notable about Taubert's music for this ode is that it ends with a half cadence whose resolution to the tonic is denied even with the onset of the next musical number, which occurs after thirteen lines of intervening text. This brief setting (No. 8a), during which the chorus reveals to Jason his children's fate, begins instead in D-flat major but ends with the same dominant of F minor that was heard at the end of the preceding chorus. This time, however, it does resolve to F—not to F minor, as we would expect, but rather to the F major of the miniature orchestral tone poem (previously discussed) depicting a triumphant Medea on the palace rooftop. The "Schlusschor" (No. 9), which sets the play's concluding anapestic lines, is also composed in F major, but whatever sense of triumph was conveyed by the preceding orchestral interlude is here undermined by frequent modal mixture, extended even to the iv-I plagal cadence with which the work concludes. This harmonic ambivalence seems to reflect at once the tragic nature of the events that have just unfolded, as well as the tone of resignation that one can detect in the chorus's statement that it is, after all, the gods who control all aspects of life and human behavior.

Ultimately, the significance of Taubert's *Medea* resides less in the music itself than in what the work represents. By largely adhering to the approach established by *Antigone*, Taubert helped to affirm the view already held by many contemporary observers that Mendelssohn's work had blazed a new trail down which others might follow. Moreover, the backing of this production by the royal court lent Taubert's composition a level of visibility and artistic legitimacy beyond what would ordinarily have been the case for a work by a relatively minor composer—and certainly beyond what would have been achieved by a similar production mounted in a school theater. The success of *Medea*, while nothing like that of *Antigone*, nonetheless provided further impetus to the budding revival of Greek tragedy on the German stage and in this way helped to lay the groundwork for the advent of still more productions of its kind.

CHAPTER FIVE | Mendelssohn and Oedipus in the Age of Christianity

THE 1845 PRODUCTION OF Sophocles' *Oedipus at Colonus*, with staging by Tieck and music by Mendelssohn, marked the third installment in a series of Greek tragedies premiered at the Prussian court theater in Potsdam. It thus formed part of a general attempt by King Friedrich Wilhelm IV to reform Prussian theater, chiefly by mounting productions of Greek dramas and Shakespearean plays. Indeed, it appears that the king commissioned the productions of *Oedipus at Colonus*, Euripides' *Medea*, and Shakespeare's *A Midsummer Night's Dream* at roughly the same time in the fall of 1842. And while Mendelssohn declined the king's request to provide a score for *Medea*, he famously composed music to *A Midsummer Night's Dream*. This production occurred in Potsdam on October 14, 1843, just one night before the Berlin premiere of *Medea*, and Mendelssohn's music would, of course, go on to become one of his most celebrated works for the stage.

By contrast, the music to *Oedipus at Colonus* failed to garner much attention. This lack of enthusiasm, however, appears more related to a waning interest in reviving ancient drama than to Mendelssohn's music, which is at least as original and compelling as that written for *Antigone* four years earlier. The overall similarity between the two works reveals that Mendelssohn had come to associate the setting of Greek tragedy with certain distinctive musical features, including frequent unison passages, choral recitative, and melodrama. Yet for all of these parallels, *Oedipus at Colonus* departs from its predecessor in two significant ways. The first of these involves the work's more pervasive use of melodrama, which stems from the unusually high proportion of so-called lyric dialogue in Sophocles' play. The second concerns the more uniformly austere character of the music written for *Oedipus at Colonus*. This austerity occasionally takes on a religious dimension through the use of what might be described as a quasi-ecclesiastical style, displayed most prominently in two chorale-like, homophonic passages that stand apart both musically and on the basis of their ritualized function. Such music not only reflects the sacred overtones of the tragedy as a whole but also symbolizes the reconciliation of an ancient pagan past with a modern Christian present that lies at the heart of this production and is enacted largely through Mendelssohn's score. In this way Mendelssohn's music resonates with the broader cultural and political aims that appear to have motivated Friedrich Wilhelm's decision to stage Greek tragedy in the first place and that may have attracted the king to a work like Sophocles' *Oedipus at Colonus*.

New Beginnings

It will be recalled that Mendelssohn had accepted the post in Berlin with great reluctance. After much bureaucratic inertia on the part of the Prussian court (and considerable indecision on his own part), he eventually agreed to a trial year during which plans for a proposed conservatory would ostensibly move forward. By the end of that year, and with no conservatory in sight, Mendelssohn remained skeptical about the prospect of having a lasting impact on musical life in the Prussian capital. So he returned to Berlin at the start of the 1842 concert season fully intending to quit his post there.[1] The king meanwhile had ceased to believe that a conservatory represented an "essential need" and instead set his sights on using Mendelssohn's talents to initiate a reform of sacred music. As he explained in a cabinet order of June 4, 1842, addressed to J. A. F. Eichhorn, the minister of religious affairs, health, and education: "My intention is directed primarily at the revival and advancement of singing in the Evangelical Church, and here would be offered the broad and adequate field of activity that Mendelssohn desires, as I intend to place him in charge of all Evangelical Church music in the monarchy."[2]

Mendelssohn, however, balked at the idea and was presented with yet another offer during a meeting with the king on October 26 at which he had planned to submit his resignation.[3] According to the terms of this new proposal, the composer would be appointed director of a cathedral choir and orchestra to be made up of the best court musicians.[4] This select ensemble would provide music for the royal cathedral and occasionally perform oratorios at court. Mendelssohn would be expected not only to conduct the group but also to compose music for it. Perhaps best of all, he would be free to reside elsewhere until assuming leadership of the ensemble. Two days after his meeting with Friedrich Wilhelm, Mendelssohn accepted the king's offer, announcing his intention to return to Leipzig and requesting that his salary be cut in half. The king agreed, issuing a cabinet order on November 22, 1842, that granted Mendelssohn the title of *Generalmusikdirektor für kirchliche und geistliche Musik* (general music director for church and sacred music) and gave the official go-ahead for the creation of this new ensemble.[5] As it turns out, the cathedral choir began singing for services in the royal chapel in the spring of 1843, though Mendelssohn did not assume the directorship until the fall of that year.

Mendelssohn's renegotiated contract had stipulated that he would fulfill various commissions from the Prussian king while awaiting the start of his new duties. Included among these requests was one to provide music for a court production of Sophocles' *Oedipus at Colonus*. Mendelssohn explained this arrangement in a letter to Karl Klingemann dated November 23, 1842, which reveals that, even after receiving the title of *Generalmusikdirektor*, the composer continued to harbor doubt concerning the king's will to follow through with his latest initiative:

> If they actually begin something worthwhile in Berlin, then I can go there in good conscience. But if they put things off, then I may just continue collecting half of my salary and maintain my current situation longer than this year, with my duties limited, as they are now, to undertaking individual projects commissioned by the king (so, for example, I am now supposed to supply music for *A Midsummer Night's Dream*, *The Tempest*, and *Oedipus at Colonus*).[6]

It was also around this time that Mendelssohn was asked to provide incidental music for Racine's *Athalie*, which ultimately premiered at the Berlin palace of Charlottenburg on December 1, 1845, one month after *Oedipus at Colonus* was first staged in Potsdam.

Mendelssohn appears to have begun preliminary work on *Oedipus at Colonus* almost immediately after being approached about the project in the fall of 1842. In a letter to his mother of November 28, he claims to have been working "in my head" on both *Oedipus* and *A Midsummer Night's Dream*.[7] He again wrote to his mother on December 11, one day before her sudden death, telling her of his plan to bring this music along with him on a visit to Berlin.[8] But at some point not long thereafter, Mendelssohn suspended work on *Oedipus at Colonus*, presumably because of the king's decision to proceed first with a production of *Medea*.[9] Serious work on the score appears to have resumed nearly two years later in the fall of 1844, leading to the completion on February 25, 1845 of a manuscript draft of the score whose whereabouts remain unknown.

Whether Mendelssohn approached the *Oedipus* project with the same level of enthusiasm he brought to *Antigone* is difficult to gauge. In a letter to Karl Klingemann written during the period when Mendelssohn was busy completing royal commissions in advance of assuming directorship of the cathedral choir, the composer expressed some reservation about taking on such endeavors. As he explained with reference to the proposed production of *Athalie*:

> If occasionally I carry out some of those musical ideas of [the king] that no one else would be happy to take on, it is because I think it pleases him and that he will then allow me to continue living where and how I am now, with the result that we both gain something in return.[10]

To what degree Mendelssohn may have viewed *Oedipus* in these terms is impossible to say, though a comment he made several months earlier in a letter to Droysen suggests a genuine willingness on his part. Writing not long after the *Antigone* premiere, Mendelssohn professed a "strong desire" to write music for the two Oedipus plays, by which he clearly meant Sophocles' *Oedipus the King* and *Oedipus at Colonus*.[11] According to a letter Mendelssohn wrote to a high-ranking Prussian official, he even completed a sketch for *Oedipus the King*, though no trace of it has survived.[12] And given that his goal at the time was to assure the king of his loyalty following his refusal to provide music for Aeschylus' *Eumenides*, it is likely that the sketch was "in his head," much as *Oedipus at Colonus* and *A Midsummer Night's Dream* had been back in November of 1842. Had Mendelssohn in fact completed a score for *Oedipus the King*, it would have allowed for the performance of Sophocles' entire Theban trilogy with music—a prospect that no doubt would have appealed to a king intent on fashioning Berlin into a center of culture and learning.

The premiere of *Oedipus at Colonus* occurred on November 1, 1845, before a select audience at the theater of the Neues Palais in Potsdam. By this time Mendelssohn had given up his court duties associated with sacred music but had agreed to continue fulfilling commissions for the king. He thus traveled from Leipzig to conduct both the Potsdam premiere and the two public performances of *Oedipus* that occurred at the Berlin Schauspielhaus on November 10 and 11. Not surprisingly, this production shared much in common with those of *Antigone* and *Medea*. The staging was again undertaken with the aim of re-creating the Greek stage—a practice that by now had become standard for such revivals. And again the choice of translation fell to Donner's recently published edition, except that this time it was used only for the choral odes and for those other parts of the play rendered musically. The remaining, mostly spoken, portions of the play employed a translation by Franz Fritze, which, unlike the Donner, used the more familiar iambic pentameter in place of the original iambic trimeter.[13] This concession to modern taste seems to have met with the general approval of contemporary observers. One critic argued that the iambic pentameter was sure to facilitate a better understanding of the play, while Ludwig Rellstab claimed that it was better suited to the German language than the ancient trimeter.[14]

As previously mentioned, the Prussian court production of *Oedipus at Colonus* and the Berlin public performances that followed roughly a week later failed to have anything like the sort of impact *Antigone* had four years earlier. This relatively cool reception seems to have stemmed in part from a growing disenchantment with the idea of reviving ancient drama on the modern stage. As a reviewer for the *Allgemeine musikalische Zeitung* put it as part of an attempt to dissuade such efforts: "Are we then ancient Greeks? No! Are all of us who nowadays attend the theater classical philologists, who have at least passed their doctoral exams? No!... Are we lacking in dramas that are based on Christian beliefs and that naturally conform to our own ideas? No!"[15]

Suggesting that the public had had its fill of these Greek revivals, this same commentator expressed the belief that Mendelssohn's music was in no way responsible for the production's lukewarm reception:

> If *Oedipus* has spawned less interest than *Antigone*, then Mendelssohn's music is not to blame, but rather the greater monotony of the play...and the fact that the public's level of curiosity in these dramatically galvanizing experiments in reviving drama [Belebungsexperimente] has already been diminished by *Antigone* and *Medea*.[16]

Indeed, while *Oedipus* generated only a small fraction of the published reports that appeared in the wake of *Antigone*, those that do exist generally find favor with Mendelssohn's music. For instance, the notoriously sharp-tongued Rellstab praised the work by saying that it bore the stamp of "nobility" not unlike Sophocles' tragedy.[17] Another reviewer claimed that whatever success the production had achieved was principally due to Mendelssohn's score.[18] It would be misleading, however, to suggest that the music was entirely immune from criticism. To cite but one example, the same reviewer who sought to absolve Mendelssohn of any responsibility for the production's reception nonetheless felt that his music would have generally benefited from a lighter orchestration, which in turn would have facilitated the listener's comprehension of the text.[19] By making such a claim, this commentator was echoing much of the same criticism that had been directed at Mendelssohn's *Antigone* three years before.

Mendelssohn himself seems to have been pleased with his music to *Oedipus*, as he told his sister Rebecka in a letter of March 25, 1845.[20] But perhaps because of the muted response to the Potsdam and Berlin productions of the play, he made no apparent effort to have the work published. Not until 1851, four years after Mendelssohn's death, did Breitkopf and Härtel finally issue the score as op. 93, first as a piano-vocal edition and then in full score the following year.[21] Unlike *Antigone*, however, *Oedipus* failed to gain a foothold in the repertory, receiving only a small handful of performances in the ensuing decades, including staged productions in Leipzig (1850) and Munich (1854) and concert performances in Leipzig that occurred in 1855, 1856, and 1873.

Sophocles' tragedy tells the story of how the blind, exiled Oedipus, with Antigone as his guide, comes upon the town of Colonus and assumes his final resting place in a sacred grove that is home to the Furies (also known as the Eumenides, or "kindly ones"). He is initially rebuffed by the chorus of town elders, who know him by reputation and fear his presence in their city. Oedipus, however, manages to convince Theseus, the king of Athens (to which Colonus belongs), to grant him a burial spot in the grove in exchange for the protection that Oedipus, through death, can provide to the city as a quasi-divine presence. Theseus in turn shields his new ally from Creon, who hopes to install Oedipus near Thebes for that city's benefit. Oedipus also rejects Polynices, who seeks his father's blessings upon the military campaign that he plans to wage against his brother Eteocles, in a bid to regain control of Thebes. Oedipus is wholly unmoved by Polynices' impassioned pleas for forgiveness, uttering the curse that leads to each of his sons dying at the other's hand (and that sets in motion the plot of *Antigone*). Following Polynices' departure, Oedipus hears a series of powerful thunderclaps (vividly depicted in Mendelssohn's score) and recognizes this as a sign from Zeus that death is at hand. Guided by a divine light, the blind Oedipus leads Theseus, Antigone, and Ismene into the grove of the Eumenides, where, offstage and with Theseus as the sole witness, he undergoes his miraculous transformation through death into the resident protector of Athens.

The choice of *Oedipus at Colonus* for the third offering in the court theater's projected series of Greek tragedies may seem strange given the play's complicated plot and relative lack of action. Indeed, many observers of the time cited this latter aspect as a significant factor in the lukewarm reception of the Mendelssohn-Tieck production. Tieck himself blamed the relatively slow pace of the drama for the production's failure to appeal to audiences in the way that *Antigone* had,[22] while a correspondent for the *Allgemeine musikalische*

Zeitung who reached essentially the same conclusion cited the play's "greater monotony."[23] This same correspondent also noted how, through its almost exclusive focus on the title character, *Oedipus* seemed at odds with modern theatrical expectations: "A crippled and blind old man who for two and a half hours alternately complains and curses with little interruption and without leaving the stage is, according to our modern dramatic standards, a sight whose embarrassing boredom no unbiased observer could deny."[24]

Even those German critics of the early nineteenth century who were strong advocates of the play had felt compelled to acknowledge its uniqueness among Sophocles' surviving output. Contrasting the poet's earlier tragedies with *Oedipus at Colonus*, Sophocles' last known work, A. W. Schlegel extolled the latter's "mature serenity and total freedom from the impetuosity and violence of youth."[25] Modern commentators, too, have generally discerned something unique about the nature of this drama. In the words of one classical scholar: "*Oedipus at Colonus* is an unusual play; in many ways it is almost unresponsive to or unknowing of features of the tragic stage that are operative in other fifth-century plays."[26] Another of its distinctive characteristics concerns its strong religious underpinnings, which include not only the miraculous transformation of the title character into a local cult figure but also several other events of religious significance. This element may have been part of the play's appeal for Friedrich Wilhelm and perhaps also for Mendelssohn, and as we shall see, the religious dimension of *Oedipus at Colonus* offers a useful framework within which to interpret the frequently sacred tone of Mendelssohn's incidental music.

Lyric Dialogue in Music

Mendelssohn adopted the same basic approach to *Oedipus* as he did to *Antigone*, no doubt having been inspired to do so by the latter's success. He thus composed "modern" music written for a sixteen-voice double men's chorus and a standard Romantic orchestra with the addition of harp. Likewise, his goal appears to have been one of "compos[ing] the mood" of each chorus or otherwise extended portion of text for which he provided music. In this case, the resulting score encompasses a brief orchestral introduction followed by ten numbers that correspond variously to the play's choral odes, its (partially) lyric exchanges between chorus and actor(s) known singly as an amoibaion, and isolated passages of spoken dialogue (see table 5.1). This last-mentioned element of the score calls to mind similar passages in Taubert's *Medea* and sets *Oedipus* apart from *Antigone*, which corresponds almost entirely to the play's

TABLE 5.1 The structure of Sophocles' play and Mendelssohn's score.

Dramatic Structure	Verse Type	Plot Synopsis	Score	Key
—	—	—	Intro.	d
Prologue	Spoken iambics	Oedipus and Antigone arrive in Colonus	—	—
Parodos (Lyric dialogue)	Sung lyrics /Chanted anapests	Finding Oedipus in a sacred grove, the elders convince him to move and then reject him upon learning of his identity	No. 1	a → A
Episode 1	Spoken iambics	Oedipus pleads for refuge	—	—
Antigone announces Ismene		Ismene arrives with news from Thebes	No. 1a	D
		The elders take pity on Oedipus	—	—
Amoibaion (Lyric dialogue)	Sung lyrics	The chorus inquires about Oedipus' infamous past	No. 2	d
Ch. leader announces Theseus	Spoken iambics	Theseus arrives to meet Oedipus		F
Episode 1 Cont.	Spoken iambics	Theseus grants Oedipus citizenship	—	—
Stasimon 1	Sung lyrics	The elders sing a hymn praising Colonus	No. 3	F
Episode 2	Spoken iambics	Seeking protection for Thebes, Creon tries to persuade Oedipus to return; Oedipus refuses	—	—
Amoibaion (Lyric dialogue)	Sung lyrics /spoken iambics	After Creon abducts Ant. and Ismene, Oedipus turns for help to the elders, who issue a call to arms	No. 4	B♭/d

(*Continued*)

TABLE 5.1 (Continued)

Dramatic Structure	Verse Type	Plot Synopsis	Score	Key
Episode 2 Cont.	Spoken iambics	Theseus and his men set out to rescue the two sisters	—	—
Stasimon 2	Sung lyrics	The elders envision the ongoing battle btw. Athens and Thebes and pray for victory	No. 5	d → D
Episode 3	Spoken iambics	Theseus returns with the sisters and delivers news that Polynices has come as a suppliant	—	—
Stasimon 3	Sung lyrics	The elders note that old age brings suffering	No. 6	g → G
Episode 4	Spoken iambics	Oedipus curses Polynices	—	—
Lyric strophes / spoken dialogue	Sung lyrics /spoken iambics	Thunder signals to Oedipus that his death is at hand	No. 7	c → C
Episode 4 Cont.	Spoken iambics	Oedipus reveals that only Theseus may know his final resting place	—	—
Stasimon 4	Sung lyrics	The elders pray for Oedipus	No. 8	A♭
Exodos	Spoken iambics	A messenger recounts Oedipus' miraculous death	—	—
Kommos	Sung lyrics	Ant. and Ism. lament Oed.'s death as the ch. responds	No. 9	d → D
Exodos Cont.	Chanted anapests	Theseus agrees to send the two sisters back to Thebes		
Choral summary		The elders urge an end to lamenting Oedipus' death		

sung or chanted verse. Because such lines of spoken text are invariably set as melodrama, they ultimately serve to contribute to the far more pervasive use of this idiom in *Oedipus at Colonus*. The primary reason for this difference between the two scores, however, concerns the uncharacteristically frequent occurrence in this play of what is generally referred to as lyric dialogue, the mostly sung, often rapid back-and-forth exchanges between the chorus and one or more actors.

Classical scholars generally agree that the playwright's daring use of this technique in his later works raised the practice to a new level. In a book that explores the significance of music within Sophoclean theater, William C. Scott suggests that "the development of the lyric dialogue into a fully integrated and powerful contributor to the drama may be the most revealing sign of growth in Sophocles' musical technique."[27] Similarly, and with reference to *Oedipus at Colonus* in particular, R. W. B. Burton concludes that Sophocles "displays in perfected form a technique used intermittently in most of his plays and exploited with increasing skill in his last three." For Burton the essence of this perfection lies in the "closer and more sustained participation of actor and chorus together in the action."[28]

What the presence of such dialogue meant for Mendelssohn from a purely practical standpoint is this: Whereas in *Antigone* the lyric verse was always assigned separately to either chorus or actor, in *Oedipus* it was frequently shared between the two in a single passage. Because Mendelssohn's approach entailed setting all of the lyric verse to music—and because he consistently set the actors' lyric lines as melodrama—the result is a score in which four of the nine individual numbers (Nos. 1, 2, 4, and 9) contain extensive passages of melodrama corresponding to the play's lyric dialogue (while a fifth piece, No. 7, includes lengthy portions of melodrama that correspond to spoken lines of text inserted between the lyric strophes). On the whole, these four numbers lack the stylistic homogeneity of the strictly choral settings, which individually tend to be dominated by a single, overriding mood. By contrast, those pieces that set extended passages of lyric dialogue are characterized by a patchwork of brief, often highly contrasting musical episodes or vignettes that reflect the changes of mood and expression resulting from the unfolding "conversation." So whereas in *Antigone* Mendelssohn mostly provided music for those emotionally and psychologically static portions of the drama, here he frequently set lines of poetry whose function it was to advance the action of the plot. As a consequence, the music to *Oedipus* seems more fully integrated into the ongoing dramatic action.

Where the choral portions of the lyric dialogue are concerned, Mendelssohn alternated freely between conventional song, recitative, and recitative-like vocal writing, with no apparent regard for whether the lines in question were originally thought to have been sung, chanted to music, or spoken without music. Rather the composer seems to have been concerned first and foremost with utilizing a form of musical delivery appropriate to both the content of the text and the disposition of the character(s) uttering it. And in those passages that feature a rapid exchange of relatively short lines between chorus and actor, Mendelssohn tended to complement the latter's melodrama with either recitative or recitative-like music for the chorus, evidently in an attempt to mitigate the potentially jarring effect of a constant back-and-forth between song and spoken text.

The first instance of lyric dialogue in Sophocles' *Oedipus at Colonus* occurs in the parodos, or choral entry ode, which is also the first number in Mendelssohn's score aside from a brief overture in D minor. The thirteen-bar overture, which Mendelssohn labels an introduction, itself represents a radical departure from the extended, bipartite overture with which *Antigone* began. It opens with an ascending unison gesture heard as the curtain rises and ends with a restatement of this same idea (example 5.1). In between, the flutes present a quiet melodic idea that, according to Mendelssohn's stage directions, is meant to accompany the arrival of Oedipus and Antigone onto the scene. R. Larry Todd has claimed that this introduction establishes the significance of the tritone—outlined in the top voice between the downbeats of measures five and six—as both a melodic and a harmonic dissonant interval that serves as a "symbol of Oedipus' defilement as an incestuous parricide" and thus plays a prominent role in the work up until the time of its "heroic transformation" near the end.[29] Yet just as important, if not more so, is the establishment of D minor, which comes to be associated with the

EXAMPLE 5.1 Mendelssohn, *Oedipus at Colonus*, introduction, mm. 1–9.

Oedipal curse and with the pain of human existence more generally, and which undergoes its own "heroic transformation" into D major at the conclusion of the play.

In the prologue that opens the tragedy, Oedipus' identity remains unknown to the lone citizen of Colonus whom he encounters, and the parodos that follows thereafter constitutes an exchange of lyric dialogue among Oedipus, Antigone, and the chorus during which the town elders attempt to learn more about this mysterious old man. The ode consists of two strophic pairs, a concluding lyric stanza known as an epode, and short passages of anapestic verse that separate all but the final two stanzas. This structural design has led the classicist William Scott to describe this song as "a strophic form struggling to contain a conversation."[30] Indeed, three of the five lyric stanzas and two of the three anapestic passages feature dialogue involving some combination of the ode's participants. The initial strophe is sung solely by the chorus, which enters searching frantically for the stranger who has dared to trespass onto the hallowed ground occupied by the Furies. Marked by short, clipped utterances and panicked questions, this stanza is set by Mendelssohn using a declamatory, mostly unison choral line that gives way to eight bars of solo recitative corresponding to the stanza's concluding five lines. The music is further characterized by a severe, at times march-like style that features repeated rhythmic patterns and the pervasive use of the minor mode (specifically A minor and E minor). Retaining the division into half choruses that he used for *Antigone*, Mendelssohn assigns the first four lines to chorus 1 and the next two lines to chorus 2, at least hinting at the idea—suggested by the text itself—that individual members of the chorus seem to scatter across the stage in search of Oedipus.[31]

In the anapestic exchange that follows, Oedipus reveals himself to the elders, who in turn comment on his wretched appearance and inquire about his identity. Here Mendelssohn sets Oedipus' lines as melodrama and employs a unison recitative-like idiom for the chorus consisting of mostly repeated notes that alternate with short motivic gestures. The entire passage, which sets eleven anapestic lines yielding nine bars of music, unfolds over a progression of major and minor triads juxtaposed against diminished-seventh chords that are clearly meant to suggest both Oedipus' pathetic condition and the elders' startled response to it. In a second lyric stanza (i.e., the antistrophe), the chorus attempts to convince Oedipus to move away from the holy ground on which he is standing, thus hoping to spare him yet further misery. Following a practice established in *Antigone*, Mendelssohn sets the antistrophe using essentially the same music as the strophe, thereby reflecting the fact that these two stanzas share the same poetic meter.

The use of lyric dialogue begins with the second strophe, during which the lines of text are divided among the chorus, Oedipus, and Antigone in what amounts to a sung conversation. In it, the elders continue to coax Oedipus out onto a rocky ledge away from the sacred grove, assuring him that no one will drive him out of Athens. Accepting Antigone's advice to abide by local custom, Oedipus follows their commands and is helped along by his faithful daughter. The pace and frequency with which these lyric lines shift from one participant to another is unlike anything Mendelssohn encountered in *Antigone*. He responds by combining melodrama for the two individual characters with a choral line that includes moments of lyricism balanced by a more declamatory, repeated-note style and that ranges in texture from unison to four-part harmony. Moreover, in nearly every case where Mendelssohn shifts the mode of vocal delivery from song to spoken text, the melodic element is transferred from the chorus to the orchestra in what appears to be an attempt at reflecting the belief that such passages would actually have been sung by the actors in ancient times. Such moments are roughly akin to the melodramatic passages in *Antigone* where Mendelssohn instructed the actor to deliver his or her spoken lines using the same rhythm as that of the instrumental accompaniment.

The ode's two strophic pairs are followed by a single lyric stanza, known as an epode, in which the elders interrogate a reluctant Oedipus and finally learn the shocking truth about his identity. Mendelssohn's setting of this lyric exchange demonstrates how his music responds to the ongoing action by reflecting the shifts in tone and emotion that occur as the parodos unfolds. Oedipus initially gives the chorus evasive answers, such as when he responds to their inquiries about his origins saying, "I have no home, strangers." The elders in turn grow suspicious, replying pointedly, "What are you keeping from me old man?" (m. 145; see example 5.2). With these words, the lyrical melodic line that dominated the previous stanza gives way to unison choral recitative, thus suggesting the elders' alarm in the face of someone unwilling to answer such a basic question. In the increasingly tense exchange that follows, the music continues to alternate between brief passages of unison choral recitative and melodrama for Oedipus, culminating in the moment when the elders infer the latter's true identity upon his mere mention of the name Laius. The shock and horror of this revelation is conveyed through a sudden *fortissimo* outburst in the orchestra, along with a choral eruption in four-part harmony that features a prominent tritone between the tenors and basses and thus would seem to support Todd's idea that this interval represents a symbol of Oedipus' spiritual uncleanliness (mm. 155–56). Mendelssohn continues to depict the elders' violent outcries in a similar fashion as Oedipus confirms

EXAMPLE 5.2 Mendelssohn, *Oedipus at Colonus*, No. 1 [parodos], mm. 145–156.

EXAMPLE 5.2 (Continued)

that he is indeed the infamous son of Laius. Only once the men order Oedipus away does the unison vocal line reappear, followed in subsequent measures by a return of the melodic lyricism heard in the previous stanza, but now reflecting the more reasoned stance assumed by the elders as they use careful logic to explain why Oedipus' revelation no longer requires them to uphold their earlier promise not to drive him out of Athens.

Mendelssohn's setting of the choral lines in this scene, by shifting from unison recitative to static four-part writing and finally to a more melodic vocal idiom, highlights the elders' rapidly changing perspectives as they move from being nervously suspicious of this stranger to finding out his identity and ultimately attempting to rid themselves of his unclean presence. This number thus offers some idea of how the composer utilized various modes of vocal utterance in response to the unusually pervasive role of lyric dialogue in Sophocles' tragedy. It also reveals that, whereas in *Antigone* choral recitative was reserved primarily for setting anapestic lines, in *Oedipus* it was routinely used to set the play's lyric verse, suggesting that in the later work Mendelssohn was more concerned with exploiting the speech-like qualities of this idiom than he was with reflecting significant changes in the poetic meter.

The end of the epode brings about a sudden move from A minor to the parallel major as Antigone pleads with the elders, in an extended passage of melodrama, to take pity on her and her father. Here Mendelssohn reintroduces in the woodwind accompaniment the tritone that was featured so prominently at the moment when Oedipus' identity was first revealed. In this case, however, the jarring quality of this interval—now presented melodically instead of harmonically—is mitigated by its resolution into a major chord upon each of its appearances. Thus Antigone is shown musically to have the effect of softening the elders' disposition toward Oedipus and of paving the way for his eventual acceptance into Athenian society. As the elders explain in the episode following the parodos, they do indeed pity Oedipus and his daughter, but they also fear recrimination from the gods and therefore repeat their demand that he depart the city at once. The chorus nonetheless continues to listen to Oedipus' pleas for compassion; and it is both his and Antigone's heartfelt appeals, together with Ismene's revelation of the new oracles concerning Oedipus' burial and his promise to stay in Athens as a protector of the city, that finally compel the elders to accept him into their community.

Those additional numbers of the score that correspond to the play's lyric dialogue (Nos. 2, 4, and 9) reveal a similar mixture of four-part writing, unison recitative-like choral passages, and melodrama for the actor(s) or chorus leader. The second such instance involves two strophe-antistrophe pairs in which Oedipus reluctantly fulfills the chorus's eager requests to learn the details of his infamous crimes (No. 2). This "duet" between Oedipus and the elders of Colonus constitutes what is known in Greek tragedy as a kommos, a song of lamentation shared between the chorus and one or more actors. Mendelssohn, of course, had already encountered two kommoi in Sophocles' *Antigone*: the lament and chorus shortly before Antigone's death, and the lament featuring Creon and the elders following the suicides of Haemon and Eurydice.

But whereas in each of those cases, the lyric stanzas were delivered by the actor and were separated by passages of non-lyric verse for the chorus, here they are shared more or less equally between the two. Thus the melodrama for the actor, instead of being set apart from the main thematic material through the use of sustained chords and short motivic gestures unrelated to the music sung by the chorus, is integrated into the unfolding musical development of the piece. This particular number consists of two contrasting halves that correspond to the first and second strophic pair, respectively. The first half of the piece takes on a dirge-like quality and features an ascending unison gesture that bears an overall similarity to the one heard in the overture. The change that occurs with the onset of the second half, marked by a faster tempo and a greater sense of urgency on the part of the chorus, seems to reflect the elders' shock upon learning that Antigone and Ismene are not only Oedipus' daughters but also his half-sisters. Also notable is the D-minor tonality of this number, which recalls the overture and helps to establish the association of this key with the horrible events described here and, by extension, with the fate to which Oedipus himself points as the reason for his tragic downfall.

A second kommos occurs toward the middle of the play as Creon, in a heated exchange with Oedipus and the chorus, carries out his threat to abduct Antigone, who also contributes to the dialogue. Having already seized Ismene, his aim is to coerce Oedipus into returning to Thebes for the safety of that city (in accordance with a Delphic oracle). At the point when Creon's guards move toward Antigone, Oedipus cries out to the citizens of Athens in a desperate plea for help, marking the onset of lyric verse and the use of meters appropriate to the intensity of the moment.[32] Thus begins a strophe shared among Oedipus, Creon, and the chorus—a strophe that both includes and is followed by lines of spoken dialogue, which in turn are followed by a corresponding antistrophe. Mendelssohn set not only the lyric and the spoken verse but also the thirteen lines of spoken iambics that precede the start of the kommos (No. 4). He did so presumably because the first of these thirteen lines marks the start of a process known as *antilabe*, whereby a single line of poetry is distributed among two or more characters, or in this case all four participants.

Mendelssohn's setting is dominated by a short rhythmic gesture that features prominent octave leaps and whose fanfare-like nature suggests a military connotation. This association, which alludes to the imminent battle between Theban and Athenian forces, is confirmed toward the end of the first lyric stanza, when the chorus employs the same octave leap as part of a call to Athens to take up arms against Creon's men. Although B-flat major serves as the governing tonic, the significance of D minor again becomes apparent. After being hinted at in the passage preceding the B-flat major call to arms, D minor emerges shortly thereafter, coinciding with the moment at which Antigone is carried off by Creon's guards. This time, however, it produces a perfect authentic cadence—the first and only one in a piece filled with half and plagal cadences—that occurs immediately after Oedipus cries out in response to witnessing his daughter's abduction and seems to affirm the link between this key and the tragic events of Oedipus' life.

Mendelssohn's score also includes a number (No. 7) with extended passages of melodrama that do not correspond to the play's lyric dialogue. In this case the chorus sings two strophic pairs, with each of the lyric stanzas separated by brief passages of spoken dialogue between Oedipus and Antigone. The effect resembles that of a kommos, and again Mendelssohn sets both the sung lyrics and the spoken iambics, the latter as melodrama. But unlike in the parodos and the two previous kommoi, Sophocles confines the lyric poetry to the choral utterances and reserves the use of iambic trimeter for the actors' lines, thus avoiding any lyric dialogue. The lyric stanzas occur in response to the exchange between Oedipus and his son Polynices, who has come to Colonus seeking his father's forgiveness along with his moral support for a military campaign intended to regain control of Thebes from his younger brother Eteocles. Oedipus, however, is unwilling to forgive the child who once ordered his exile and sends him away with a curse meant to ensure that each son perishes at the other's hand. As one recent commentator has noted, this severing of the bond with his sons "was an exceptional measure for any Greek father, and underlines the magnitude of the dishonor his sons have paid him."[33]

For its part, the chorus begins by pondering Oedipus' curse, but at the end of the first strophe and in two of the three lyric stanzas that follow, focuses its attention on the flashes of lightning and ever-louder peals of thunder that signal Oedipus' imminent death. The opening, more reflective part of the initial stanza is set by Mendelssohn using a slow, funereal theme in C minor that features a prominent tritone leap near the outset (example 5.3a). The first rumbling of thunder, depicted by a timpani roll that swells from pianissimo to fortissimo while accompanied by a rhythmic figure in the horn, brings about a faster tempo and a unison choral outcry, which in turn are followed by a triumphant fanfare-like gesture in C major and a frightened plea from the elders ("Hilf, Zeus!"). The two C-major chords to which the chorus sings these words are followed by a repetition of this plea, now using a diminished-seventh chord. The lightning and thunder indicate that Oedipus' death is near and thus mark the beginning of his heroic transformation into a local cult figure. Oedipus makes it clear in an iambic passage shared with Antigone that he fully understands the import of these signs. As William Scott has noted: "The onset of thunder and lightning is actually the most welcome and blessed moment of Oedipus' life. He will be released from suffering, and the powers of heaven will recognize him as a special man."[34]

The chorus, on the other hand, remains unaware of the storm's significance and is fearful of its consequences. This outlook explains both the elders' outcry on a diminished-seventh chord and the musical transformation that occurs at the start of the antistrophe. Here the funereal theme heard at the outset of the piece is presented in a new guise: faster, louder, and with full orchestra in place of strings (example 5.3b). In other words, Mendelssohn is clearly providing the listener with a sonic depiction of the storm, and in accordance with longstanding conventions surrounding such representational music, includes frequent tremolos, timpani rolls, and diminished sonorities along with darting figures in the strings and a chromatic ascent meant to suggest the presence of violent winds. Following another spoken exchange between Oedipus and Antigone, this depiction resumes in the second strophe and is echoed in part in the corresponding antistrophe, which ends in C major but with elements of modal mixture as the elders call out for Theseus' quick arrival in accordance with the wishes of Oedipus.

Yet another kommos toward the end of the play involving Antigone, Ismene, and the chorus encompasses what Scott describes as "the most

EXAMPLE 5.3A Mendelssohn, *Oedipus at Colonus*, No. 7, mm. 1–5.

EXAMPLE 5.3B Mendelssohn, *Oedipus at Colonus*, No. 7, mm. 46–52.

expressive usage of lyric dialogue in Sophoclean drama."[35] This kommos comes in the wake of Oedipus' mysterious death and consists of two—or, in Donner's rendering, three—strophic pairs that feature the two sisters mourning the loss of their father. Mendelssohn's setting of this sung dialogue (No. 9) marks a return to D minor along with the introduction of a lament-like, appoggiatura-laden theme that is heard several times throughout the piece. When compared with other numbers in the score that set extended passages of lyric dialogue, this one is unusual insofar as the proportion of melodrama to conventional song is significantly higher. That is, melodrama makes up nearly two-thirds of this piece, or roughly the inverse of the other three settings of lyric dialogue (Nos. 1, 2, and 4). As a result, the orchestra presents most of the main thematic material accompanying the spoken text.

Apart from engendering the frequent use of melodrama in Mendelssohn's score, the pervasiveness of lyric dialogue in *Oedipus at Colonus* appears to have inspired the composer to make at least one other major adjustment in his approach to setting Greek tragedy. Whereas in *Antigone* Mendelssohn had relied on different modes of vocal utterance—conventional song, recitative, and melodrama—to highlight distinctions between lyric and non-lyric poetry, here the presence of such contrasting idioms is less likely to indicate a change in poetic meter. The reason for this shift concerns the sheer number of lengthy lyric passages that are shared between actor and chorus. A case in point is the exchange previously discussed during which the chorus presses Oedipus to recount the details of his horrific crimes (No. 2). While the initial strophe opens with the chorus addressing Oedipus, the corresponding antistrophe begins with Oedipus' reply and thus occasions the use of melodrama. Yet in both instances, the same D minor theme is heard, sung in the first stanza by the chorus and played in the second by the orchestra as Oedipus delivers his text.

This instrumental restatement offers perhaps the most persuasive evidence anywhere in Mendelssohn's two Sophoclean settings that the composer generally viewed melodrama as a substitute for the missing Greek song in those instances where the lyric verse would have originally been sung by one of the actors. As in the case of *Antigone*, this substitution functions as both a proxy for the unrecoverable ancient music and a surrogate for what might otherwise have been a sung rendering of the poetry had actors with trained singing voices been used for the two productions for which Mendelssohn composed music. This passage also underscores the degree to which Mendelssohn, even more so in *Oedipus* than in *Antigone*, relied on strophic form as a way of suggesting the metrical identity between stanzas—and thus as a way of evoking an important structural element of ancient Greek tragedy.

Hearing the Sacred

The four remaining numbers of Mendelssohn's score (Nos. 3, 5, 6, and 8) correspond to the play's four choral odes, or stasima. Compared to those that set passages of lyric dialogue, these pieces typically feature a narrower range of tempos and stylistic references. They tend rather to evoke a single musical character and in this way recall Mendelssohn's aim of "composing the mood" of each chorus in *Antigone*. The difference here, however, is that the music maintains a more consistently serious and elevated means of expression. To be sure, both works display a certain austerity, but whereas *Antigone* includes pieces rooted in broadly popular idioms such as the unaccompanied part-song and the march, *Oedipus at Colonus* generally avoids such musical types in favor of evoking a more elevated, quasi-religious tone. And even on those few occasions when it does feature more secular references, including the use of march-like music in the composer's setting of the second stasimon (No. 6), these passages lack the air of simplicity and *Volkstümlichkeit* that characterized, for example, the "Ode to Man" in Mendelssohn's setting of *Antigone*. Thus the music of *Oedipus* is in some sense aligned with that of *Athalie*, which was written around the same time and which, as Douglass Seaton has noted, "invokes a 'religious' spirit within the broader Romantic style."[36] Of course, in *Athalie* this reference seems wholly appropriate to the Old Testament story dramatized by Racine. It is perhaps because of this biblical context that Mendelssohn's *Athalie* achieves a more overtly religious character through the use of hymn-like choruses, cantus firmus textures, and the quotation of a familiar Christmas chorale, while the "pagan" score for *Oedipus at Colonus* relies on a more generalized evocation of the sacred.[37]

By writing music that was even more austere than that of *Antigone*, Mendelssohn appears to have been responding to the particularly strong religious underpinnings of Sophocles' final tragedy. The play's sacred character is apparent from the outset and goes beyond the frequent references to divine power and influence that are typical of Greek tragedy. For example, in the prologue, when Oedipus first sets foot in the sacred grove of the Eumenides and asks his daughter about the location upon which he has stumbled, Antigone responds by noting: "This ground is sacred—that much I can clearly tell." And when subsequently Oedipus prays to these same deities, he explicitly acknowledges that his arrival in Colonus had been foretold by an oracle of Apollo.

Sophocles' tragedy also features several ritual moments that highlight its religious dimension. Toward the beginning of the play we witness Oedipus, hands outstretched, delivering a lengthy prayer of supplication to the Eumenides. Similarly, when the town elders finally take pity on Oedipus, they instruct him in sacred rituals meant to atone for trespassing on holy ground. Because Oedipus is too old and feeble to perform this act of contrition, the duty falls to his daughter Ismene. The ritual itself is enacted offstage, but the detailed description provided by the chorus, including a full recitation of the requisite prayer, momentarily casts the elders in the role of priestly intermediaries. According to Cynthia Gardiner, who argues that this passage underscores the elders' piety and reverence, "It is as if the ritual were being performed before us, as if the chorus [itself has] the authority to purify Oedipus."[38]

The play's culminating dramatic event is also religious in nature. Oedipus' miraculous transformation through death from pathetic outcast to resident guardian of Athens symbolizes his role as savior and his newfound status as a quasi-divine hero who is destined to become an object of cult worship. With his earthly remains safely deposited in the Eumenidean grove, Oedipus literally becomes a part of the sacred landscape from which he was initially excluded as an unclean and unwelcome presence. The divine nature of this transformation is revealed to the spectator at the moment when the blind Oedipus, who began the play wholly dependent on others for guidance and instruction, now triumphantly leads the way to his final resting place: "Follow me, O my children, come this way. I stand revealed at last, look, a strange new role for me—I am your guide as you were your father's.... This is the way they lead me on, Hermes the Escort of the Dead, Persephone, Queen of the Dead."[39]

German commentators of the nineteenth century frequently acknowledged the play's religious character. Friedrich Schlegel found something intrinsically spiritual in the poet's approach to this work, drawing a contrast between Sophocles' attempt to portray Athens as a center of law and humanity and a similar attempt on the part of Aeschylus in his *Eumenides*: "The patriotic and liberty-breathing Aeschylus has recourse to a judicial approach and the pious Sophocles to a religious one, including even the consecration of Oedipus in death."[40] Along similar lines, an anonymous critic who reviewed the 1845 Prussian court production made the claim that "underlying *Oedipus* is a religious element, from which the character [of Oedipus] emerges as a glorification of Greek religious belief."[41] And in a more informal context, a letter written to Mendelssohn by his close friend Karl Klingemann expressed confidence in the composer's ability to capture the "profound religious feeling" of Sophocles' tragedy.[42]

The religious dimension of Sophocles' play, though not specifically Christian, may nevertheless have appealed to King Friedrich Wilhelm IV, a devout Pietist whose broader cultural and political agenda entailed the creation of a patriarchal Christian-German state. Moreover, it is likely that Tieck suggested a proto-Christian reading of the work similar to his interpretation of *Antigone*, at least judging from his claim that *Oedipus* possessed an "inkling of Christianity."[43] One can also imagine that, in the same way Tieck referred to Antigone as a Christian martyr and compared her to Mary Magdalene, he drew a parallel between Oedipus and Christ, both of whom experience, through death, a transformation from painful and humiliating earthly existence to divine savior. For his part, Mendelssohn perhaps sensed a loose parallel between the story of Oedipus, whose burial in Colonus depends on his acceptance of local custom and the bestowal of citizenship, and the many German-Jewish intellectuals like himself who may have felt compelled to conform to a society rooted in the beliefs and rituals of Christianity.

Perhaps the most conspicuous examples of the quasi-sacred tone displayed by this work involve two separate chorale-like passages that occur in the first two stasima (Nos. 3 and 5). In each case, this music appears unexpectedly in the midst of a choral ode and coincides with the chorus's direct appeal to some deity. The first such instance occurs in the initial stasimon, a hymn to Colonus sung by the elders to welcome Oedipus as the town's newest resident. Having learned of the protection that a deceased Oedipus would provide Athens, Theseus bestows on him full citizenship. He thus promises to protect Oedipus against Theban forces intent on removing him and entrusts his care to the elders, whereupon they sing their ode. The first strophic pair praises the natural beauty of Colonus: its white soil, dark ivy, singing nightingales, and beautiful flowers that dot the landscape. Using the same music for both strophe and antistrophe, Mendelssohn employs a simple hymn-like melody in F major with a sustained accompaniment that evokes the sound of an organ (example 5.4).

In the second strophic pair, the focus shifts to the larger metropolis of Athens and its most precious gifts from the gods: the unique and indestructible olive tree, a gift from Athena, and, most important of all, the city's association with horses and seafaring, for which praise is given to Poseidon. The onset of the second strophe is met with new thematic material, greater rhythmic and harmonic activity, and the start of an extended *accelerando*—perhaps meant to suggest a growing excitement on the part of the elders as they describe Athens' abundant blessings. The corresponding antistrophe opens with the same music, but after just six measures begins to deviate from the

EXAMPLE 5.4 Mendelssohn, *Oedipus at Colonus*, No. 3, mm. 9–16.

preceding stanza. Instead of moving almost immediately to the subdominant (B-flat major), the antistrophe opens by briefly tonicizing B-flat and then quickly initiating a move back to the tonic, after which an eight-measure chorale-like passage appears, characterized by total homophony in the voices and orchestra, a simple diatonic progression, and uniform rhythms (mm. 129–136; example 5.5).

EXAMPLE 5.5 Mendelssohn, *Oedipus at Colonus*, No. 3, mm. 129–138.

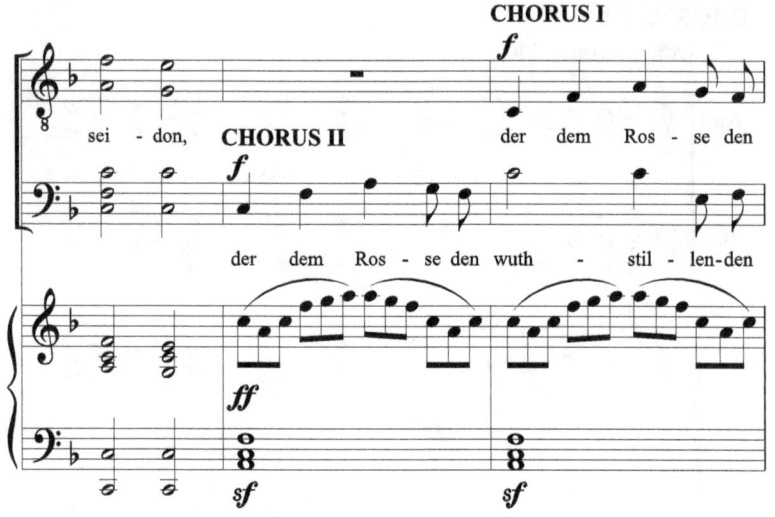

EXAMPLE 5.5 (Continued)

Line 710 O Kronos' Sohn, du hobst es ja
Zu diesem Preis, hehrer Gott Poseidon,
Der dem Rosse den wuthstillenden Zügel
Am ersten umwarf auf diesen Wegen.

O, son of Cronus, you enthroned [this land]
in such glory, exalted Lord Poseidon,
who was the first in these parts
to control horses with the taming bit.

This music coincides with two lines (ll. 710–711) that, in Donner's translation, directly address Poseidon using the second-person pronoun and thus constitute the only instance in this ode where a god is addressed as such. Moreover, this passage is set in relief through the use of a texture that contrasts markedly with that of the music surrounding it. The measures leading up to this point include a repeated triplet figure in the strings that gives way to more static rhythms at the onset of the "chorale," and those immediately following it feature a return to the opening thematic gesture of the piece, heard in imitation between the two choruses (mm. 137–138). Still further weight is lent to this chorale-like passage by the six-measure dominant pedal that precedes it. This increase in tension, which is underscored by an orchestral crescendo from piano to fortissimo, culminates in the arrival on the tonic F major, highlighting not only the textural and rhythmic shift that occurs at this point but also hinting at the impassioned nature with which the chorus seems to address these words of praise to Poseidon.

A similar chorale-like passage occurs in the play's second stasimon (No. 5), during which the chorus envisions the ongoing Athenian military campaign to rescue Oedipus' daughters from Theban soldiers. Prevented by age from taking part in the battle, the elders express their wish to join the fighting and in the final stanza offer up a prayer for victory that begins with an invocation of Zeus as the omnipotent, sovereign ruler of the gods. The first strophic pair features music in D minor that possesses a distinctly martial character and at

EXAMPLE 5.6 Mendelssohn, *Oedipus at Colonus*, No. 5, mm. 115–127.

EXAMPLE 5.6 (Continued)

times seems to evoke the galloping of horses. By contrast, the music of the second strophe, which includes several iterations of a heroic ascending-fourth gesture, turns to the parallel major and takes on a triumphant quality, perhaps as a way of foreshadowing an Athenian victory.

Mendelssohn's setting of the corresponding antistrophe retains this general tone, but opens with a largely unaccompanied passage for full chorus that is reminiscent of a Protestant chorale (mm. 115–127; example 5.6). This passage sets the first three lines of the prayer uttered to Zeus, while its fourth and final line is set in a similar fashion but with a less uniform rhythm and a continuous orchestral accompaniment throughout (mm. 128–134). The ascending fourth in the orchestra that precedes the chorale-like music and punctuates the ends of the first two phrases provides a clear motivic link to the previous stanza, thus evoking a sense of strength and heroism that here can be ascribed to the power of Zeus. Likewise, what follows the chorale passage constitutes a return of thematic material first presented in the second strophe, which in turn is followed by an expansive coda-like section with imitative writing that further exemplifies the sacred patina covering the work as a whole.

In each of these two instances, Mendelssohn's aim was to use chorale-like music to create a sense of ritual for those moments in Sophocles' play—or at least Donner's rendering of it—when the chorus directly addresses one of the many gods invoked throughout the tragedy. The composer's association with the chorale is, of course, well known. Aside from completing several chorale cantatas in the 1830s, he also employed traditional Lutheran chorales in such works as the "Reformation" Symphony, *St. Paul*, and the *Lobgesang*, while in others, including the Piano Trio in C Minor and *Elijah*, he devised his own. Although critics and scholars have not always look favorably upon these choices, most agree that Mendelssohn's goal was to lend his music a self-consciously religious tone.[44] In the case of *Oedipus*, the chorale-like music not only helps to convey the "profound religious feeling" that Klingemann detected in the play but also invokes a "modern" Christian tradition that reaches back to Luther and includes the sacred music of J. S. Bach. In other words, Mendelssohn uses music to impose a feeling of ritual on the utterance of a collective prayer by momentarily tapping into the power of the Protestant chorale as a devotional and liturgical symbol with strong cultural resonances. Moreover, these chorale-like passages can be understood as part of the composer's attempt to lend a conspicuously Christian element to an otherwise pagan drama—in effect translating ancient pagan rituals into modern Christian ones. In this way his music engages in a strategy similar to the one that led Tieck to propose a Christian reading of *Antigone* (and perhaps also *Oedipus*) while at the same time resonating with Friedrich Wilhelm's attempts to transform the Prussian capital into the cultural centerpiece of his envisioned Christian-German monarchy.

The two remaining stasima set by Mendelssohn assume an elevated, quasi-sacred character but without any obvious musical emblems of the kind encountered in the first two stasima. In the play's third stasimon, which occurs after the revelation that Polynices has come as a supplicant seeking forgiveness from his father, the chorus muses on the pain and suffering that accompanies old age, indirectly invoking Oedipus as evidence of life's downward trajectory. Somewhat unusually, this ode consists of three lyric stanzas: a matching strophe-antistrophe pair followed by a third, independent stanza. Mendelssohn responds by setting each of the two stanzas that make up the initial strophic pair to the same music, employing an entirely unison vocal line in G minor with frequent repeated notes and a sparse orchestral accompaniment.

By contrast, the final stanza—labeled a "Schlussgesang" in both Donner's translation and Mendelssohn's score—turns to the parallel major and introduces new music that is mostly written in four- or five-part harmony. Moreover, this music strikes a markedly brighter, more affirmative tone than the austere, almost dirge-like music of the first strophic pair, and it does so despite the fact that the elders continue to dwell on the loneliness and despair that comes with old age. And yet the chorus is mistaken when it refers to such despair as an inevitable outcome of one's later life, at least insofar as they are referring specifically to Oedipus. As William Scott has pointed out, Oedipus does not "find himself overcome by the waves of trouble foreseen by the chorus at the close of its ode."[45] Indeed, Oedipus is ultimately able to transcend mortal weakness through his transformation into a semi-divine cult figure and protector of Athens. By concluding his setting with a G-major passage tinged with only the occasional hint of modal mixture, Mendelssohn seems to be pointing ahead to Oedipus' miraculous death and suggesting his triumph over the pain and suffering that ordinarily comes in the final phases of life. He is also, of course, foreshadowing the work's larger modal shift from D minor to D major, a move that itself reflects Oedipus' heroic transformation through death.

The fourth and final stasimon occurs immediately after Oedipus departs the stage, led by divine guidance to the appointed place of his death. With Theseus, Antigone, and Ismene following his lead, the chorus is left to sing a short two-stanza ode in which they commend Oedipus to the gods of the underworld. Mendelssohn's setting of this prayer (No. 8), which includes some of the most beautiful music in the entire work, features lush four-part writing in A-flat major scored for TTBB soloists in the first stanza with the addition of full chorus in the second. This opulent writing evokes the rich tradition of German part-song and, within the limited context of Mendelssohn's music to Greek tragedy, recalls the "Ode to Eros" from *Antigone*, which was scored exclusively for soloists and also set a single strophic pair using essentially the same music for each stanza. But whereas the "Ode to Eros" is predominantly unaccompanied, the prayer for Oedipus includes a mostly string accompaniment that contributes to the lush texture. Another notable difference concerns the far more frequent presence of modal mixture in the *Oedipus* chorus, perhaps intended to achieve a certain lament-like quality. One example of this tendency occurs when the elders invoke the god Aidoneus (better known as Hades), the twofold iteration of whose name employs the unison, repeated-note idiom encountered elsewhere in the score and is punctuated by a minor tonic and dominant chord, respectively. Both the use of an orchestral accompaniment and the presence of modal mixture serve to undermine the association of this music with the secular part-song, which was often unaccompanied and generally lacked the sort of harmonic complexity found here. In this way, Mendelssohn succeeds in maintaining the elevated tone that characterizes the music of *Oedipus* as a whole.

It may be recalled from the above discussion of lyric dialogue that the work's final number corresponds to a lengthy kommos for Antigone, Ismene, and the chorus followed by a series of anapestic lines that bring the play to its conclusion. This anapestic passage, set initially as melodrama for Antigone and Theseus, begins with the entrance of the latter, who tells the two sisters to stop weeping and reminds them that, for Oedipus, death was a welcome gift. Refusing Antigone's request to see her father's grave (lest Athens be denied the protection promised by Oedipus), Theseus agrees to help her and her sister return to Thebes so that they may attempt to prevent the bloodshed between their two brothers. At this point the chorus utters the final lines of the play, directed at the two sisters and given below in Donner's translation:

> So laßt denn ab, und der Klag' Ausruf
> Weckt länger nicht mehr:
> Dies Wort ist heilig und wahrhaft!

> Thus let us cease lamenting, and raise
> the cry of sorrow no longer.
> These words are holy and true!

Mendelssohn set these lines as a sixteen-bar *adagio maestoso* intended to convey the triumph of Oedipus' transformative death, the first seven bars of which are shown in example 5.7a. This sense of triumph is conveyed not only by the character of the music but also by its D-major tonality, which, from the standpoint of both this number and the work as a whole, represents the heroic transformation of D minor into the parallel major—a move that was already foreshadowed by the four numbers in the score that followed a similar trajectory from minor to major (Nos. 1, 5, 6, and 7).

This final passage, in both its feels and its function relative to the work as a whole, seems vaguely reminiscent of the concluding *allegro maestoso assai* of the "Scottish" Symphony. Perhaps even more significantly, it also seems to contain faint echoes of the "Hallelujah" chorus from Handel's *Messiah*, with which it shares its key (example 5.7b). Intentional or not, this allusion hints

EXAMPLE 5.7A Mendelssohn, *Oedipus at Colonus*, No. 9, mm. 67–73.

EXAMPLE 5.7B Handel, *Messiah*, "Hallelujah Chorus," mm. 38–40.

at the pervasiveness of the elevated, quasi-sacred tone that runs throughout this work. And to the extent that it was deliberate, this musical reference may have been Mendelssohn's way of suggesting that, just as Christ died to redeem humanity, so Oedipus' death casts him as a "savior" for the city of Athens. Seen from this vantage point, the conclusion of Mendelssohn's *Oedipus* offers yet another instance of how the work's evocation of the sacred is marked as specifically Christian in nature.

Between Christian and Pagan

Aside from both the religious elements of the play and the sociopolitical agenda of Friedrich Wilhelm, Mendelssohn's impulse to infuse this music with an element of the sacred (read: Christian) appears to have stemmed from a more broadly aesthetic aim of reconciling ancient Greek civic and cultural values with those of modern Europe. As we saw in the first two chapters, such an objective was in many ways a defining feature of the eighteenth- and nineteenth-century German attempt at appropriating classical antiquity. In a provocative essay exploring the composer's aesthetic views, Leon Botstein suggests that we look to the Berlin architect Karl Friedrich Schinkel for clues to understanding the origins of Mendelssohn's neoclassical outlook. Botstein claims that, particularly in his formative years, Mendelssohn appears to have been influenced by Schinkel's celebration of the Greek civic ideal through modern German architecture, and he draws a parallel between the ways in which these two men "bridged overt neoclassicism with a newer Romantic sensibility."[46] As Barry Bergdoll has argued, Schinkel viewed architecture as the expression of a cultural and ethical imperative geared toward achieving "a synthesis between the daily civic life of the ancients... and the spirituality of Christianity."[47] Botstein echoes this point and uses it to suggest a fundamental affinity between these two early nineteenth-century figures: "The project of a synthesis between the classical humanism of antiquity and modern German spirituality that defined Schinkel's work... are mirrored in Mendelssohn's tireless engagement with music as a civic, religious, and political enterprise."[48]

This sort of engagement with music is wholly evident in Mendelssohn's two settings of Sophoclean tragedy, as is the quest for some meaningful form of reconciliation between ancient and modern. These aesthetic goals, which reflect a general neo-humanist stance characteristic of many German artists and intellectuals of the early nineteenth century, provide a framework for understanding the evocations of Christian ritual and musical traditions found in Mendelssohn's score to *Oedipus at Colonus*. Just as one might view Schinkel's classically inspired Altes Museum of 1830—strategically placed adjacent to both the royal palace and the central Protestant cathedral in Berlin—as emblematic of a desired synthesis between ancient (pagan) and modern (Christian) civic and religious values, so too one might regard Mendelssohn's *Oedipus at Colonus* as a sonic manifestation of this same tendency. Moreover, as we shall see in the following chapter, even as the trend of staging Greek tragedy with music moved southward to Munich in the early 1850s, the same confluence of political, cultural, and religious concerns that so decisively shaped its emergence in Protestant Prussia would continue to inform its later development in Catholic Bavaria.

CHAPTER SIX | Lachner and the Emergence of a New Athens

O**N NOVEMBER 28, 1851**, the Royal Court and National Theater of Munich staged a much-anticipated production of Sophocles' *Antigone* in celebration of the fortieth birthday of King Maximilian II. Like the Prussian court production a decade earlier, this one featured Mendelssohn's by now widely known music and also entailed an effort to re-create the ancient playing space. This ambitious undertaking by the recently installed court theater director Franz von Dingelstedt (1814–81) brought together some of Munich's most distinguished artists and intellectuals, including the court composer Franz Lachner (1803–90), who directed the music; the renowned architect Leo von Klenze (1784–1864), who led the stage reconstruction and created the set; the painter Wilhelm von Kaulbach (1805–74), who designed the costumes; and the classical philologist Friedrich Thiersch (1784–1860), who served as scholarly advisor and made changes to the German translation by Johann Jakob Donner.

Despite—or perhaps because of—the many similar performances of *Antigone* that had occurred in Germany and elsewhere over the past decade, this production generated much excitement in the Bavarian capital. On the day of the premiere, the *Bayerische Landbote* published the first of a five-part installment that addressed, among other things, the expectations surrounding the upcoming performance and the significance of Sophocles' play.[1] The anonymous author of these incisive essays noted in a supplement to the December 2 issue that many of those who attended the sold-out premiere were also present at the encore of November 30, and that tickets for a third performance were already sold out.[2] By all accounts, the production was a stunning success. A correspondent for the *Allgemeine Zeitung* (Augsburg) claimed that it had surpassed all others through its "meticulousness and authenticity" [Fleiß und Treue], adding that it was certain to live on in the annals of local theater for some time to come.[3] In a second report that appeared two days later, the author marveled at the audience's response to the two-and-a-half-hour performance: "Never before has one seen the public here watch a theatrical production with more heartfelt suspense, more rapt attentiveness, or more circumspect calm."[4] Another reviewer described the audience's reaction as "dignified" and "solemn," and compared exiting the theater at the end of the performance to leaving a church service.[5]

Many contemporary observers viewed this production as a manifestation of the reformist stance adopted by Dingelstedt, who had been appointed director of the Munich court theater earlier that same year.[6] In a review of the encore performance for the *Neueste Nachrichten*, the author described Dingelstedt as the long-awaited agent of reform for spoken theater in Munich.[7] The subsequent issue featured yet another discussion of *Antigone*, this one followed by a consideration of all the productions staged at the court theater that month. As a result of the theater's "insightful" leadership, the author contends, nearly all of the eighteen theatrical and operatic representations performed in November were of "classic" works, by which he appears to mean simply a dramatic or literary work of the highest caliber.[8] For at least one critic, the production of *Antigone* held the promise of lasting theatrical reform in Munich. Aligning this production more with opera than with spoken theater, this author issued a call for the performance of all three plays comprising Sophocles' Theban trilogy (*Oedipus the King*, *Oedipus at Colonus*, and *Antigone*), and suggested, somewhat prophetically, that Lachner compose music for *Oedipus the King*. The author went on to make the bold claim that such an undertaking would provide the foundation for a complete transformation of modern opera, though unfortunately this point is never elaborated upon further.[9]

Apart from Dingelstedt's ostensible goal of theater reform, the Bavarian court production of *Antigone* would have resonated with the sustained and highly visible efforts on the part of the previous king, Ludwig I, to shape Munich into a "New Athens." Among the results of this project were several neoclassical structures that helped to redefine the Munich landscape and symbolized a vital link between ancient Greece and a Bavarian culture increasingly viewed from within as an important component in the creation of a pan-German national identity. The present chapter explores the revival of Greek tragedy in Munich in light of the city's unique relationship to both ancient and modern Greece. It is this relationship that ultimately provides a key to understanding the enthusiasm surrounding the 1851 *Antigone*, as well as the impulse to stage an original production of *Oedipus the King* the following year.

Not unlike the case of Friedrich Wilhelm IV's Prussia, the ties between Bavarian and Greek culture were rooted to a large degree in the desire of a highly cultivated monarch to transform his seat of power into a shining beacon of German art and learning. In comparison to his Prussian counterpart, however, Ludwig I had pursued this project in a manner that more overtly fostered a cultural identification with the Greeks, and it was his example that made such a lasting impression on his son, Maximilian II, under whom the revival of Greek tragedy would occur. Maximilian's appointment of Dingelstedt as director of the court theater played a crucial role in finally bringing about the performance of Greek tragedy in Munich and can be viewed as part of the new king's attempt to continue along the path established by his father.

Even more important than the 1851 Munich production of *Antigone*—at least where the larger German revival of Greek tragedy is concerned—was the production exactly one year later of Sophocles' *Oedipus the King* with music by Franz Lachner. Although Lachner's approach is heavily indebted to Mendelssohn's, his willingness to regularly provide music for those parts of the play not originally sung or chanted results in a score that is more closely aligned with the traditional understanding of incidental music. In other words, even as Lachner employed melodrama and choral recitative in a manner that was by now customary for music written to accompany such revivals of Greek tragedy, he looked to these musical devices less as a means of evoking aspects of ancient drama and more as a way of creating a sense of heightened drama in the midst of an otherwise spoken passage of text. Lachner's *Oedipus the King* is thus not unlike Taubert's *Medea*, insofar as both works underscore the degree to which music for Greek stage revivals had emerged as a quasi-independent genre with a set of conventions that had grown increasingly removed from their original aims. Moreover, like Mendelssohn's settings of classical drama but to an even greater degree, Lachner's music is firmly rooted in a sacred idiom, the aim of which is not only to reflect the elevated nature of Greek tragedy but also to effect a general reconciliation of the ancient Greek religious values at the core of Sophocles' tragedy with the Christian ones upheld by nineteenth-century German culture.

'Athens on the Isar'

The link in the nineteenth century between Greece and Bavaria owes much of its strength to the cultural and political aspirations of Ludwig I. Initially as crown prince and then as king from 1825 until his abdication of the throne in 1848, Ludwig waged a relentless campaign to transform Munich from a sleepy, provincial capital with barely 50,000 residents into an artistic and cultural center on par with such vibrant European cities as London, Paris, and Rome. This quest was no doubt inspired in large part by the city's newfound status as a royal seat. Not until 1806, through an alliance with Napoleon, was the Wittelsbach dynasty granted control over Bavaria, which then became a kingdom. As Ludwig once declared, his hope was to create a city such that it would be impossible to think of Germany without also thinking of Munich.[10] A key element of this ambitious project involved the erection in both the capital and elsewhere in Bavaria of grand buildings and monuments that drew from an array of historical styles.

The centerpiece of this immense architectural program was the Ludwigstrasse, an expansive boulevard that juts out from the royal palace in what constitutes a northward expansion of the city beyond its old medieval walls.[11] Originally conceived by the architect Klenze, it was lined on either side with civic, religious, and residential structures built beginning in 1816 according to plans by Klenze himself and the architect Friedrich von Gärtner. Klenze was responsible for the large apartment buildings in neo-Renaissance style that sprang up on the mostly residential southern end of the street. Gärtner, who essentially took over work on the Ludwigstrasse starting in the late 1820s, was commissioned to design several public or semi-public buildings on the northern end of the street, including the Ludwigskirche (1829–44) and the Bavarian State Library (1832–43). These and a host of other adjacent buildings were designed in a Romanesque Revival style known in Germany as the *Rundbogenstil*, or round-arched style, which grew in popularity over the next several decades and was embraced by influential German architects in search of a national style.[12]

Many of the structures built under Ludwig I were neoclassical in design and thus reflect his attempt to turn the Bavarian capital into a veritable "Athens on the Isar," as some observers at the time described the city. Ludwig himself is reported to have said, "I will not rest until Munich looks like Athens."[13] To accomplish this task, he turned to Klenze. Appointed by Ludwig as *Hofbaumeister* in 1816, Klenze shared with the then-crown prince an intense devotion to Greek antiquity. In a letter from 1817, he wrote to Ludwig explaining that, "Just as Palladio became great and immortal through an inspired adaptation of Roman architecture to the exigencies of his own time and country, I shall attempt to do likewise with the works of the Greeks."[14]

One of Klenze's first projects in Munich was the Glyptothek (1816–30), a sculpture gallery open to the public that featured an elegant neoclassical facade appropriate for its vast display of antique pieces. Soon thereafter followed the Alte Pinakothek (1826–36), designed in a neo-Renaissance style and built to house the Wittelsbach collection of paintings, which was also accessible to the public. Like Schinkel's Altes Museum (1830) in Berlin, these institutions formed part of a new state-sponsored effort to educate the growing bourgeois public through aesthetic representation—in this case filtered through a historical consciousness marked by a desire to appropriate the legacy of past cultural achievements. That both the Glyptothek and the Altes Museum were neoclassical in design suggests the degree to which this endeavor was bound up with neo-humanist aims of erecting a modern German culture on the foundations of an ancient Greek artistic and cultural ideal.

Ludwig also turned to Klenze for the creation of several public monuments intended not only to glorify Bavaria and its reigning dynasty but also to foster a sense of Bavarian and ultimately German identity. At Ludwig's prompting, the Munich Academy announced a competition in 1814 for the design of, among other structures, a German national monument. Ludwig had specified that it be "in the purest antique style, in accordance with the most beautiful patterns of the ancient Greek temple."[15] The idea for such a monument came in 1807, when Ludwig was filled with nationalistic fervor during a visit to French-occupied Berlin.[16] He immediately began soliciting plans for a monument—to be known as the Walhalla—that would display the busts of Germany's most celebrated political, cultural, and religious figures. Eager to see several submissions, Ludwig came up with the idea of a competition, though no formal winner was ever declared. The Walhalla was eventually built near the city of Regensburg between 1830 and 1842 according to a design by Klenze modeled on the Parthenon of Athens. Set amid a picturesque landscape on a site perched high above the Danube, the Walhalla features a lavish marble interior that contains the busts of such notable German figures as Dürer, Gutenberg, Goethe, Schiller, Handel, Mozart, and Beethoven, along with a host of important rulers.

Similar monuments followed, most of whose origins date back to the king's time as crown prince. Both the Feldhernnhalle (Field Marshall's Hall, 1841–43), built by Gärtner at the southern end of the Ludwigstrasse, and the Ruhmeshalle (Hall of Fame, 1843–54), designed by Klenze and erected on a slope overlooking Munich's Theresienwiese, explicitly celebrated the achievements of an increasingly influential Bavaria. The former was built in honor of famous commanders in the Bavarian army and clearly evokes the fourteenth-century Loggia dei Lanzi in Florence, while the latter houses the busts of famous Bavarians within the walls of an imposing neoclassical structure in front of which stands a colossal bronze statue of a female Bavaria.

Yet another monument commissioned by Ludwig, the Befreiungshalle (Hall of Liberation, 1842–63), was built to commemorate the Wars of Liberation against Napoleon. Begun by Gärtner but completed by Klenze in the form of a classically inspired rotunda, it was erected in the countryside near the town of Kelheim, not far from the Walhalla, on a hill overlooking the confluence of the Danube and Altmühl rivers. Related to such memorial structures were the monumental gates that Ludwig had built in Munich. Gärtner's Siegestor (Victory Gate, 1843–52), dedicated to the Bavarian army, marks the northern end of the Ludwigstrasse and recalls the Arch of Constantine in Rome. Adjacent to the Glyptothek is Klenze's Propyläen (1846–60), which he modeled on the Propyläen of the Athenian Acropolis and which stands as a memorial to the Greek War of Independence fought between 1821 and 1830.

The monuments commissioned by Ludwig, and to a lesser degree the public museums established during his reign, made significant contributions to a burgeoning sense of German national identity. By commemorating important people and events, these structures reminded Germans of their collective heritage and shared historical past. The neoclassical architecture characteristic of so many of them additionally served to underscore the widely perceived affinity between Greek and German culture, while at the same time affirming Germany's self-appointed task of redeeming the modern world through its extraordinary cultural achievements. The fact that, in 1814, Ludwig had insisted that his proposed German national monument be built in imitation of a Greek temple offers perhaps the strongest evidence that German identity was being fashioned to a considerable degree out of the spirit of ancient Greece. He later revealed his belief in the broader cultural significance of the Walhalla when he explained that it was created in order that "the German might emerge from it more German and better than when he arrived."[17] Such projects can ultimately be seen as part of a larger trend in the decades after Napoleon's defeat aimed at raising the level of cultural and historical consciousness by openly celebrating the German legacy in both the artistic and political realms.

As we have seen, Ludwig's own efforts along these lines were fueled partly by a cultural nationalism born of the threat to German sovereignty posed by Napoleonic rule. Yet, like Prussia's Friedrich Wilhelm IV, he keenly recognized the need to create a strong monarchical tradition and win a certain measure of popular support. His extensive building campaign and his decision to establish public museums are to be understood as attempts to gain popular appeal for a fledging monarchy at a time when European rulers were involved in the task of carefully restoring elements of the old political order.[18]

Indeed, Ludwig was as much concerned with cultivating a specifically Bavarian identity as he was a broadly German one.[19] His challenge on this front was to reconcile local and regional allegiances with his notion of a more centralized state, all the while fostering loyalty to both the German and the Bavarian *Vaterland* at a time when one's identity as, say, a Prussian, a Saxon, or a Hanoverian generally ran far deeper than one's identity as a German in a roughly national sense. Monuments such as the Ruhmeshalle and the Siegestor, which were built as tributes to Bavarian cultural and military achievements, became symbols of a new Bavaria. Ludwig also sought to protect the kingdom's interests against the dominance of Austria and Prussia within the German Confederation, and in this sense, his goal of establishing Munich as the center of German culture can be seen as an attempt by Catholic Bavaria to undermine the nationalist claims of Protestant Prussia.

By placing so much of his focus on the creation of new buildings and memorials, Ludwig contributed indirectly to an ongoing controversy concerning the relationship of contemporary architecture to the architecture of various historical eras. In 1828, the architect Heinrich Hübsch (1795–1863) published a pamphlet titled *In welchem Stil sollen wir bauen?* (*In What Style Should We Build?*) that reverberated widely and became the source of much subsequent debate.[20] In it, he rejected the "lifeless imitation of classical antiquity" in favor of a *Rundbogenstil* rooted in his conception of architecture as a functional art defined by the limitations of materials, technology, climate, and cultural values specific to a given time and place.

More important than his own prescriptions for modern German architecture, however, is the perspective that his work reveals. Hübsch was essentially responding to the rise of historicism, which for architecture meant that the normative classicism of the late eighteenth and early nineteenth centuries had begun to face increasing competition from other past forms including Gothic, Renaissance, and even Egyptian styles. Architects could now choose from a vast array of available styles rather than conforming to a single dominant style, as had traditionally been the case. As James Garratt has pointed out, this situation bears a striking parallel to the field of music, in which composers began to experiment in the early part of the nineteenth century with imitating and in some cases combining a range of previous musical styles, most notably those of the Renaissance and Baroque eras.[21] The question "in what style should we compose?" would have been of particular relevance to a composer involved in the revival of Greek tragedy, especially since the productions being staged were marked by such a strong historicist impulse.

As we have seen, the buildings commissioned by Ludwig I during the first half of the nineteenth century were variously designed in accordance with classical, Romanesque, and Renaissance principles, among those of other periods. Indeed, Ludwig's Munich was often singled out as a living monument to architectural history. As one commentator put it, writing in 1845: "Whoever strolls around Munich...has the best opportunity to become acquainted with the entire history of architecture from the present back to Egyptian art. This stone artistic atlas remains constantly in view."[22] In contrast to Hübsch, Ludwig embraced a view of architecture whereby all historical styles retained some validity, though he appears to have favored that of ancient Greece, which he once described as the "throne of eternal, unparalleled art."[23] It was undoubtedly Ludwig's enthusiasm for ancient Greece that cemented his bond with Klenze, for whom Greek architecture constituted a universal norm.[24] In Klenze's words, "There is only one true art and that is the art of the Greeks."[25]

Although he never fulfilled his lifelong desire to visit Greece, Ludwig's time in Italy fueled his passion for classical culture and helped to lay the foundation for the crown prince's robust philhellenism in response to the Greek War of Independence (1821–30).[26] Unlike many of his royal counterparts, Ludwig openly backed the cause of Greek liberation from the Ottoman Empire.[27] In 1821, Crown Prince Ludwig assumed the role of royal protector for the Munich *Griechenverein*, one of many groups established throughout Europe to help organize efforts in support of the Greek cause. Although his father had been reluctant to do so, Ludwig provided both financial and military support to the Greeks after he ascended the throne in 1825. The three major European powers, England, France, and Russia, eventually became involved in the conflict, siding with the Greeks out of self-interest and ultimately helping to ensure a Greek victory. The three powers finally determined that Greece should be an independent state under their protection and with a monarch of their choosing from among the ruling dynasties of Europe. After the refusal of both Prince Leopold of Saxony-Coburg and Ludwig's brother Prince Karl, Ludwig began to advance a case for his second son Otto, who eventually assumed the Greek throne in 1832 at the age of seventeen, reigning for some thirty years. Thus did King Ludwig's ardent passion for ancient Greek culture and his intense devotion to the cause of Greek liberty manifest itself in a strong political and cultural bond between a rising Bavaria and a newly independent Greece under the immediate control of a Wittelsbach.

Greek Tragedy as Cultural Reform

In 1848, amid revolutionary unrest in Europe, King Ludwig I of Bavaria abdicated the throne to his son Maximilian II. Maximilian, like his father, was a cultured intellectual who once quipped that he would have become a professor had he not been destined for the crown. The new king initiated several ambitious projects that, while reflective of his own personal taste and political agenda, were undertaken in the same spirit of cultural reform embraced by Ludwig I. As early as 1832, Maximilian had proposed the idea of erecting a building of national significance on a site in Munich overlooking the Isar River. His self-professed aim was to create something that would "enhance the people's national and monarchist sentiments," and by the time he assumed the throne, this generalized vision had morphed into the idea of an educational institution whose mission would be to further the intellectual development of Bavaria's most promising young students.[28]

After rejecting initial plans for the Maximilianeum, as the building would come to be known, King Maximilian sponsored an international design competition in 1850. His call for a structure that combined the architectural achievements of the past with aspects of the Gothic style in particular to create an original, essentially Germanic style outlined the tenets of what would later come to be known as the *Maximilianstil*. Work on the Maximilianeum began in 1851 in accordance with plans by the architect Friedrich Bürklein and dragged on until 1874—a full decade after King Maximilian's untimely death, prior to which he had announced major changes to Bürklein's original design.[29]

The year 1851 also saw the groundbreaking for what would eventually become the Maximilianstrasse, a broad avenue in central Munich lined with buildings commissioned by the new king that reflected both his desire to foster a German national style and his preference for Gothic architecture in favor of the classical style so beloved by his father. Despite this difference in taste, Maximilian continued to lend generous sums of money to Ludwig's many unfinished building projects, bringing about the completion of some of the latter's most defining contributions to the Bavarian landscape, including the Befreiungshalle, the Ruhmeshalle, the Pinakothek, and the Siegestor.

King Maximilian also turned his attention to furthering the cultural development of Bavaria in the years following his accession to the throne. Thus he enticed several well-known cultural figures—mostly poets who have since fallen into obscurity—to accept positions at the Bavarian court, of whom Dingelstedt is a notable example. He also appointed several esteemed scholars to the University of Munich, which Ludwig had moved from Landshut to the Bavarian capital in 1825. In 1852, Maximilian established the Germanisches Nationalmuseum in Nuremberg and, three years later, the Bayerisches Nationalmuseum in Munich. Both offer examples of the way in which he attempted to foster a sense of Bavarian and German national identity in hopes of raising Bavaria's cultural status within the collective consciousness of a German *Kulturstaat*.

To this end, King Maximilian turned his attention to the court theater, and on the advice of one his most trusted advisors, looked to Dingelstedt as a potential director.[30] The first known mention of this prospect comes in a letter to Dingelstedt dated October 18, 1850, written by his friend Gustav Kolb, editor of the venerable *Allgemeine Zeitung*. It reads in part: "In Munich these days, questions are focused on you and whether you would be inclined to take over the direction of the local court theater. King Max, who hopes to appoint famous poets to his court and distinguished scholars to the university, would also like to include the theater among his reform efforts."[31] In December of that year, Dingelstedt traveled to Munich to oversee the production of one of his own works, and on the last day of the month, he received an official offer from the court to assume the directorship of the theater for a provisional period of three to five years. He arrived in Munich late the following month and assumed his post amid increasing controversy between those who supported his appointment and those, mostly conservative Catholics, who opposed it because of the liberal tone of his early works—tensions that would continue to plague and eventually derail his six-year tenure at the Bavarian court.

King Maximilian II clearly viewed the theater as one of the most effective ways to attain his goal of furthering Bavaria's collective *Bildung*. As he explained in a letter of December 21, 1851 to the philosopher Friedrich Schelling, he sought to elevate the theater by "gradually bringing the best ancient and modern works to [the stage]."[32] Such an objective is to be understood in light of the generally unfavorable view of the Munich court theater shared by many Germans in the decades leading up to Dingelstedt's appointment. During this period, its repertory of spoken drama was stale and unimaginative, consisting of popular French plays in German translation supplemented by a steady diet of works by minor Viennese and in some cases Bavarian playwrights. It was not until 1849 that the theater first performed Shakespeare, and prior to that, only six works of Goethe and ten of Schiller had been staged, totaling just over 100 performances. In 1850, a Munich correspondent for the Leipzig periodical *Europa* accused the court theater of choosing its repertory based solely on a work's potential for financial success, claiming that "no new play or opera is ever put before us until all of Germany has had its fill of it."[33] Nor was the level of execution particularly high. As the actor Carl Seydelmann concluded of the court theater following a brief residency in 1835: "It is irresponsible just how badly the available resources are being put to use."[34]

The king and his circle hoped that Dingelstedt would breathe new life into the court theater, though the task before him was no easy one. Wilhelm Dönniges, the royal confidante who had initially suggested Dingelstedt, explained to him that he should expect, at best, indifference from that segment of the Munich public not already hostile toward him. He went on to say: "Munich is generally much less interested in the theater than Vienna, Berlin, or Dresden. Your job is to arouse this interest, to establish a strong foothold for the theater, to gain a following among the personnel, to secure guest [performers] and new recruits, and to present new works."[35]

For his part, Dingelstedt had had little direct involvement with the theater up to this point in his career and was in many ways an unlikely choice. Born in Hesse in 1814, he had studied theology at the university in Marburg but decided against joining the clergy, instead becoming a teacher and pursuing a literary career on the side.[36] In 1836, he accepted a teaching post at a Gymnasium in Kassel, where he began to sympathize with the goals of the Young Germany movement and came into contact with some of its most prominent representatives, including Heinrich Heine, Heinrich Laube, and Karl Gutzkow. Due in large part to the increasingly satirical nature of his poetry, Dingelstedt was transferred to Fulda in 1838, but only three years later resigned from service to the Hessian state altogether. That same year he published his best-known work, a collection of highly satirical and politically charged lyric poems known as the *Lieder eines kosmopolitischen Nachtwächters (Songs of a Cosmopolitan Night Watchman)*. Dingelstedt subsequently turned to journalism, spending time in Augsburg, Paris, London, and Vienna, and writing frequently about the theater. Then, in 1843, he was appointed librarian and official reader to the king at the court of Württemberg in Stuttgart, where he remained until accepting the post in Munich.

Dingelstedt's strategy for reforming the Bavarian court theater appears to have been one of balancing the existing repertory with stage works of the highest caliber, both past and present. In April of 1851, roughly two months after arriving in Munich, he staged a production of Friedrich Hebbel's *Judith*, followed one month later by a production of the comedy *Der geheime Agent (The Secret Agent)* by the popular German writer Friedrich Hackländer. These two works, each by a respected contemporary playwright, paved the way for Dingelstedt's even more ambitious production of *Antigone* in the fall of that year. Dingelstedt continued along this path in 1852, mounting not only a production of Sophocles' *Oedipus the King* but also such celebrated works as Schiller's *Wallenstein*, Goethe's *Iphigenie* and *Egmont*, Calderon's *The Doctor of His Own Honor*, and Racine's *Phaedra*, in addition to five plays by Shakespeare, including *Romeo and Juliet* and *A Midsummer Night's Dream*.

As far as we can tell, the impulse to stage Greek tragedy originated with Dingelstedt himself, who evidently saw it as a way of publicly declaring his intention to initiate theatrical reform. Dingelstedt later recalled of his experience in Munich: "Only once I had brought *Antigone* to the stage...did I really feel like I was firm in the saddle with a steady hold of the reins."[37] He was undoubtedly aware of the success garnered by the Prussian court production of the play and in particular by Mendelssohn's music, and he presumably felt that a successful production of *Antigone* along similar lines would call attention to the theatrical reform underway in Bavaria. Dingelstedt may have also detected a certain irony in the fact that, despite its strong cultural and political ties to Greece, Munich remained one of the few major cities in Germany where a production of *Antigone* had yet to occur. It was perhaps because of Munich's reputation as an "Athens on the Isar" that Dingelstedt felt compelled to make his own contribution to the German revival of Greek tragedy by staging a production of *Oedipus the King*—the one work in Sophocles' Theban cycle for which no recent score existed.

Liberating Mendelssohn

The Munich production of *Oedipus the King* was conceived along the same lines as the court performance of *Antigone* staged one year earlier. Dingelstedt turned to Donner's translation of the play, which had appeared in 1850 in a newly revised third edition. Yet at what appears to have been the instigation of Thiersch, the renowned classicist who served as scholarly advisor to the production, several passages of the Donner were replaced with ones taken from a translation first published in 1835 by the Leipzig philologist Johannes Minckwitz.[38]

Sophocles' play, the events of which precede those of *Oedipus at Colonus* and *Antigone*, dramatizes Oedipus' stunning fall from power and influence. As an infant, Oedipus had been left to die in the elements by his parents King Laius and Queen Jocasta of Thebes in an attempt to avoid fulfillment of a prophecy that the child would one day murder his father. Oedipus, however, was rescued by the king and queen of Corinth, with whom he lived until learning from the oracle at Delphi that he was destined to kill his father and marry his mother. Believing that this prophecy referred to the only parents he had ever known, Oedipus exiled himself from Corinth and while traveling on the road from Delphi met and killed a stranger (actually Laius) and his companions following an altercation. Thereafter he arrived in Thebes, which was suffering at the time under the grips of the monstrous Sphinx. Oedipus solved the riddle of the Sphinx and spared the city from ruin, in return for which he was rewarded not only with its throne but also the hand of its recently widowed queen, with whom he fathered four children: Eteocles, Polynices, Ismene, and Antigone. At the outset of Sophocles' *Oedipus the King*, Thebes is once again suffering under a plague, this time for harboring the murderer of Laius. As the oracle at Delphi makes clear, the only solution is to find and then kill or expel the murderer, and it is during the course of the play that Oedipus comes to learn that the stranger he once killed was his father Laius, and that his wife is in reality his own mother. This revelation leads him to gouge out his own eyes, while Jocasta responds by committing suicide. At the end of the play, Oedipus is shown begging Thebes' new ruler, his brother-in-law Creon, to watch over his daughters and cast him out of the city so that he might wither away in the mountains outside of Thebes, just as his parents had intended years ago.

In what by the 1850s had become customary for such revivals of Greek drama, the stage of the Munich court theater was reconstructed along ancient lines, in this case with the help of the architect Klenze. Unusual for this production, however, were the number of extras, totaling no less than thirty-eight. Many of these roles, which included priests, servants, members of the king's retinue, and Thebans young and old, were given to dancers employed by the court ballet. One of the advantages of such a large cast was the ability to stage massive crowd scenes (such as the gathering of supplicants before the royal palace), which had become a hallmark of Dingelstedt's directorial style.[39] In line with this blatant concession to modern taste—Sophoclean drama would have used no more than three actors—was a similar expansion of the chorus, which comprised twenty performers instead of the traditional fifteen or, in the case of Mendelssohn's stage music, sixteen. Like Mendelssohn, Lachner restricted his chorus to male singers split evenly between tenors and basses and divided, according to ancient practice, into two half choruses. He also employed the same conventional orchestra as Mendelssohn, though with the rather unusual substitution of basset horn in place of clarinet and with an expanded percussion battery.

The king's choice of Lachner to provide the music for *Oedipus the King* was surely influenced by the fact that the composer had conducted the 1851 production of Mendelssohn's *Antigone*.[40] Born in 1803 to a musical family in the Bavarian town of Rain am Lech, Lachner had arrived in Munich in 1822 and settled there permanently in 1836 after spending time in Vienna and Berlin. Not long thereafter, he was appointed conductor of both the royal opera and chapel choir, and he soon established himself as one of the most influential musicians in Munich. In January of 1852, Lachner was granted the title *Generalmusikdirektor*—the first such title to be granted in Bavaria—as incentive to turn down a lucrative offer from the Vienna Court Opera. As Ulrich Konrad has suggested, Lachner may have viewed the request to write music for *Oedipus* as an opportunity to justify his recently conferred title.[41]

Lachner generally adopted Mendelssohn's approach to setting Greek tragedy and in so doing helped to further solidify the idea of such music as belonging to an autonomous genre with its own set of conventions. He looked specifically to Mendelssohn's *Antigone* as a model. Not only was this work by far the more popular of Mendelssohn's two Sophoclean settings, but it was also known to Lachner from his role as conductor for the 1851 Munich production. In addition to scoring his work for men's chorus and a conventional orchestra, Lachner also followed Mendelssohn's lead in employing a frequently unison vocal line along with a predominantly syllabic setting of the text. Likewise, he incorporated extended passages of choral recitative and melodrama, though unlike Mendelssohn, he appears to have done so without much concern for highlighting significant changes in the play's poetic meter. To a greater degree than either Mendelssohn or Taubert, Lachner made liberal use of melodrama as a means of heightening the dramatic action. His score thus includes several extended passages of melodrama that correspond to otherwise spoken verse. In this sense his work is more closely aligned with the traditional notion of incidental music, according to which the composer is generally free to set to music any part of the script deemed appropriate.

One notable example of such "free" melodrama occurs toward the end of the play, when a messenger arrives to deliver the horrifying news of Jocasta's suicide. In an obvious attempt to intensify the dramatic impact of this announcement, Lachner provides music for nearly the entire exchange between the messenger and the chorus, including the former's vivid description of Oedipus' self-mutilation (No. 10). Beginning with the statement that Jocasta is dead, the messenger's lines are punctuated by orchestral interjections that lend greater weight to the words being spoken, to which the chorus responds with recitative-like music. As the messenger begins his graphic narrative of Jocasta's suicide and Oedipus' own shocking actions, the accompanying music alternates between soft, sustained tremolos heard beneath the words and a series of vigorous motivic ideas played in between them, such as the descending chromatic idea that first appears in measure 22 of example 6.1. It is impossible to say for certain whether or not Lachner

EXAMPLE 6.1 Lachner, *Oedipus the King*, No. 10, mm. 14–30.

EXAMPLE 6.1 (Continued)

was aware that such passages deviated from Mendelssohn's model of restricting melodrama to lines of anapestic or lyric verse. Yet a mere glance at the metrical index included along with Donner's translation would have made it apparent which portions of the play were originally intended to have been sung and which were meant to have been spoken.

In another departure from Mendelssohn's model, Lachner includes a brief instrumental number that, like the overture, exists apart from the musical demands of the play (i.e., in accordance with what was known of ancient practice). The piece labeled No. 2 comprises a march that occurs immediately after the overture and is meant to accompany Oedipus (and his retinue) as he walks onto the stage to address the massive crowd that has gathered around the altar of the royal palace. Scored for flutes, basset horn, trumpets, cymbals, triangle, and tambourine, it clearly evokes the Turkish Janissary music that had long been used by composers to suggest military *topoi* and that in this case points to Oedipus' power as the King of Thebes while also hinting at the otherness of ancient Greece. Typical of a march, this music consists of short repeated gestures, pervasive dotted rhythms, and simple, mostly tonic-dominant harmonies, amounting to a mere twenty-eight measures centered on the key of C major. What distinguishes this piece from the even shorter number that accompanies Ismene's entrance in Mendelssohn's *Antigone* (No. 2a) is that, whereas Mendelssohn was prompted by a passage of anapestic verse whose function was to call attention to the arrival of the character, Lachner composed music to coincide with a moment in the play for which no text exists at all.

Yet, as with Taubert's *Medea*, the similarities of Lachner's *Oedipus* to Mendelssohn's settings of Greek tragedy far outweigh the differences. Perhaps the clearest manifestation of Lachner's indebtedness to his younger colleague comes in the overture to *Oedipus the King*, which in many ways recalls that of *Antigone*. Both works include an overture in C minor that opens with loud, dotted-rhythm gestures followed by a sudden drop in the dynamic level and the onset of a contrasting thematic idea heard in the strings. Moreover, the contrasting material in Lachner's score shares a similar melodic and rhythmic contour with Mendelssohn's and also features the use of imitative counterpoint (example 6.2; cf. example 2.1). These common traits suggest that Lachner was self-consciously alluding to Mendelssohn's *Antigone*, presumably as a way of both paying homage to and aligning his own score with what was seen at the time as a groundbreaking work in a new genre of stage music.

But whereas Mendelssohn's overture consists of a slow section and a fast one that can be described roughly as portraits of Creon and Antigone, respectively, Lachner's overture employs a tripartite scheme (ABA'). The middle section, which takes on the guise of a development, begins by presenting the opening material in the relative major, now heard in combination with dotted-rhythm gestures in the strings that evoke the French overture style. This reference not only lends the music a distinctly Baroque flavor that conjures up associations with the past, but it also hints at the grandeur and majesty of Oedipus as the ruling King of Thebes and thereby suggests the

Adagio quasi andante

EXAMPLE 6.2 Lachner, *Oedipus the King*, overture, mm. 1–12.

heights from which he will fall over the course of the play. Despite beginning in the relative major, this middle section quickly initiates a move to F minor, with the result that the only genuine respite from the minor mode of the overture comes toward the end of this middle section during a quiet passage in A-flat major that prepares for a return to the tonic and, along with it, a restatement of the plaintive theme presented in measure five.

Because of its almost exclusive use of the minor mode, as well as its motivic emphasis on both an ascending and descending semitone gesture, the overture to *Oedipus the King* is marked by an even more relentlessly somber and tragic character than that of its apparent model. The slow, solemn nature of the music heard in the A section (and its return) is clearly intended to foreshadow the stunning downfall of Oedipus and to suggest the pain and suffering that it brings to those around him. Thus, for example, the five-measure dominant pedal (mm. 17–21) that occurs near the outset of the piece and that manifests itself as a steady drumbeat of quarter notes played by pizzicato low strings and timpani creates a sense not only of the funereal but of the inexorability of the tragic fate that Oedipus seeks in vain to escape. Yet the establishment of such a dark mood represents only one of two significant tasks accomplished by the overture that set the tone for the remainder of the work. The other concerns a general tendency to gesture toward the music of the past, as we saw with the reference to the French overture. This general stylistic orientation lends the work a certain archaic quality, which in turn hints at the historical remoteness of ancient Greece itself.

Aside from its overture, Lachner's *Oedipus* includes fourteen additional numbers that correspond to the play's five lyric odes and two kommoi and that, as we have seen, also set extended passages of otherwise spoken iambic trimeter (see table 6.1, p.188).[42] Lachner's score generally lacks the stylistic diversity of Mendelssohn's *Antigone*, revealing instead a more relentlessly austere character. Thus while Mendelssohn composed choruses rooted in both sacred (or quasi-sacred) and secular idioms, Lachner generally avoided obvious stylistic references to the latter (the brief march discussed above being one of only a few notable exceptions).

The result is a work whose overall aesthetic is firmly aligned with that of elevated, quasi-sacred genres such as the oratorio and the cantata. This orientation was not lost on commentators of the day. As one reviewer for the *Allgemeine Zeitung* explained: "Concerning the general character of Lachner's music, it is no more Greek than that of Mendelssohn, but rather, in its melodic counters, harmonic progressions, and cadential formulae, is distinctly Christian and sacred."[43] One such example occurs in Lachner's setting of the parodos (No. 3), to be discussed later in more detail. Here, in the midst of the chorus's plea for divine intervention, the composer includes a hymn-like passage that invokes a religious spirit reminiscent of certain passages in Mendelssohn's *Oedipus at Colonus* (example 6.3).

On the one hand, the sacred overtones of Lachner's music can be seen as evidence of an attempt to suggest the gravity of Sophocles' play and the elevated nature of Greek drama more generally. On the other hand, this inclination seems to reflect the important role that religion plays in this tragedy in particular. For example, the lengthy parodos constitutes a prayer to the gods to deliver Thebes from its collective suffering, while several of the remaining stasima include references to the omniscience of the gods, the everlasting nature of divine law, the truth of the oracles, and the importance of religious worship. As the classical scholar R. W. B. Burton has noted with regard to the play's chorus of Theban elders: "Besides their loyalty to Oedipus and their devotion to their community, they emphasize and maintain the strong religious tone which is established in the prologue."[44] Moreover, not unlike Mendelssohn's use of music in *Oedipus at Colonus*, Lachner's sacred idiom can also be understood as an attempt to express the play's religious character through the medium of a "Christian" musical language and thus in some

EXAMPLE 6.3 Lachner, *Oedipus the King*, No. 3, mm. 61–68.

sense to translate the pagan values at the core of this ancient drama into distinctly modern terms.

Perhaps because he was more concerned with the evocation of a general, overarching mood—or because he viewed his score principally as a means of heightening the dramatic action—Lachner made no apparent effort to convey the play's poetic meter. To be sure, the mostly syllabic setting of the text produces a work in which the larger rhythmic values typically correspond to the "longs" and the smaller ones to the "shorts" of Donner's metrical translation (and, by extension, Sophocles' poetry). Yet nowhere does Lachner maintain the sort of rhythmic consistency that we observed in parts of Mendelssohn's *Antigone*. Nor does he attempt to convey fundamental shifts in the poetic meter through a calculated use of recitative or melodrama. Thus, whereas Mendelssohn typically restricts the use of choral recitative and melodrama to either anapestic verse or lyric verse assigned to individual actors, Lachner

TABLE 6.1 The structure of Sophocles' play and Lachner's score.

Dramatic Structure	Verse Type	Plot Synopsis	Score	Key
—	—	—	No. 1	c
Oedipus enters			No. 2	C
Prologue	Spoken iambics	The oracles make clear that Laius' killer must be caught to end the plague on Thebes	—	—
Parodos (chorus enters)	Sung lyrics	The chorus prays for Thebes to be freed of its plague	No. 3	d → D
Episode 1	Spoken iambics	Oedipus vows to find Laius' murderer	—	—
		Oed. and the chorus agree to consult the seer Tiresias	No. 4	d → D
		After being named the murderer by Tiresias, Oed. suspects Tiresias and Creon in a plot to unseat him	—	—
Stasimon 1	Sung lyrics	The chorus imagines the killer fleeing the gods and expresses its support for Oedipus	No. 5	g → G
Episode 2	Spoken iambics	Creon denies wrongdoing as Oed. calls for his death	—	—
Jocasta enters		Jocasta calls for calm and for Oed. to be rational	No. 6	b♭
Kommos	Sung lyrics /spoken iambics	The chorus convinces Oed. to spare Creon and affirms its support for Oed. as Jocasta asks what transpired		
Episode 2 Cont.	Spoken iambics	Jocasta reveals a detail of Laius' murder that leads Oed. to suspect himself as the killer	No. 6 cont. (three isolated lines of Oed. and chorus)	B♭/f

(*Continued*)

188 | THE POLITICS OF APPROPRIATION

TABLE 6.1 (Continued)

Dramatic Structure	Verse Type	Plot Synopsis	Score	Key
Stasimon 2	Sung lyrics	The chorus extols the law of the gods	No. 7	f
Episode 3	Spoken iambics	It is revealed that Oed. was not the son of Polybus	—	—
Episode 3 Cont.	Spoken iambics	Oed. seeks his true identity despite Jocasta's wishes	No. 8	c
Stasimon 3	Sung lyrics	The chorus wonders if Oed. is of divine parentage		g♯ /E
Episode 4	Spoken iambics	A shepherd approaches	No. 8 Cont.	g♯ → E
		Oedipus' true fate is finally revealed	—	—
Stasimon 4	Sung lyrics	The chorus reflects on Oed. and on man's unhappiness	No. 9	c
Exodos	Spoken iambics	Report of Jocasta's suicide and Oed.'s mutilation	No. 10	c♯
Kommos	Chanted anapests / spoken iambics	Seeing Oedipus, the chorus expresses horror	No. 11	f
	sung lyrics	Oedipus and the chorus lament his fate	No. 12	b♭ → f♯
Cont. dialogue	Spoken iambics	Oed. curses his life	—	—
		Creon arrives and Oedipus pleads for banishment	No. 13	b
		Oed. begs Creon to care for his daughters	No. 14	g
Choral summary	Chanted trochaics	The moral: Success and joy can vanish in an instant	No. 15	c

employs these forms of delivery primarily as a means of setting otherwise spoken text, as we saw with his use of melodrama to accompany the report of Jocasta's suicide and Oedipus' self-mutilation.

On still another occasion, Lachner includes an isolated eleven-measure passage of unison choral recitative in his setting of the play's first stasimon (No. 5). He does so despite the fact that the entire ode consists of lyric, or sung, meters and thus would seem not to warrant any change in the mode of delivery employed by the chorus. In this ode, the elders imagine the as-yet-unknown murderer of Laius being feverishly pursued by a host of vengeful gods, and they express their puzzlement at the seer Teiresias' seemingly implausible indictment of Oedipus as the killer of Thebes' former king.

The passage of recitative included in this setting corresponds to eight lines in which the chorus explains that it knows of no such feud, past or present, between the families of Oedipus and Laius that would lend credence to the prophet's accusation. While Lachner's use of recitative gives the impression of a sudden outburst or change in perspective on the part of the chorus, there is nothing inherent in the poetry to suggest such a shift. Rather, the unexpected onset of recitative—accompanied in characteristic fashion by sustained chords in the strings—appears to have been calculated to bring about a temporary halt in momentum and thus to lend greater weight to the climactic final stanza, which follows immediately thereafter. This fourth stanza (i.e., the second antistrophe), in which the elders express their support for Oedipus and recall the good that he has done for Thebes, marks a shift from the predominantly minor mode of the preceding three stanzas to the G-major tonality with which the piece concludes. As such this final stanza suggests the elders' hope that Oedipus might rescue the city from the brink of disaster, just as he did when he solved the riddle of the Sphinx.

A Fate Transformed

As previously mentioned, Lachner's score generally reveals less variety than either of Mendelssohn's two settings of Greek tragedy. But perhaps for this very reason, Lachner's music to *Oedipus the King* is characterized by a more tightly knit construction through the presence of a single recurring thematic idea—a strategy not employed in any of the works we have considered thus far. This theme, which we shall dub the "fate theme" for reasons soon to become apparent, first appears at the outset of the second strophe of the parodos, or choral entrance ode (No. 3; example 6.4a). It consists of two distinct segments: a falling major third followed by a descending half- and

EXAMPLE 6.4a–e Lachner, *Oedipus the King*—the "fate" motive and its transformations: (a) No. 3, mm. 72–75; (b) No. 3, mm. 78–83; (c) No. 9, mm. 2–4; (d) No. 11, mm. 3–6; (e) No. 12, mm. 21–24.

whole-step (labeled "x"), and a stepwise ascent from scale degrees three to six followed by a final semitone descent ("y"). The words to which this theme is sung encapsulate the overall sentiment of the ode and hint at the widespread suffering that afflicts Thebes ("Oh, gods, countless are the pains that I suffer"). For, as we learn in the play's prologue, the city has been devastated by famine, disease, and death as the result of unwittingly harboring Laius' killer. The elders, for their part, remain unaware of the reason for this suffering as they fervently pray to Apollo, Athena, Artemis, and Phoebus to deliver Thebes from its plight.

Following the initial appearance of the fate theme, the first half of this idea ("x") is immediately transformed into a descending melodic gesture that outlines a tritone in conjunction with the elders' specific reference to the sickness that plagues Thebes (example 6.5b). And when shortly thereafter they point to the rash of deaths brought on by childbirth, the chorus sings a pair of interlocking tritones that would seem to indicate the immediate association of this interval—heard several times throughout this number—with Thebes' collective grief. The melodic tritone occurs frequently in subsequent numbers as well, where it appears to be used by Lachner as a general emblem of the pain and suffering associated not only with the curse on Thebes but also with Oedipus' tragic fate.

Although he has yet to realize it, Oedipus himself is ultimately responsible for the plague on Thebes, whose suffering is tied inextricably to his own fate, or rather his futile attempt to avoid it; ergo the decision to label the recurring theme that first appears in the parodos the "fate theme," the later transformations of which are also loosely connected to the idea of fate as it exists in Sophocles' play. Notwithstanding its many iterations in the parodos, this theme is not heard again until the beginning of the fourth stasimon, more than halfway through the entire work (No. 9; example 6.4c). Here it constitutes not so much an obvious restatement but rather another subtle transformation, in this case resembling the tritone version of "x" that occurred in the parodos and that itself marked a slight transformation of the initial part of the fate theme. This motivic idea, shorn of its tritone, functions as a motto-like introductory theme that sets the mood of this number and establishes its tonality but is not heard again in this particular chorus. The text sung to this theme—roughly translated as "Oh, you race of mortals!"—forms part of the elders' explanation that no mortal being is truly happy, least of all Oedipus. The chorus is reacting to the shocking revelation of Oedipus' true relationship to Laius and Jocasta, and it points to his fate as proof that happiness is merely fleeting. Representing the moment at which the chorus first articulates a revised view of a king once held in such high regard, this ode marks a significant turning point in the drama. In the previous stasimon, the elders had expressed a fervent belief that Oedipus was of divine parentage, whereas now they feel compelled to say to him: "I wish I had never laid eyes on you." As William Scott has noted, "[The elders] now realize that the story of Oedipus is that of all humans; the events of the play reconfigure as they are seen to be but the record of the day on which Oedipus learns that he is only another ephemeral, afflicted mortal."[45]

The fate theme returns several times in No. 11, where it serves as the main melodic material for a brief number that corresponds to several anapestic lines uttered by the chorus in response to seeing the freshly blind Oedipus. Most appearances of the theme, including the one heard at the outset of the work, constitute an intervallic expansion of the original form combined with elements of rhythmic diminution (example 6.4d). The expansion of the initial descending gesture ("x") by a semitone (to E-natural within the context of F minor) creates a tritone between those notes on the downbeat of bars four and five, thus again embedding this symbolic interval into the work's single recurring motivic idea.

Perhaps more so than any other occurrence of the theme, this one makes the strongest case for an association with the idea of fate, occurring as it does in conjunction with the elders' opening line, "O gräßliches Loos für Menschen zu schau'n!" (What a horrible fate for one to behold!). The onset of anapestic verse at this point in Sophocles' play reflects not only the general shock and horror on the part of the elders in response to the events that have unfolded but also their bemusement surrounding the question of what source of divine power could possibly have brought such sorrow and misfortune to a once great man. The emphasis is less on Oedipus and his actions than on the unseen forces at work in the lives of human beings, most prominently fate and its attendant mysteries.

As many nineteenth-century German commentators were quick to point out, the notion of fate and its inescapability is at the heart of Sophocles' play and provides an important key to understanding the work. Writing in the wake of the Bavarian court production of *Oedipus the King*, a correspondent for the *Allgemeine Zeitung* described the play as "belong[ing] to those ancient tragedies in which the idea of fate in a pagan sense is expressed most blatantly and most forcefully."[46] The author went on to claim that the Greek concept of fate stands completely opposed to the modern Christian worldview and ultimately serves as an impediment to fully appreciating Sophocles' play.

Speaking in more general terms, a correspondent for the same periodical—perhaps even the same critic—noted in a separate review of the Lachner-Dingelstedt production: "The main character in Greek tragedy is the predetermined fate that crushes the [play's] hero."[47] As this author points out, several of the most eventful moments in Oedipus' life, including his killing of Laius and his victory over the Sphinx, have occurred before the first word of the play is ever uttered. As such, Sophocles' tragedy is concerned not so much with Oedipus' actions themselves but with his inability to comprehend that those actions were the very ones foretold by the oracles. However great his accomplishments and however high his standing among mortals, Oedipus is ultimately powerless to alter his destiny as determined by the divine truth of Zeus' law.[48]

The fate theme makes one final, fleeting appearance in Lachner's setting of the kommos that occurs toward the end of the play (No. 12). Heard only once near the beginning of the piece in a fashion that resembles its immediately preceding appearance, its purpose here is to establish a sense of continuity with the previous number. In this kommos, Oedipus laments his fate in a series of lyric stanzas to which the chorus generally responds with terse spoken lines in iambic trimeter. The stark contrast between Oedipus' sung lines and the chorus's spoken responses suggests the king's sudden alienation from the city elders—and, by extension, from Thebes itself. As we might expect, Lachner sets Oedipus' lyrics as melodrama and employs a predominantly unison line for the brief choral responses.

The second such response, however, brings about the sole use of recitative in this number, and it is here that we encounter a clear reference to the fate theme, albeit in yet another transformation of its original guise (example 6.4e). At this point, the chorus responds to Oedipus' description of being enveloped in a cloud of darkness (both literally and figuratively) by noting that he suffers doubly from both emotional anguish and his self-inflicted physical wounds. In other words, it links both mind and body together with Oedipus' cruel fate, and thus the notion that the melodic theme heard at this point is associated with the idea of fate would seem to be affirmed. But perhaps even more importantly, the appearance of this theme creates a direct link to the preceding number. This connection is significant because, despite being identified with two separate numbers (Nos. 11 and 12), these two pieces occur as part of an extended musico-dramatic complex that encompasses six nearly continuous numbers in Lachner's score (Nos. 9–15) and corresponds to the play's final stasimon and the immediately ensuing exodus (cf. table 6.1 above).

The first break in this lengthy passage comes at the conclusion of No. 12, at which point Oedipus delivers a purely spoken monologue further dwelling on his unspeakable crimes and his violent reaction to learning of their true meaning. Nos. 9–12 can therefore be regarded as a kind of sub-complex in which Oedipus and the chorus attempt to come to terms with his actions, highlighting the sheer power of fate and the inability to escape it. It is likely for this reason that the fate theme—last heard in the parodos—appears in each of these pieces except No. 10, which, as we have seen, focuses not on Oedipus or the chorus but on the messenger whose scene is set to music.

Thus in much the same way that Oedipus' fate is known from the outset of the play but affirmed only toward the end of it, so too the fate theme is presented early on in Lachner's work but is not developed until much later.

The two numbers that follow this sub-complex (Nos. 13 and 14) mostly set a lengthy spoken (i.e., iambic) exchange between Oedipus and Creon during which the former pleads with the latter to banish him from Thebes and watch over his two young daughters, Antigone and Ismene. (His sons, Oedipus reasons, are male and thus can care for themselves.) With the exception of a brief passage sung by the chorus in No. 13 and about two dozen lines of dialogue that Lachner refrained from setting altogether, this spoken exchange is rendered entirely as melodrama. This decision offers still further proof of the composer's willingness to set otherwise spoken portions of text to music. The last seven lines of the play, which some scholars have argued were a later addition by someone other than Sophocles, provide the text for what Lachner labels the work's "Schlußchor" (No. 15).[49] Written for the chorus in trochaic tetrameter and addressed to the inhabitants of Thebes, these lines present the moral of the play by pointing to the once-mighty Oedipus as an example of how happiness can so quickly vanish. Lachner's setting of this passage includes march-like music in C minor that features an entirely unison vocal line together with a predominantly unison orchestral accompaniment including cymbals and tambourine. The relentless C-minor tonality clearly recalls the severity of the work's overture while suggesting the unmitigated tragedy with which the play concludes.

On the whole, the 1852 production of *Oedipus the King*, and in particular Lachner's music for it, met with a positive reception. This success immediately laid the groundwork for a proposed Munich performance of the Theban trilogy on three successive nights that would feature the music of both Mendelssohn and Lachner. Undoubtedly with such a goal in mind, a performance of *Oedipus at Colonus* with Mendelssohn's music took place at the court theater on January 19, 1854, though this production met with only modest success. In contrast to the sold-out houses to which *Antigone* had played for eager Munich audiences three years before, the theater in this case was only sparsely filled in what perhaps was a sign of the waning interest in the performance of Greek tragedy on the part of local theatergoers.[50]

For his part, Dingelstedt pressed on with plans to stage the Theban trilogy in the summer of that year, but it was not meant to be. With Munich suffering from the effects of a cholera epidemic, it was determined that such a production would be inappropriate. This decision was made in no small part because those who attended the first rehearsal sensed an eerie parallel between their present reality and the first scene of *Oedipus the King*, in which a throng of desperate Thebans gathers at the steps of the royal palace to plead for Oedipus' help in lifting the plague on the city. The inability to bring Sophocles' Theban trilogy to the Munich stage is in many ways a fitting metaphor for the precipitous decline in the German performance of Greek tragedy with music. Although performances of Mendelssohn's *Antigone*—both on and off the stage—would continue to take place throughout the nineteenth century, the trend that it represented gradually faded from view. Yet the significance of ancient Greece remained, particularly in Germany. Artists and intellectuals of the mid-nineteenth century continued to search for ways of appropriating aspects of ancient Greek culture. Of these attempts, perhaps none was more important for the development of German Romantic music than Richard Wagner's efforts to distill the essence of Greek tragedy into his "artwork of the future"—a monumental task fraught with cultural and aesthetic implications, and one that is addressed in the following chapter.

CHAPTER SEVEN | The Wagnerian Turn

RICHARD WAGNER'S INTEREST in the Greeks has been the subject of serious scholarly inquiry for more than a century. One of the earliest book-length studies on the topic, by George Wrassiwanopulos-Braschowanoff, appeared in 1905 in the form of a published dissertation submitted to the Friedrich-Alexander University in Erlangen under the title *Richard Wagner und die Antike*. In it, the author explores the composer's relationship to Greece as a decisive factor in shaping his cultural and artistic outlook, noting at the outset of the work: "It is a well-known fact that the ancient Greek world exerted a major influence on Wagner's overall intellectual and aesthetic-philosophical development."[1] He goes on to claim that Wagner is "perhaps the most noble and most genuine of antiquity's spiritual offspring ever to have arisen from the fertile ground of neoclassical Germany."[2]

Such a sentiment, though clearly up for debate, corresponds to the view held by many late nineteenth-century observers (including at one point Friedrich Nietzsche), for whom Wagner seemed to possess an almost mystical ability to channel the inimitable spirit of ancient Greece through the medium of music.[3] Wrassiwanopulos-Braschowanoff cites, among other things, Wagner's mid-century reform essays, his notion of the *Gesamtkunstwerk*, and the creation of the Bayreuth Festspielhaus as evidence of the composer's lifelong affinity with the Greeks. He also points to several of the operas, including those of *Der Ring des Nibelungen*, which he offers as proof of Wagner's philosophical treatment of mythology and his fundamentally Aristotelian approach to drama.[4]

Two years after this study appeared, Robert Petsch became the first of many scholars to directly link Wagner's *Ring* to a particular work of Greek tragedy.⁵ Whereas previous scholars, including Ernst Meinck and Wolfgang Golther, had identified elements of the *Ring* that were derived from or at least shared a unique kinship with Greek mythology and in some cases Greek drama, Petsch was far more specific.⁶ He claimed that Wagner had adapted aspects of plot and character from Aeschylus' partially extant Prometheus trilogy—or more accurately, the reconstruction, translation, and commentary issued by Johann Gustav Droysen in 1832 and again in 1841. A dozen years after Petsch's work appeared, the subject of Wagnerian opera and its connection to Greek tragedy was taken up more generally by Pearl Cleveland Wilson in a published Columbia University dissertation of 1919 and then again in 1931 by Arthur Drews, who echoed many of Petsch's claims concerning the link between Aeschylus and the *Ring* cycle.⁷ Much of this work, however, remained obscure, and it was not until the postwar era that the question of Wagner's relationship to the Greeks came into sharp focus, beginning with a series of three lectures delivered at Bayreuth between 1962 and 1965 by the German classicist Wolfgang Schadewaldt.

Published in 1970, Schadewaldt's work built on the foundations established by Petsch and would eventually prove to be the most influential treatment of the topic for late twentieth-century scholars of Wagner.⁸ Schadewaldt delivered his lectures at the invitation of Wagner's grandson Wieland, who, as director of the Bayreuth Festival, was leading the postwar effort to rehabilitate the institution in the wake of its damning association with Hitler and the National Socialist regime. In this context, Wieland Wagner's self-conscious decision to play up the Greek influence on his grandfather's operas through the classically inspired stage design and costumes of productions such as his 1952 *Ring* can be seen as an attempt to impose a more sanitized and universal character upon the traditionally Germanic—or at least Northern European—nature of the work.⁹

For his part, Schadewaldt presented a detailed case for the by-then familiar argument that Greek antiquity had shaped Wagner's overall aesthetic outlook, influenced his approach to drama, and inspired the idea for a festival theater rooted in the principles of inclusiveness and a spiritual devotion to art. He also argued, as Petsch had, for a direct link in several instances between the plots and characters of ancient Greek literature and those of Wagner's mature operas. Thus he identified, among other examples, a fundamental similarity between the title character of *Der fliegende Holländer* and Homer's Odysseus, both of whom share a sense of longing for home. Yet the work most heavily indebted to the Greeks, according to Schadewaldt, was the *Ring*. Here he echoed the claim made by Petsch that key elements of this tetralogy were decisively influenced by Aeschylus' Prometheus trilogy (about which more later).

Schadewaldt divides Wagner's artistic and intellectual engagement with Greek antiquity into three distinct phases of the composer's life. The initial phase encompasses Wagner's youth and adolescence in Dresden and Leipzig and spans the period from roughly 1822 to 1827. Basing his account on the often exaggerated claims made by Wagner in his autobiography, *Mein Leben*, Schadewaldt discusses the composer's early classical studies under the influence of Julius Sillig, his favorite teacher at the Dresden Kreuzschule, and his uncle Adolf Wagner, a philologist and noted translator of ancient Greek works. Schadewaldt's relatively uncritical view of Wagner's recollections from this period ultimately helps to perpetuate the myth surrounding the composer's self-proclaimed affinity for classical studies and the Greeks in particular. Thus, for example, Schadewaldt repeats Wagner's claim that, upon transferring to the Nikolaischule in Leipzig, he had already translated twelve books of Homer into German from the original Greek—an achievement that is hard to reconcile with the fact that he was also at that point held back a year in his studies. Moreover, as John Deathridge has recently pointed out, Schadewaldt fails to take into account the composer's own subsequent admission in *Mein Leben* that he never fully mastered ancient Greek.[10]

The second phase that Schadewaldt identifies is said to coincide with Wagner's stay in Paris between 1839 and 1842. During this time, he forged a close friendship with Samuel Lehrs, a philologist whose interests extended beyond classical antiquity to German culture of the distant past. Lehrs guided Wagner in his renewed attempts to read Greek works in the original, and he also helped to stimulate Wagner's interest in the historical sources that would later play a role in *Tannhäuser*, *Lohengrin*, and *Die Meistersinger*.

The third and most important phase of Wagner's Hellenism—what Schadewaldt refers to as his "breakthrough"—is identified as beginning in Dresden in the summer of 1847. It was at this time that the composer undertook an intensive program of reading the many works (in translation) of ancient Greek literature and history that formed a significant part of the vast personal library he had begun amassing upon his appointment as Kapellmeister to the Saxon court in 1843. Thus he read works by, among other ancient writers, Aeschylus, Aristophanes, and Plato, as well as those of modern historians, including Barthold Georg Niebuhr, Edward Gibbon on Roman history, and Droysen on Alexander the Great and the Hellenistic period in Greek culture.[11]

Also among the items in his library, which was left behind when he fled Germany and eventually forfeited to a creditor, were translations of

Euripides, Sophocles (by J. J. Donner), Pindar, Homer, and Herodotus.[12] According to Wagner, the work that had the most lasting influence on him was Aeschylus' *Oresteia*, the impact of which he called "indescribable."[13] He went on to say of this trilogy, which he read in Droysen's translation, that it decisively shaped his ideas about drama and the theater, having left him "in a state of transport from which I have never really returned to become fully reconciled with modern literature."[14] Schadewaldt, like so many others before and after him, rightly points to these claims as evidence of the degree to which the Greeks influenced Wagner's thinking at this time in his life. Indeed, it is as a result of this "breakthrough" third stage of Wagner's Hellenism, Schadewaldt maintains, that Greek-inspired themes, plots, characters, and ideas began to manifest themselves in his prose essays, as well as in his creative output.

Perhaps owing to his authority as a classical philologist, Schadewaldt's views on Wagner and the Greeks were highly influential in the decades following the publication of his Bayreuth lectures. Most notably, the classicist Hugh Lloyd-Jones and the literary scholar Ulrich Müller, in individual essays on the subject of Wagner's relationship to classical antiquity, reveal a considerable debt to Schadewaldt, in each case adopting his tripartite scheme outlining the composer's Hellenistic influences.[15] On the face of it, this division seems reasonable enough, especially insofar as it roughly mirrors the early-middle-late classification so frequently encountered in biographical accounts of important artistic figures.

Yet, because of its chronological organization and its teleological emphasis on the third-period "breakthrough," this model has the unintended effect of portraying Wagner's engagement with the Greeks in the years around 1850 as the inexorable culmination of a lifelong interest in classical antiquity. In other words, it tends to emphasize the biographical elements of Wagner's life at the expense of investigating the cultural context that appears to have given rise to his overall concern for Greek antiquity and, more specifically, to the intense devotion that surfaced in the late 1840s and would profoundly influence his thinking for years to come. Rather than considering the unique role of ancient Greece in German thought from the mid-eighteenth century onward as a factor shaping Wagner's Hellenism, Schadewaldt and others following his lead instead take for granted the composer's abiding interest in the Greeks, tracing it back to his formative years as a promising young student. By doing so, they unwittingly validate the arguments made by Wagner and many of his late nineteenth-century acolytes that the composer was naturally endowed with some sort of special affinity for ancient Greek culture.

In what follows I argue that a crucial dimension to understanding the context of Wagner's relationship to the Greeks is the widespread popularity enjoyed by the 1841 *Antigone* and, in particular, Mendelssohn's music for it. Wagner's mid-century writings make clear that his core argument concerning the rebirth of Greek tragedy in a modern Germanic guise was to a considerable degree conceived as a reaction against the trend of reviving ancient drama in the manner represented by the Mendelssohn-Tieck *Antigone*. Rejecting its premise of faithfully re-creating the past, Wagner set out to undermine this effort and to replace its brand of classicism with one of his own as a way of lending artistic legitimacy to his ambitious plans for reforming modern opera.

To be sure, a fair number of scholars—among them Schadewaldt—have noted Wagner's antipathy toward this production, though on the whole they have underestimated the extent to which it colored his thinking about Greek tragedy and its relationship to modern drama. This relative lack of attention may stem in part from the fact that scholars dealing with Wagner's appropriation of the Greeks have generally failed to recognize the 1841 *Antigone*'s cultural resonance throughout the remainder of the decade and even into the 1850s. Nor have such commentators typically acknowledged the anti-Semitic thrust of Wagner's critique of this production. Thus the present chapter outlines the basic contours of the composer's notoriously vicious anti-Semitic attacks in an effort to show that his rejection of *Antigone* was infused with the same overall spirit.

Not only does this chapter highlight the manner in which the Prussian court production of *Antigone* shaped some of the most pivotal ideas presented in Wagner's mid-century reform essays; it also argues that elements of the *Ring* were likewise influenced by the composer's attempt at reclaiming the Oedipus myth for his own classicizing aims. Most notably, the key figure of Brünnhilde bears a striking parallel to Antigone, insofar as both characters help to bring about a destruction of the existing social order. In his lengthy discussion of the Oedipus saga in *Opera and Drama*, Wagner himself points to the redemptive nature of Antigone's actions and appears to regard this figure as a general model for Brünnhilde and her redemptive function. To be clear, the purpose of the present chapter is not to explore the theme of Wagner and the Greeks to its fullest extent, a topic that has already been the subject of several book-length studies.[16] Rather, my aim is to redefine our understanding of Wagner's Hellenism by demonstrating that some of his principal notions concerning the Greeks were rooted in a sense of personal and professional rivalry with Mendelssohn and a desire to capitalize on the

German legacy of ancient Greece in much the same way as the 1841 Prussian court production of *Antigone*.

Wagner's Greeks

Wagner's reform essays, completed during the initial years of his Swiss exile, represent the clearest manifestation of his interest in the Greeks. In the first of these, *Art and Revolution* (1849), he points to ancient Greece as the wellspring of all modern European art, claiming that any attempt to come to terms with the latter must necessarily begin with a consideration of the former.[17] Singling out classical tragedy as the highest achievement of Greek culture, Wagner paints a stark contrast between ancient and modern art, a contrast that in his mind stems from certain basic distinctions between the two periods. Ancient Greece, represented above all by Athens in its prime, is seen as the embodiment of a free, communal spirit—a harmonious society in which individuals are at one with themselves, each other, and the world around them. Modern Christian society, on the other hand, is characterized by individualism, self-loathing, and alienation from nature.

These notions are clearly rooted in the German idealist thought of such figures as Schiller and Hegel, whose views on Greece strongly colored those of Wagner. As we have seen, such views grew out of a tradition of German Hellenism that stretches back to Winckelmann. Wagner affirmed the importance of this legacy when he claimed in a collection of essays published in 1878 under the title "What is German?" that "the idea of antiquity dates from the middle of the previous century, that is, from the time of Winckelmann and Lessing."[18] His larger point here is that, through its natural affinity with ancient Greece, Germany has played a crucial role in shaping the modern European cultural landscape, first by appropriating the Greek spirit and then by disseminating it in the form of a universalizing German culture.

The fundamental problem with modern art, however, is that it has ceased to be public in character. Wagner contends that art in ancient Greece was the purest reflection of the harmony that existed between the state and the individual and between man and nature: "For the Greeks, [art] resided in the public consciousness, whereas today it resides solely in the consciousness of individuals, as opposed to the unconsciousness of the public as a whole."[19] As a *Gesamtkunstwerk* that embodied a harmonious union of all the arts, Greek tragedy was the highest manifestation of this tendency and, as such, gave full artistic expression to the public consciousness of a free and unified society.

Accordingly, its performance occurred within the framework of a religious festival that appealed to the entire populace:

> [The Athenians] streamed away from the state assemblies, from the forum, the country, ships, from military camps, from the most distant regions, thirty-thousand together filling the amphitheater in order to see the most profound of all tragedies, that of Prometheus, to gather together before the most powerful works of art, to understand themselves, grasp their own actions, to come together with their essence, their comradeship, their god, in the most intimate unity and to be together again in the finest, deepest tranquility, when a few hours before there had been restless excitement and distinct individuality.[20]

By stark contrast, the basis of modern art is commerce, insofar as the artist's primary objective is to earn money (and here Wagner is thinking especially of the contemporary stage). Thus modern works are performed in private palaces and opulent theaters, where they serve to entertain the wealthiest members of society and function principally as a release from the pressures of modern industrial life. One devastating result of this circumstance is that the genuine nature of ancient Greek artistic creation has been reduced in modern times to mere "craftwork" [*Handwerk*].[21]

In Wagner's view, the deplorable state of modern art is ultimately traceable to the downfall of Greek tragedy. The demise of this previously unified artwork caused its various component parts—music, dance, poetry, and the visual arts—to develop in unnatural isolation from one another. In *Art and Revolution* and *Artwork of the Future*, also completed in 1849, Wagner envisions a return of the total artwork that must, however, be preceded by what he calls "the great revolution of mankind."[22] The successful completion of this revolution, which Wagner hoped for even after—or especially after—the failure of the 1848–49 revolutions, would mean the overthrow of existing political and economic structures and the advent of a free, utopian society. This society in turn would give rise to a perfect artwork created in the spirit of ancient Greek drama.[23] Such radical thinking clearly reflects the composer's sympathies with the liberal Young Hegelian movement and the socialist reform ideas of Pierre-Joseph Proudhon, and also points to his own personal association with the anarchist Mikhail Bakunin.[24]

Nowhere in his writings, however, does Wagner advocate a return to the conditions of ancient Greece. As he explains in *Art and Revolution*, "We do not want to become Greeks, for we know what the Greeks did not—and that which they did not know was the very reason for their downfall."[25] The fundamental problem with ancient Greek society was that it rested on the institution of slavery, which ultimately led to its failure. As Wagner explains, "The [Greek] slave...has exposed the nullity and the fleeting nature of the beauty and strength unique to Greek manhood, and has shown for all eternity that beauty and strength, as attributes of public life, can only be lasting blessings when they become the gifts of all mankind."[26] Moreover, the slavery that existed in ancient Greece has simply come down to us in a different form; the ostensibly free individual of modern bourgeois society is in reality a slave to capitalism and the demands of a monetary world. By pointing to slavery as the foundation of Greek culture, Wagner distances his own view of the Greeks from the more idealized one represented by Winckelmann. The latter had deliberately avoided the topic, despite his claim that the essence of Greek art stemmed partly from the unique freedom that was characteristic of ancient Greek society. The revolution that Wagner envisions will bring about genuine freedom, because machines will be used to perform the work that presently enslaves mankind. The result will be a new world order built on a foundation of love and freedom for *all* human beings.[27]

The *Gesamtkunstwerk* to which these circumstances give rise will be the artistic expression of this newfound unity. Not only will it reunite the individual arts torn asunder by the downfall of Greek tragedy, but it will be rooted firmly in the spirit of the *Volk*. For Wagner, the *Volk* represents "the embodiment of all those who experience a common need" and who recognize the inherently collective nature of what would otherwise be perceived as an individual need.[28] For, ultimately, only the *Volk* acts in accordance with genuine need, whereas those individuals divorced from this collectivity are driven by artificial and egoistic desire. Thus only the *Volk* can bring about the redemption of mankind and fulfill the promise of a long-awaited revolution. After all, it was the common man and not the intellectual elite who served as the driving impulse behind every worthwhile human creation, of which the "artwork of the future" was to be no exception.[29] In reality, of course, the unified artwork that Wagner has in mind is none other than his own novel reinterpretation of traditional opera, or what has come to be known simply as "music drama." The blueprint for this new conception of opera is provided in the most extensive of Wagner's reform essays, *Opera and Drama* (1851), in which the composer discusses at length such particulars as poetic meter, text-setting, and the role of the orchestra.

As Dieter Borchmeyer has rightly noted, Wagner's notion of a *Gesamtkunstwerk*—a term he uses only sparingly in the reform essays—should be regarded less as an aesthetic ideal and more as a sociopolitical one within the context of his larger utopian vision.[30] Wagner's use of the term therefore should not be understood to mean a complete artwork in the sense that opera combines music, poetry, dance, and elaborate scenery, which, after all, is quite conventional for the genre. Rather, its usage implies a "cultural vision" (to borrow Borchmeyer's phrase) defined by an artistic unity that mirrors the social and political unity of a society redeemed by the advent of a new world order.

To further complicate matters, this notion of a "total artwork" is distinct from the one invoked by Wagner when he describes music drama as the reunification of the "purely human" arts of dance, poetry, and music. With that he means something like the absolute integration of mimic, linguistic, and musical dimensions that characterized ancient Greek drama, an idea suggested by the Greek word *mousike*.[31] The first of these two definitions—which coincides with Wagner's actual use of the term and with which we are mostly concerned in the discussion that follows—grows out of the composer's ideal of Greece as a harmonious society that offers a stark contrast to the overall division and disunity characteristic of the modern world. And it is for this reason that he largely abandoned such thinking after his discovery in 1854 of the resolutely pessimistic philosophy of Arthur Schopenhauer.

Reform versus Revival

As familiar as many of the ideas in these landmark essays are, it is easy to overlook the extent to which they were formulated in response to the tremendous success of the Mendelssohn-Tieck *Antigone* and the trend of reviving Greek tragedy that it represented. Wagner's first clear reference to this production occurs in the second part of *Opera and Drama*, where he notes with disdain:

> A talented poet, who as a creative artist had never found the ability to master any sort of material for the true drama, convinced an absolute monarch to command his theater-intendant to stage an *actual Greek tragedy* with fidelity to ancient [practices], for which a famous composer was compelled to provide the necessary music.[32]

Here Wagner is invoking the 1841 *Antigone* as evidence of the misguided path taken by contemporary theater. In the pages leading up to this remark, Wagner makes the argument that modern drama has developed along two parallel historical paths, each erroneous in its own way and each ultimately a reflection of man's alienation from both nature and himself. On one side is the novel, an embodiment of the bourgeois spirit that has been unnaturally adapted for the stage; and on the other side is Greek drama, which has been misappropriated above all by French classical dramatists concerned solely with "imitation and repetition."[33]

Associating the former path chiefly with Shakespeare and the latter with Racine, Wagner obviously regards the Mendelssohn-Tieck *Antigone* as the logical yet unfortunate continuation of the Racinian impulse toward imitating Greek tragedy in an outward fashion:

> In the face of modern life, this *Sophoclean drama* proved to be a crass, artistic white lie, a sham wrapped in artistic poverty to mask the falsehood of our entire artistic enterprise, a fabrication that attempted to paper over with all manner of artistic pretext the genuine need of our time. Yet the one plain truth that this tragedy could not help but reveal is this: that *we possess no* [genuine] *drama and nor can we.*[34]

In other words, this production shied away from the aesthetic demands of the present age by relying solely on ancient form and content. While Racine and other French classical tragedians are deserving of scorn for their repeated efforts at adapting Greek tragedy in an artificial and imitative fashion, Tieck, Mendelssohn, and others behind the Prussian court production of *Antigone* are guilty of a far worse offense. For they did away entirely with the idea of adaptation and instead made a futile attempt to present Sophocles' play as it would have been presented in ancient times (thus Wagner's emphasis on the words "Sophoclean drama" in the above quotation). The fact that Wagner makes these remarks without ever mentioning by name *Antigone*, Mendelssohn, or Tieck suggests the degree to which this phenomenon had permeated the German cultural consciousness of the 1840s and '50s.

Wagner issued a similar critique—albeit in far more subtle fashion—in his semi-autobiographical work of 1851, *A Communication to My Friends*. Here the composer ridicules the idea of taking a work written for a democratic Athens and simply transplanting it to the modern European court without any attempt at rendering it more appropriate for its modern context. The reference is obviously to the 1841 *Antigone*, and Wagner's sarcastic remark that some modern aesthetic theorists actually believe in the possibility of such a direct transplant is a clear denunciation of this mindset.[35] Wagner further mocks this belief when he notes that some of his contemporaries are of the opinion that, like a fine wine, a dramatic work of art will gain something by having been locked away in the metaphorical cellar for centuries on end, and that it is actually more apt to be understood by a modern audience than by its original one.

In light of such references to the Mendelssohn-Tieck *Antigone*—and in light of the production's larger cultural and artistic significance—certain passages in the reform essays take on new meaning. In *Art and Revolution*, for example, Wagner declares in regard to the future development of art: "We have to accomplish something completely different than simply re-creating Greek antiquity. Indeed, the foolish restoration of a pseudo-Greek form of art has already been attempted—for, what has *not* been attempted by artists on commission?"[36] Judging from its immediate context, this remark appears to be aimed at the French neoclassicism of Racine and Corneille, whom earlier in the essay Wagner had accused of hypocrisy for writing plays that, while based on ancient notions of freedom and political virtue, ultimately served to glorify the image of King Louis XIV. Yet this comment is almost certainly aimed as much—if not more—at the two "commissioned" artists responsible for the court production of *Antigone*, which in its own way served to enhance the public image of the Prussian king.

Wagner also seems to have this production in mind when he states with pointed emphasis that the unified and totally integrated work of art yet to arise "cannot be *reborn* but rather must be *born anew*."[37] Not "slavish restoration," he continues, but only genuine revolution will bring forth such a work. In short, Wagner's statements concerning the Mendelssohn-Tieck *Antigone* are intended to highlight its artificially imitative and academic nature. This production thus forms a vital component of Wagner's critique aimed at the appropriation of ancient drama in the manner of Racine, and it quickly becomes apparent that the composer's intention is to portray this misguided endeavor in self-conscious opposition to his envisioned "artwork of the future," which is to be a modern-day embodiment and not a mere re-creation of classical tragedy.

Wagner's ultimate objective here is to delegitimize this production—and the trend that it represents—in hopes of paving the way for his own modern re-conceptualization of Greek tragedy (i.e., Wagnerian music drama). As we have seen, Wagner claims that what emerges will be a *Gesamtkunstwerk* in the mold of ancient Greek drama. In reality, however, Wagner's post-1850 operas are no more a synthesis of music, poetry, and dance than any number of operatic works from the period—and in certain instances appear even less so.

Yet the fact remains that Wagner used Greek tragedy and the notion of a total artwork as an aesthetic construct upon which to develop his groundbreaking ideas for operatic reform. In this way his thinking is aligned with several generations of German intellectuals for whom the ancient Greeks represented an original source of moral and artistic perfection. As Carl Dahlhaus shrewdly noted, "The *Gesamtkunstwerk* that Wagner proclaimed in his writings around 1850 was less the result of a real operatic tradition than of a utopian one whose arena was not the stage but all of aesthetic theory."[38]

Moreover, Wagner seems eager to exploit the cultural trope of ancient Greece as a way of lending artistic legitimacy to his own operatic ambitions, and from this perspective, these ambitions have more in common with Friedrich Wilhelm's endeavor to stage ancient drama than the composer ever would have acknowledged. Greek tragedy becomes for Wagner an aesthetic ideal according to which modern art falls woefully short. But recognizing the impossibility of ever truly recapturing this art form, Wagner instead establishes the goal of capturing its spirit while at the same time dismissing any attempt at what he regards as mere imitation.

As we saw in the opening chapter, this same strategy was employed by German literary critics of the late eighteenth century who rejected French neoclassical tragedy as a pale imitation of the original and advocated a German brand of classicism more attuned to the essence of Greek drama. And though Wagner, too, takes aim at the French neoclassicists, his vehement opposition to any sort of wholesale attempt at imitating Greek tragedy also constitutes the rejection of a strand of Hellenism associated above all with Winckelmann, who had argued that the only path to modern greatness lay in the imitation of the ancients. In contrast to Winckelmann and others who seemed to harbor faith in an eventual return to the glories of ancient Greece, Wagner remains adamant that such a return is neither possible nor desirable. His comments on the 1841 *Antigone* can be understood as an effort to link the production to precisely this sort of outdated, "naïve" form of Hellenism. Thus when Wagner describes the Mendelssohn-Tieck *Antigone* as "an artistic white lie," he is attacking above all its aim of vainly trying to recover a lost past. He is also implicitly aligning himself with the more historicist outlook on ancient Greece espoused by such scholars as Droysen, Böckh, and the philologist Karl Ottfried Müller, whose works Wagner had read. His imagined artwork of the future will not only stand opposed to the overall aesthetic principles governing an undertaking such as the 1841 *Antigone*, but it will also be erected on a sounder intellectual footing.

The widespread association of *Antigone* with the Prussian court only served to amplify Wagner's distaste for the 1841 production. In his reform essays, the composer places much of the blame for the sad state of modern art on the wealthiest members of society, in particular the aristocracy. He argues that, during the Renaissance, the guiding hand behind the individual arts that once comprised Greek tragedy became that of monarchs, princes, and other wealthy nobles who commissioned works for their own entertainment or, worse yet, their own glorification.[39] By increasing the demand for art, these patrons were essentially responsible for the extent to which the different arts developed independently of one another, and thus they played a part in further alienating these forms from the original Greek unity.

Moreover, as artists grew increasingly concerned with meeting these demands, they drifted farther away from the creation of genuine art. Indeed, when Wagner asks, in the midst of indirectly attacking the Mendelssohn-Tieck *Antigone*, whether there is anything that commissioned artists will *not* do, he seems to be implying that this production—like the tragedies of Racine and Corneille—was undertaken only because those involved in leading the creative effort were paid for their talents (and in each case by a ruling monarch).[40] With Louis XIV foremost in mind, Wagner elsewhere notes the irony of a powerful and wealthy ruler exploiting the "free" art of a democratic Athens for his own personal and political benefit.[41] Despite Wagner's own employment at the Saxon court, and despite his willingness to have his operas performed at royal courts across Germany, he remained emphatic in his belief that the artwork born of the "great revolution of mankind" would be shaped not by the aristocracy or a wealthy leisure class but by the spirit of the *Volk*.

A Target of Opportunity

One of the main targets of Wagner's attack on the 1841 *Antigone* was Mendelssohn, toward whom he harbored both personal and professional resentment. Although Wagner never mentions the composer by name, he surely would have recognized that any reference to the Prussian *Antigone* would have immediately called to mind Mendelssohn's celebrated and widely known incidental music. Perhaps not surprisingly, many of the specific criticisms directed at Mendelssohn and his music for *Antigone* dovetail with the ideas upon which Wagner based his notorious anti-Semitic critique of Jewish composers, most notably Mendelssohn and Meyerbeer. Mendelssohn is thus implicitly portrayed as a composer who not only lacks the means to fully comprehend the true German spirit but also the ancient Greek one with which it shares such a strong affinity.

Exactly how Wagner came to know Mendelssohn's *Antigone* is unclear. It is possible that he attended one of the performances at the Berlin Schauspielhaus in April of 1842, during which time Wagner was in the Prussian capital to discuss a possible performance of *Der fliegende Holländer*. This scenario, however, seems unlikely because, despite visiting Mendelssohn during this trip, he mentions nothing about the Berlin production in any of his writings. It seems more likely that Wagner witnessed the 1844 Dresden production of the play at the Saxon court, for which he was then serving as Kapellmeister.

This production opened on April 12 and was staged eight additional times that year.[42] It not only featured Mendelssohn's music but also a stage reconstructed along ancient lines, in this case with help from the noted architect Gottfried Semper.

Although Wagner never mentions having seen this production, he does make reference to it in *Mein Leben*, where he recalls an evening spent at the Dresden home of the famous soprano Wilhelmine Schröder-Devrient in the company of, among others, Gaspare Spontini and Heinrich Heine. He describes how, after dinner, Schröder-Devrient inquired if Spontini, along with Heine, wished to attend the nearby performance of *Antigone*, adding that the authentically classical stage design was sure to be of interest to him. Reluctant at first, Spontini finally agreed, only to return a short time later and to announce "with a condescending smile" that his own *Olympie* (1819) was more authentically classical than anything he had seen that evening. Wagner's account continues:

> Heine recounted to us that, shortly after he and Spontini had entered the virtually empty gallery, [Spontini] had turned to him at the beginning of the Bacchus chorus [No. 6] and said: "It's [like] the Berlin Singakademie, let's go." Through the opened door a beam of light had fallen on a hitherto unnoticed and solitary figure behind one of the pillars; Heine had recognized Mendelssohn and concluded at once that he had overheard the master's remark.[43]

As with so many of Wagner's recollections, this one should be taken with a grain of salt. For one thing, there is reason to question just how short a period of time elapsed between the departure of the two men and their return, given that the Bacchus chorus is the penultimate number in Mendelssohn's score and would have occurred toward the end of the production. Moreover, while this anecdote is ostensibly meant to offer insight into Wagner's relationship with Spontini, it seems to be used more as a way of portraying Mendelssohn's *Antigone* in a negative light. And for those who would argue that such a claim is reading too much into a personal, anecdotal reminiscence, it should be noted that as late as 1872—seven years into work on *Mein Leben* and more than thirty after the Prussian court premiere of *Antigone*—the composer saw fit to publicly disparage Mendelssohn's music to Greek tragedy. In an open letter to Nietzsche written on June 12, 1872, Wagner explains that, although he was naturally inclined to envy Mendelssohn's thorough classical education, he was stunned to find that, even with such training, Mendelssohn had failed to recognize the folly of applying precisely *his* musical style to the performance of Sophoclean tragedy. This was all the more puzzling, argues

Wagner, "since despite my own lack of expertise, I still had more respect for the spirit of antiquity than [Mendelssohn] appears to have had."[44]

Such a remark affirms that Wagner's earlier criticism was aimed as much at Mendelssohn's *Antigone* as it was the underlying aesthetic of the production for which it was conceived. Ultimately, though, Wagner's aim was not only to undermine the success of this music but also to challenge its supposed reflection of the Greek spirit—and, by extension, Mendelssohn's presumed affinity with the Greeks. Thus Wagner implicitly links Mendelssohn to the imitative and naïve form of classicism that he had associated with Racine and that, at least for some intellectuals of the time, was also tied to Winckelmann and the late eighteenth century.

As previously mentioned, Wagner's rejection of the 1841 *Antigone* resonates with his anti-Semitic beliefs, especially insofar as Mendelssohn is the intended target of both attacks. Wagner's clearest expression of his anti-Semitic stance came in the essay *Judaism in Music*, published in 1850 under the pseudonym K. Freigedank and reprinted in 1869 under the composer's own name. In it, Wagner attempts to show that the "Judaization" of contemporary art has resulted in its marked decline. His essential argument is that the Jews, as a foreign race, are alienated from the European cultures into which they have sought assimilation and thus are incapable of creating genuine art. They are capable, however, of imitating such art in a trivial and superficial manner by constructing a patchwork of "various forms and styles of every master and of every age."[45] Here Wagner points specifically to Mendelssohn, whom he claims had successfully mimicked the largely formal language of Bach but was unable to penetrate the depths of the highly individual, expressive, and "purely human" language of Beethoven.[46]

Wagner's goal is not so much to dismiss Mendelssohn's output or deny his musical ability as it is to label him a composer of the second rank, barred from the pantheon of great German composers by his Jewish heritage. Indeed, Mendelssohn offers a case of a Jewish musician who was endowed with extraordinary talent and afforded the finest education, but who nevertheless failed to even once "bring forth that deep, heart-rending effect upon us that we expect from art."[47] According to Wagner, his elegant and polished style may serve to entertain or to engage one's intellect, but it remains incapable of profoundly touching the human soul. As Wagner explains: "The educated Jew has gone to unimaginable lengths to remove all the obvious signs of his more lowly fellow believers, in many cases even finding it appropriate to employ Christian baptism as a means of washing away every trace of his origin."[48] Yet ultimately, Wagner concludes, such individuals are unable to forge any sort of meaningful bond with mainstream society, except through a connection with the money controlled by certain Jews.

Thus the artistic content of a work produced even by someone as talented and cultured as Mendelssohn is destined to be trivial and imitative in nature. According to Wagner, music lends itself more than any other art form to imitating the genuine language spoken by the greatest masters in the field, an act that he likens to a parrot mimicking human speech in a manner devoid of appropriate feeling and expression. In Mendelssohn's case, his remarkable talent made it relatively easy to imitate the outward form of whichever musical style he happened to choose as a model, but it was insufficient to propel him down the path established by Beethoven—the very path down which Wagner was now intent on traveling.

This essay represents one of several attempts by Wagner beginning around the middle of the century to publicly discredit Mendelssohn's music by portraying it as superficial in nature.[49] Aware of the extraordinary popularity and prestige that Mendelssohn enjoyed leading up to the time of his death, Wagner was motivated in this pursuit largely by a self-serving desire to establish himself as the sole legitimate heir to the Beethovenian legacy and thus as the standard-bearer of musical progress. This latter notion resonated with ideas of social and political advancement associated with the revolutions of 1848, which, although mostly unsuccessful, were thought by those in progressive circles to have been a harbinger of radical new developments in composition.

In this context, Wagner and other like-minded artists construed Mendelssohn's music as symbolic of the conservative, restoration-era politics against which the revolutionary aims had been directed. Moreover, as John Michael Cooper has noted, the overall transformation beginning around mid-century from a dialectical to a more linear view of history lent support to the idea that Mendelssohn's over-reliance on the music of the past was an indication of his reluctance to embrace an aesthetic of originality and forward-looking modernity.[50] Such developments helped to lay the foundation of a critical outlook whereby Mendelssohn's music was thought to lack the kind of individuality and expressive power that characterized the music of a composer like Beethoven or even Wagner.

As the voluminous literature on the composer's anti-Semitism has documented, Wagner's attitude toward the Jews grew out of a German tradition of anti-Semitic thought that found expression in the writings of such influential figures as Karl Marx and the theologian Bruno Bauer.[51] A convincing case has also been made that the tirade unleashed rather unexpectedly in 1850 owes much of its intensity to the jealousy and resentment directed toward the figure of Giacomo Meyerbeer, who is subjected to an even more searing critique than

Mendelssohn.[52] Although Wagner does not mention Meyerbeer by name, he clearly has him in mind when he notes that the unnamed composer under discussion "writes operas for Paris and sends them touring around the world."[53] Wagner's negative feelings toward Meyerbeer can be traced back to his initial stay in Paris, during which time the latter was riding high on the success of *Les Huguenots* (1836) while the former was barely eking out a living and trying to cope with his own frustrated operatic ambitions. Similarly, Wagner's attack on Mendelssohn can be explained at least partly by personal envy and resentment, considering that Mendelssohn was among the most celebrated living German composers in the late 1830s and early 1840s at a time when Wagner was struggling to get his career off the ground.

Although Wagner had criticized the music of these two composers prior to writing *Judaism in Music*, he had never systematically linked such criticism to their Jewish origins. Wagner's claim that the music of Jewish composers was superficial provides an obvious parallel to his views on the Mendelssohn-Tieck *Antigone*, which he believed had imitated the external form of Greek tragedy without conveying its true essence. And he clearly has a figure like Mendelssohn in mind when he argues that, because the educated Jew has betrayed his own origins and yet cannot fully assimilate into any other culture, he is necessarily denied access to the spirit of the *Volk* that animates all genuine art.[54] Mendelssohn's *Antigone* therefore lacks this vital connection and is completely unlike the *Gesamtkunstwerk* that Wagner outlines in the Zurich essays.

Finally, when Wagner asks in *Art and Revolution* just what it is that artists will not do on commission, he seems to be disparaging not only the "foolish restoration" of Greek tragedy but also the capitalist system that he and others associated above all with Jews. In *Judaism in Music*, Wagner repeatedly links Jews to the pursuit and control of money in modern European society, claiming near the outset that what the great artists of past centuries "had wrought with all-consuming effort, the Jew today converts into an art-commodity-exchange."[55] Viewed in this light, his criticism aimed indirectly at the royal commission of *Antigone* can be seen as an attempt to draw an implicit connection between Mendelssohn and the single-minded pursuit of wealth ascribed to Jews.

Ultimately, Wagner's rejection of the 1841 *Antigone* constitutes an attempt to exclude Mendelssohn, and to a lesser degree Tieck, from the legitimate pursuit of appropriating ancient Greek tragedy in the name of modern German drama. Mendelssohn, of course, is doubly indicted for his role in this artistic travesty. Not only is he complicit in the "white lie" of re-creating classical drama in a purely imitative fashion, but he compounds the offense by lending to this effort a facile and superficial musical style that, because of its composer's Jewish origins, is powerless to plumb the depths of Sophocles' timeless poetry. Just as in *Judaism in Music* Wagner sought to lay exclusive claim to the legacy of Beethoven by rejecting the music of Mendelssohn (and Meyerbeer), so too his earlier attack on the Mendelssohn-Tieck *Antigone* staked a claim to the likewise contested legacy of ancient Greece.

Reclaiming the Greek Legacy

By the time he wrote *Opera and Drama* in 1851, Wagner had become concerned not only with delegitimizing the Prussian revival of Greek tragedy but also with reclaiming the mythic significance of Sophocles' *Antigone* for his own reform goals. In the second part of this lengthy essay, Wagner offers a detailed analysis of the Oedipus myth as it is rendered by Sophocles in *Oedipus the King* and *Antigone* and by Aeschylus in *Seven against Thebes* (Sophocles' *Oedipus at Colonus* is referenced only in passing). His ostensible aim is to underscore the enduring power of myth by revealing how the Oedipus saga enacts "the entire history of mankind from the beginnings of society to the necessary downfall of the state."[56] Yet given the many parallels between the story of Oedipus and Wagner's retelling of the Nibelung myth in the *Ring*—some of which have yet to be acknowledged—his discussion of the former can also be seen as an attempt to construct a sociopolitical interpretive framework within which to understand the operatic tetralogy that would eventually grow out of *Siegfrieds Tod*, on which he was working at the time.

Wagner's interpretation of the Oedipus myth is based on his fundamental belief that society, as a collective entity that prizes order and established custom, necessarily encroaches on the will of the individual, who is prone to change and instability. As he explains:

> The outlook of society, so long as it fails to fully understand the essence of the individual and the manner in which it has itself arisen out of this essence, is a limiting and restrictive one, and it becomes ever more tyrannical to precisely the degree that the animated and innovative essence of the individual, propelled by an instinctive urge, challenges established custom.[57]

Wagner also claims that the ancient Greeks wrongly ascribed to the power of fate such instinctive yet ultimately disruptive behavior on the part of the individual. Rather, he tells us, this behavior constitutes simply the natural, unconscious action of the individual colliding with the more arbitrary and artificial character of societal convention. And it is precisely this sort of collision that defines the central events of the Oedipus myth.

Thus when Oedipus unwittingly murdered his father Laius, he was merely acting in self-defense against a potential threat to his own existence. Likewise, when he accepted the Theban throne and the hand of its widowed queen in return for solving the riddle of the Sphinx and saving the city from imminent destruction, he was again exercising a natural human impulse. Not until Oedipus' kinship to Laius and Jocasta was revealed did society (along with Oedipus himself) view his actions as a perversion of the customary relations between members of a family unit. Based on instinctive feelings concerning children's love for their parents and the distinction between sexual and familial love, the parameters of these relations had evolved over time into rigid societal conventions, of which Oedipus was in clear violation.

Wagner, however, argues that, because Oedipus never established the ties of familiarity out of which these boundaries naturally arise, his actions toward Laius and Jocasta are determined by his unconscious, human instinct and are thus undeserving of condemnation. The relationship between Oedipus and his mother was in no way a crime, least of all a crime against nature. Indeed, how could it have been if nature saw fit to bless this union with four healthy children, one of whom was Antigone, the very embodiment of "purely human" love and compassion?[58]

In recent decades, a handful of scholars have argued that Wagner's discussion of this incestuous relationship reveals something about his understanding of the incest motif in *Der Ring des Nibelungen*.[59] Wagner, it seems, viewed the union between the Volsung twins, Siegmund and Sieglinde, not as a violation against nature but against social morality. Moreover, this relationship between brother and sister, like Oedipus' marriage to his mother, produced a healthy offspring—in this case Siegfried, whose status as a redemptive agent bears a certain parallel to the role played by Antigone in the Oedipus saga.

When Wagner refers in an 1851 letter to "Wotan's struggle with his own inclination and with custom (Fricka)," he is clearly identifying Fricka as an allegory of societal convention.[60] As such, she acts as the guardian of wedlock and defends Hunding's cause against the adulterous twins, while at the same time expressing shock and outrage at the incestuous nature of their relationship. As Wotan explains to Fricka in Act II of *Die Walküre*: "It is always convention that is the only thing you can understand, but what concerns my mind is that which has never happened before." Here we find the manifestation of Wagner's opposition, outlined in *Opera and Drama*, between the natural, ever-changing will of the individual and the artificial, unbending consciousness of society as represented in the opera by Fricka.

Moreover, just as Oedipus and Jocasta succumb to the weight of societal judgment—she by committing suicide and he by mutilating himself—so too the love of Siegmund and Sieglinde must ultimately be sacrificed in the name of Fricka's honor.

Wagner's discussion of the Oedipus myth eventually focuses on Antigone and the crucial role that she plays in bringing about the necessary destruction of the state. He first explains how the bureaucratic state emerged imperceptibly out of society, adopting the latter's ethical laws to such a degree that the state became the abstract embodiment of convention. In other words, the state is characterized by a general adherence to established custom and a desire to preserve the status quo. It in turn acts as a destructive force on society by opposing the unconscious, instinctive human feelings to which, paradoxically, it owes its very existence.

Wagner then turns to that part of the Oedipus myth corresponding to Aeschylus' *Seven against Thebes* and Sophocles' *Antigone* in order to illustrate how the state effectively destroys society. Following Oedipus' exile from Thebes, his two sons, Eteocles and Polynices, had agreed to share the throne by alternately ruling for a year. But once the first year had passed, Eteocles refused to give up the crown, in response to which Polynices enlisted the aid of several allies and advanced on his native city. The two brothers battled and killed one another, leaving Creon to assume the throne (and setting the stage for the events depicted in *Antigone*). Wagner chastises the Theban public for supporting Eteocles' bid to retain the throne. He concludes that society, having grown accustomed to his reign, placed such a characteristically high value on maintaining existing conditions that it was willing to overlook his violation of a sworn oath. For similar reasons, the Thebans raised no objection to Creon's decree against burying the traitorous Polynices, as this prohibition was aimed at punishing an act that, while in some ways justifiable, had nonetheless undermined the stability of the state.

For Wagner, this outlook on the part of the public revealed the extent to which the "purely human" impulse of the individual had fallen victim to the more narrow-minded, self-serving interests of society. So entrenched was the collective desire for calm and stability that even those ethical conventions that once had compelled Oedipus to blind himself and Jocasta to take her own life were being increasingly disregarded. Wagner further concludes: "Wherever this ethical consciousness came into conflict with societal practice, it severed itself from the latter and established itself firmly as *religion*, whereas practical society molded itself into the *state*."[61] Thus religion became the main province of morality, whereas in the realm of the state, usefulness became the new standard by which one's actions were judged.

As a result of this fundamental separation between church and state, society was able to justify its moral transgressions by appealing to the religious sphere for absolution or by simply transferring its guilt to the representative of the state. So, for example, the Theban polis could support Eteocles in the interest of maintaining the status quo, safe in the belief that the gods would inflict their own brand of justice on the perpetrator himself. Thebes likewise turned a blind eye to the moral crime responsible for setting all of these turbulent events in motion, namely Laius' decision to have his infant son murdered in order to avoid fulfillment of the prophecy that this child would one day grow up to kill him. Wagner reasons that the public would have been more pleased had the murder actually been carried out, so that it could have avoided altogether the disturbance caused by Oedipus. Through its lack of moral outrage and its collective failure to act, society placed "calm and order" above an adherence to the instinctive, human sentiment that suggests a father should sacrifice his life for that of his child and not the other way around.[62]

Crumbling beneath the weight of immorality fueled by habit [Gewohnheit] and aversion to change, society found itself in need of a free, self-determining individual who would reintroduce a genuine, instinctively human morality. Creon made it clear through his decree that he favored the interests of the state over a steadfast allegiance to the ethical laws of humanity. Antigone, however, stood up in sole opposition to the state, defying Creon's order out of love for Polynices. But, as Wagner argues, the love she displayed was not familial love (*pace* Hegel) and certainly not sexual love, but rather a pure love born out of compassion for another human being, or what Wagner calls "purely human love" [reiner Menschenliebe].[63] Moreover, Antigone's love was also a "fully conscious" one. She was aware of the potential consequences of her actions and yet recognized the need to act. This awareness of love's redemptive power and her willingness to act in the face of self-destruction—what Wagner describes as the "consciousness of the unconscious"—makes Antigone the embodiment of purest love and thus the perfect human being. This view of Antigone, it is worth noting, departs markedly from Hegel's celebrated interpretation of Sophocles' play as a collision between two equal moral powers.

Through her purely human love, Antigone reveals to society the unethical nature of its own outlook. She not only convicts Theban society for passing judgment on Oedipus, Jocasta, and Polynices while ignoring the sins of Laius and Eteocles, but also serves as a force of redemption for humanity itself by bringing about the symbolic destruction of the state. In other words, her actions reveal the power of love to destroy the existing world order and usher in a new one defined by the presence of instinctively ethical human beings.

As a further testament to love's influence, Wagner points to the example of Haemon, who took his own life out of love for Antigone and in so doing reawakened within Creon his consciousness as a father. In the same way that Creon, the personification of the state, embraces his own humanity through the death of his son, so too is the state destroyed in the name of love so that, through death, it might once again represent life. As Wagner proclaims at the end of his extensive analysis of Antigone, adding emphasis to underscore the centrality of these words to his broader argument: *"O holy Antigone! On you I now call! Let your banner wave so that beneath it we might destroy and yet redeem!"*[64]

Tellingly, one of the most overt references to the 1841 *Antigone* that Wagner makes in the reform essays comes immediately following this passage. He notes with considerable irony that when a certain poet, longing to see a "perfect art form," convinced the reigning monarch to call for the performance of a Greek tragedy, the choice fell on none other than *Antigone*. He goes on to point out that, though the ostensible aim was to present the highest representative of Greek drama, it so happened that this work also portrayed the destruction of the state. Noting how much this production pleased the "learned old children" at the Prussian court, Wagner compares them to Mephistopheles, who, toward the end of Goethe's *Faust*, witnessed roses being showered down from on high by a host of redeeming angels, only to be gripped by feelings of lust and desire toward the angels themselves. According to Wagner, those who witnessed the 1841 *Antigone* likewise failed to recognize the import of the moment. What should have revealed to them the power of Antigone's purely human love and its potential for redeeming mankind instead merely appealed to their academic nature and whetted their appetite for subsequent re-creations of ancient drama characterized by a cold and fussy philological impulse.

Insofar as *Opera and Drama* paved the way for what would eventually become *Der Ring des Nibelungen*, Wagner's attempt to claim ownership of *Antigone* in the face of the successful Mendelssohn-Tieck production lends considerable weight to the idea that Sophocles' play served as one of the main influences on the composer's retelling of the Nibelung myth. Scholars have traditionally looked to the works of Aeschylus as potential models for the *Ring*, perhaps taking into consideration the composer's own admiration for this poet. As we saw above, Petsch appears to have been the first commentator to claim a substantial link between Wagner's *Ring* and Aeschylus' partially extant Prometheus trilogy, prompting a number of scholars after him to do the same.

Scholars have pointed in particular to the resemblance between *Prometheus Bound* and *Die Walküre*. Both of these works feature a principal character—Prometheus in one case and Brünnhilde in the other—who is confined to a remote place as punishment for disobedience to the ruler of the gods. Moreover, both figures also come to the aid of a female character (Io and Sieglinde, respectively) whose descendant will one day set them free. In contrast to those scholars who have looked for parallels between the *Ring* and the Prometheus trilogy are those who have identified Aeschylus' *Oresteia* as an important model. Chief among this group is Michael Ewans, who has argued that Wagner borrowed not only the content of Aeschylus' trilogy but also aspects of its overall form and pacing.[65]

Surprisingly little attention, however, has been devoted to exploring similarities between the *Ring* and the Oedipus myth, especially in light of Wagner's extensive discussion of the latter. Dieter Borchmeyer was one of the first scholars to point out this connection, arguing that perhaps the most striking link between the two is the incest motif as it is manifested in the figures of Oedipus and Jocasta, on the one hand, and Siegmund and Sieglinde, on the other.[66] Borchmeyer suggests that Wagner's analysis of the Oedipus myth was intended to show the affinity, from both the perspectives of form and content, between *Antigone* and what at the time was known as *Siegfrieds Tod*, later to become *Götterdämmerung*:

> That there was originally an analogy between the "decline of the state" at the end of Sophocles' tragedy and the twilight of the gods at the end of the *Ring*, and that both of these are symbolic pointers to that mythical state of the world when, at the end of time, political domination is no more, ought... to be self-evident, in spite of later attempts by Wagner to reinterpret the tetralogy in the light of Schopenhauerian metaphysics.[67]

Borchmeyer further maintains that both the Sophoclean and the Wagnerian interpretations of the two myths presuppose a future state in which the individual will transcend such external forces as fate or societal convention in order to become wholly free and self-determining—though in this case he comes perilously close to projecting Wagner's own reading of the Oedipus myth onto Sophocles' rendering of it.

Not long before Borchmeyer's work appeared, L. J. Rather outlined a different set of parallels between Wagner's *Ring* and the story of Oedipus.[68] Rather claimed that Wagner's Siegfried was in many ways analogous to the figure of Antigone in that both were products of an incestuous union and both assumed the role of savior. In Wagner's conception of the *Ring*, "the savior-hero Siegfried would replace the savior-heroine Antigone, both representative of the liberated and perfected human beings of the future."[69]

Like Antigone, Siegfried accomplishes the crucial task of supplanting the existing world order and paving the way for a new one that will exist on a higher plane. Wagner himself described Siegfried as "the [human being] of the future whom we desire and long for but who cannot be made by us, since he must create himself on the basis of *our own annihilation*."[70] But, as Rather points out (and as Wagner once suggested in a letter to August Röckel), the perfect human being that emerges in the *Ring* is in actuality not Siegfried but rather an amalgam of Siegfried and Brünnhilde, each of whom alone proves unable to carry out the act of redemption necessary to bring about a satisfactory resolution of the events set in motion by Alberich's theft of the Rhine-gold.[71] Rather sees this abstract "Siegfried-Brünnhilde" as Wagner's attempt to reconcile the male and female principles, a process that replicates on some level the sought-after union of word and tone characteristic of the composer's operatic reform project.

Rather also points to several additional, albeit less fundamental, similarities between Wagner's *Ring* and the Oedipus legend. For instance, he points out that, just as Oedipus fails to recognize the stranger who obstructs his path as his father, so too is Siegfried unaware that the meddlesome old man who attempts to bar his way in Act III of *Siegfried* is in fact his grandfather. Moreover, in much the same way that Oedipus, who is unwittingly headed toward a union with his mother, kills Laius, Siegfried shatters Wotan's spear while making his way toward Brünnhilde, whom he initially takes to be his mother.[72]

Historian Mark Berry, in a recent book on politics and religion in the *Ring*, suggests in passing several links between the Oedipus myth and Wagner's tetralogy. Like Borchmeyer and Rather, he detects a basic parallel between the incestuous relationship of Oedipus and Jocasta and that of the Volsung twins, pointing to the healthy offspring that arise from these unions and citing Wagner's claim in *Opera and Drama* that sexual love serves to break the narrow bonds of family life and to expand into wider human society.[73]

Elsewhere Berry maintains that Wotan's stance toward his subjects is similar to that of Sophocles' Creon. Here he has in mind Creon's belief that a secure "ship of state" is crucial to a peaceful existence, and he sees this attitude reflected in Wotan's clearly arduous task of "state-formation" among a highly diverse and hierarchical society comprising Nibelungs, giants, gods, and mortals.[74] Berry also draws a comparison between the figures of Antigone and Brünnhilde. Pointing to Wagner's argument that Antigone acts out of purely human love, Berry concludes: "Brünnhilde, who understood nothing of politics, acts through necessity, both internal and political, through sympathy or purest human love."[75] Brünnhilde's "self-annihilation and her love-curse upon oaths" signals the end of Valhalla and the effective destruction of the state, just as in Wagner's reading of the Oedipus myth Antigone's actions destroy the Theban state.

Berry's remarks on the subject, although made only in passing, come closest to identifying what I argue is a fundamental affinity between Sophocles' Antigone and Wagner's Brünnhilde—an affinity that can be seen as part of the composer's attempt to reclaim the legacy of Greek tragedy from the successful Mendelssohn-Tieck *Antigone*. Wagner's fascination with the Oedipus myth—and with the figure of Antigone in particular—is evident from the attention it receives in *Opera and Drama*. We also know from the diary of his wife Cosima that he was equally gripped by Sophocles' celebrated tragedy based on this character. According to an entry from August 18, 1878, Wagner read aloud the passage in *Opera and Drama* that centers on Antigone, in response to which Cosima expressed her admiration for Sophocles' play and elicited the following response from her husband: "I was completely obsessed with [Sophocles' *Antigone*] at the time, I could not have composed a single note of music, so absorbed was I in it."[76] This self-described obsession may help to explain Wagner's repeated references to the 1841 production of the play, and at the same time lends further credence to the idea that he conceived of the main female protagonist in his operatic tetralogy as a virtual reincarnation of Sophocles' timeless heroine.

What binds Antigone and Brünnhilde together as spiritual kin is the role that each plays in bringing about redemption through love, or more precisely, through "purely human love." We have seen that, in Wagner's interpretation of the Oedipus myth, Antigone's determination to bury Polynices is rooted not in the love of a sister for her brother (as many commentators have suggested), but rather stems from the sort of human compassion that transcends all familial, cultural, social, and political ties. So whereas for Hegel, who views this play as a conflict between the spheres of public and private, Antigone functions primarily as a defender of the "unwritten and everlasting laws of the gods," for Wagner, she embodies above all the spirit of her memorable line: "I was born to join in love, not hate—that is my nature."[77]

Both Wagner's libretto for the *Ring* and, more importantly, the music set to it indicate his concern for demonstrating that Brünnhilde's actions are motivated by the same purely human love that drove Antigone to openly defy Creon's decree. Thus Brünnhilde's violation of Wotan's command to protect Hunding in battle against Siegmund grows out of compassion for the latter. When she initially confronts Siegmund in the so-called "Annunciation of

Death" scene that occurs in Act II of *Die Walküre*, she declares that she will be carrying the soon-to-be-slain hero off to Valhalla in accordance with Wotan's wishes. Yet Brünnhilde takes pity on Siegmund after he states his intention of giving up Valhalla's eternal bliss out of love for Sieglinde. Accused by Siegmund of being "unsympathetic" [fühllose], she responds using the leitmotif heard when she first laid eyes on the hero at the outset of the scene: "I see the distress that gnaws away at your heart, I feel the hero's holy sorrow." She then says that she will protect Sieglinde, in response to which Siegmund proclaims that, if he is to die, he shall first kill his sister-bride. Brünnhilde in turn feels compelled to reveal that Sieglinde is carrying his child, and it is in conjunction with these lines that the orchestra intones a fragment of the leitmotif first associated with the instinctive love of the Volsung twins for one another. The presence here of the love motif (as it is often called) can be understood as both an evocation of the "blissful" love that has resulted in the unborn child stirring in Sieglinde's womb and a representation of Brünnhilde's love for the Volsungs, which will be directed most fervently toward Siegfried. Brünnhilde ultimately determines to protect both Siegmund and Sieglinde, but she is thwarted in this task by Wotan. As she reveals toward the end of the opera, her decision was motivated by love and her desire to fulfill Wotan's inner will. "My own instinct told me to do only one thing," she explains to Wotan, "to love that which you loved."

Wotan himself later acknowledges Brünnhilde's significance as an agent of love and redemption. In the guise of the Wanderer, he informs the earth goddess Erda in the final act of *Siegfried* that Brünnhilde, the child they share together, will be awoken by Siegfried and will redeem the world through her actions. His words are initially accompanied by an orchestral presentation of a motivic idea that is associated throughout the cycle with love (example 7.1) and that Deryck Cooke has identified as an emblem of "love in its totality," calling this theme "one of the central and most fertile ideas in the *Ring*."[78]

Brünnhilde's act of redemption is the culminating event of the cycle and its final opera, *Götterdämmerung*, which offers perhaps the strongest evidence of a fundamental affinity between Antigone and Brünnhilde. It is here we come to realize that only Brünnhilde's self-annihilation can bring about the downfall of the gods and usher in a new world order. Siegfried, of course, also has a chance to return the ring to the Rhinemaidens, but refuses after he perceives their warning about its curse as a threat. He possesses neither the love nor the understanding required to perform the necessary deed. For her part, Brünnhilde initially dismisses Waltraute's plea in the first act of *Götterdämmerung* to give up the ring, explaining that it was given to her by Siegfried as a "pledge of love" [Liebespfand]. Even upon learning that only through this

EXAMPLE 7.1 Wagner, *Siegfried*, Act III, sc. i.

action will Valhalla's despair come to an end, Brünnhilde responds unequivocally that she will never renounce love and never allow it to be taken from her by the gods. She utters these words to the leitmotif associated with the renunciation of love, a thematic idea first heard in Act I of *Das Rheingold* as the Rhinemaiden Woglinde explained to Alberich the sacrifice required of anyone wishing to obtain the gold. Brünnhilde's devotion to Siegfried is thus presented here as the polar opposite of Alberich's fateful love curse; whereas Alberich renounced love in order to win the gold out of which he fashioned the ring, Brünnhilde, who already possesses the ring but acknowledges it only as a symbol of love, refuses to part with it.

Brünnhilde is made wise only through Siegfried's death, whereupon she recognizes the need to return the ring to its rightful owners. As she states near the end of the opera: "The innocent one had to betray me so that I should become a wise woman." At last she understands and appreciates the redemptive role that she must play, and she readily accepts this responsibility. Thus she tells Grane, her trusty steed, that her bosom burns with desire to embrace Siegfried, and she exclaims in her final line, just before leaping into the all-consuming flames, that she blissfully greets her departed husband. Just as Antigone knowingly risked her life to ensure Polynices' passage to the underworld, so too does Brünnhilde willingly sacrifice herself in order to follow Siegfried into death. Yet, as Brünnhilde makes clear, her actions also cleanse the ring of Alberich's curse and bring about the ultimate destruction of Valhalla—the latter representing an obvious parallel to the symbolic destruction of the state that Wagner ascribed to Antigone. The almost exclusive focus in the final moments of the opera on the motif that Wagner once dubbed the "Glorification of Brünnhilde" affirms her importance to the composer as a figure whose willing death, like that of Antigone, constitutes the expression of a "purely human" love.

Wagner's conviction that, through this love, Antigone brought about the downfall of the state clearly resonates with some of the revolutionary ideas that he espoused during the 1840s and '50s. It will be recalled, for example, that the "great revolution of mankind" envisioned by Wagner was supposed to herald the advent of a new world order based on a foundation of love and freedom. As scholars have often pointed out, the *Ring* can be understood as a dramatization of such revolutionary aims, with the fall of Valhalla symbolizing the collapse of the contemporary social and political order. Insofar as this is true, the figure of Antigone seems to have provided the composer with a model of the kind of selfless and compassionate individual necessary for instigating such momentous change. The fact that the Sophoclean play based on this character had recently come to the forefront of European culture through a highly influential albeit, in Wagner's mind, misguided production must have affirmed for him the lasting importance of this drama and the artistic significance of appropriating elements of it in a work that aimed to breathe the spirit of Greek tragedy into the soul of modern opera.

To be clear, it would be a mistake to say that the *Ring* was somehow a response to the Mendelssohn-Tieck *Antigone*. Rather, what the above observations seek to reveal is that Wagner formulated many of his aesthetic ideas in light of this successful production, and that these ideas in turn informed elements of his approach to both the music and text of his tetralogy. The role of Brünnhilde as a source of redemption can be linked to Wagner's attraction to Antigone, which itself reflects a general obsession with the Greeks. Other similarities of the *Ring* to the Oedipus saga, as well as its grounding in Germanic myth, point to the composer's desire to create a music drama that embodied the essence of classical tragedy. Finally, Wagner's repeated references to the 1841 *Antigone* as a wrongheaded attempt to "authentically" re-create Greek tragedy make it clear that he viewed his own effort to capture the spirit of ancient drama in direct opposition to the undertaking of Mendelssohn and Tieck.

A great irony of Wagner's stance against this production is that one of the key elements of his operatic reform, the use of Stabreim in the librettos for the *Ring*, bears a striking similarity to a defining aspect of the "ancient" musical language devised by Mendelssohn for *Antigone*. Wagner's decision to replace traditional end-rhyme with an alliterative rhyme scheme characteristic of medieval German poetry contributed to a departure from conventional four-bar phrasing that resulted in a relationship between text and music not unlike that of Mendelssohn's *Antigone*. There, it may be recalled, Mendelssohn's attempt to convey the poetic meter often generated uneven phrases stemming from the irregular line lengths of Donner's metrical translation. In Wagner's case, the greater flexibility of line lengths and syllabic stresses typical of Stabreim allowed the composer to organize portions of his score in accordance with musico-poetic periods in which the music responds to the poetry by creating "open" forms that are marked by the frequent occurrence of uneven phrasing. The suggestion here is not that Wagner set out to imitate Mendelssohn, but rather that both works are rooted in a kind of "ancient" aesthetic whereby the poetic conventions of a distant past give rise to a musical approach that departs from the contemporary norm in some fundamental way.

Ultimately, the attention that Wagner devoted to criticizing the Mendelssohn-Tieck *Antigone* suggests the broad cultural and aesthetic significance of this production around the middle of the nineteenth century. It also underscores the continuing relevance of ancient Greek culture at a time when many educated Germans were still attempting to come to terms with the broader political implications of the failed revolutions of 1848–49. As for Wagner's own mid-century views of ancient Greece, they seem to have been colored as much by the then-current trend of reviving Greek tragedy with music as by the tenets of a German Hellenism that, although rooted in the eighteenth century, had left an indelible mark on the nineteenth century as well.

CHAPTER EIGHT | Epilogue
The Decline of a Genre

DESPITE THE SUCCESS of the 1841 *Antigone* and other productions like it, the revival of Greek tragedy with music failed to have a significant impact on artistic developments of the later nineteenth century. The compositions to which this trend gave rise gradually fell into obscurity, while the genre of stage music that they represented proved unsuccessful at becoming the mainstream alternative to traditional opera that some early observers had predicted it would. And to the degree that such works were composed at all during the second half of the nineteenth century, they were invariably undertaken by minor composers, typically for productions in school theaters.

To be sure, the practice of staging ancient drama with the aid of music was destined to be somewhat esoteric given the relative unfamiliarity with Greek tragedy on the part of most theatergoers. This was essentially the point made by A. B. Marx when he expressed his objection to this trend in his influential text on nineteenth-century music. With the Mendelssohn-Tieck *Antigone* foremost in mind, Marx called the restoration of Greek tragedy "an undertaking unsuitable for our time and void of living interest, however highly it may have been extolled by zealous philologists, or by the members of that 'highly refined' society, which is continually on the lookout for something new and classic."[1]

Indeed, it appears as if the "learned" nature of these productions often served as an obstacle to their success. Reviewing an 1870 performance of *Antigone* that occurred in Hamburg, a local correspondent for the *Allgemeine musikalische Zeitung* explained the audience's lukewarm response by noting: "Our city probably belongs among those places that are least suited to take pleasure in such a restoration of ancient taste; there is simply more *Bildung* required than one should expect to find here."[2] Others viewed the inevitable association of this trend with the (Prussian) royal court as one of the principal reasons for its failure to find broad public appeal. As the music critic and historian Friedrich Chrysander, writing in 1876, claimed of Mendelssohn's *Antigone*: "From the beginning it was a glittering and original private undertaking, and so it remains today."[3]

Another factor behind the genre's failure to capture the public's long-term imagination appears to have been the rise of Wagnerian opera in the second half of the nineteenth century. On this point, the later reception of Mendelssohn's *Antigone* proves instructive. In stark contrast to the early, mostly favorable reviews of the music, those that appeared in roughly the last quarter of the century tended to be highly critical and even dismissive of the work. Of course, this change in outlook occurred partly as a result of shifting aesthetic tastes, and in many ways mirrors the overall reception of Mendelssohn's music. Nevertheless, the widespread dissemination of Wagner's artistic theories and the popular notion that his music dramas represented the modern embodiment of Greek tragedy helped to create an atmosphere in which Mendelssohn's *Antigone* was increasingly viewed as having failed to meet the demands of reconciling modern music with ancient drama.

As we saw in the previous chapter, the idea of Wagnerian music drama as a *Gesamtkunstwerk* conceived in the spirit of Attic tragedy was one that originated with Wagner himself in the reform essays completed around 1850. He would later come to distance himself from the sociopolitical overtones of this claim, but musicians and critics in the ensuing decades began increasingly to discuss his post-1850 operas with reference to the "total artwork" that the composer had equated with ancient Greek tragedy.[4] Most famously, Friedrich Nietzsche claimed in *The Birth of Tragedy*, published in 1872 with a dedication to Wagner, that the latter's music dramas signaled the modern advent of classical tragedy.

Dismissed by the academic establishment but received favorably by the public, Nietzsche's work underscored the association of Wagnerian opera with Greek tragedy, however tenuous this link may have been in reality. Within this changing cultural and musical landscape, Mendelssohn's *Antigone*—itself once celebrated for having captured the spirit of Greek tragedy—was now frequently described as inadequate, irrelevant, or, at best, utterly misguided. Although these later critics rarely mention Wagner by name, they appear to have been implicitly judging *Antigone* against a Wagnerian standard when they concluded, in essence, that Mendelssohn's music was not integral to the effect of the whole.

So whereas critics of the 1840s might have faulted one or another aspect of Mendelssohn's score, those of the later nineteenth century frequently questioned the very idea of writing music for a Greek tragedy. The Hamburg correspondent mentioned above deemed the use of music in the performance of Greek tragedy "superfluous," in that "a mere reading of the original or even of a good translation provides the cultured individual with a much deeper and purer enjoyment of these works."[5] An anonymous critic writing for the *Musikalisches Wochenblatt* reached a similar conclusion, proclaiming in response to a Viennese performance of 1872 that combined Mendelssohn's music with an abridged version of Sophocles' play: "The unhealthiness of this artistic genre—the decoration of ancient tragedy with modern music—was felt by every impartial observer to be more embarrassing than ever."[6]

The Hamburg correspondent had attributed the ineffectiveness of the production directly to Mendelssohn's music: "One may regret the audience's unresponsiveness but must also concede that at the basis of this disapproving stance lies the right sentiment, for Mendelssohn did not adhere to the proper path in his use of music as a way of reviving Greek drama."[7] Unfortunately, the author never elaborates on this "proper path" except to say that, in order for such productions to gain broad appeal, the music would have to become more Greek. Criticizing Mendelssohn's score in a similarly vague fashion, a critic for the *Allgemeine musikalische Zeitung* who reported on the 1873 Munich court production of *Antigone* remarked that often the music was "completely inappropriate," though this reviewer at least noted a favorable response on the part of the audience.[8]

One of the harshest critiques leveled against Mendelssohn's work came in response to a production of *Antigone* that took place in 1881 at the Vienna Court Opera. A critic for the *Allgemeine musikalische Zeitung* claimed that the production's musical component constituted nothing more than "a frequently disturbing and obtrusive ornamentation," adding that the melodramatic portions of the score seemed especially so in relation to the "colossal proportions of the plot" [*Riesengestalten der Handlung*].[9] Lamenting the general lack of knowledge surrounding Greek music, this critic went on to describe the composer's effort as "almost purely dilettantish." Once again the implication is that the music should somehow be more Greek, though presumably not in such a way that it attempts to imagine the sound of ancient music. By characterizing Mendelssohn's music as ornamental, the author seems to be suggesting its insignificance relative to the drama and thus its failure to assume the same importance that music was thought to have assumed in ancient Greek tragedy. Such a stance is qualitatively different from that taken by early commentators who, when criticizing Mendelssohn's music as "un-Greek," were claiming not that it was ornamental in the face of the drama, but rather that it seemed to overwhelm the ancient poetry.

With one notable exception, these later commentators refrain from making any explicit reference to Wagner. Yet the language they employ frequently recalls the composer's own criticism of Mendelssohn's music and suggests a viewpoint influenced by a Wagnerian aesthetic. By characterizing the music to *Antigone* as decorative and calling the work "dilettantish," these critics appear to have been decrying the very "grace" and "cheerfulness" that earlier ones saw as a reflection of the ancient Greek spirit, embodied above all in Mendelssohn's setting of the "Ode to Man." Insofar as this is true, these later claims also reflect a general move away from a Winckelmannian view of antiquity, one that appears to have been taken almost for granted during the early part of the century. Nietzsche's *Birth of Tragedy*, with its emphasis on the Dionysian elements of ancient Greek culture, itself signaled a growing inability to sustain faith in Winckelmann's idealized portrayal of the Greeks.

For most late nineteenth-century critics confronting Mendelssohn's *Antigone*, the work's naïve character was more of a liability than an asset, associated as it was with an increasingly outdated view of Greek antiquity. Or to frame the issue in Nietzschean terms: Mendelssohn's music, with its concern for conveying text and meter through what might be called a refined simplicity, was blind to the Dionysian element inherent in Attic tragedy and thus was negatively associated with the Apollonian. Wagner's music, on the other hand, with its sensual nature and rich, chromatic language, was rooted precisely in this Dionysian impulse and therefore breathed the spirit of classical tragedy in a way that Mendelssohn's work simply did not. Moreover, the view of Mendelssohn's *Antigone* as somehow lacking or superfluous resonates with Wagner's anti-Semitic critique of the composer as a mere imitator of other, more profound musical styles. And it is perhaps worth recalling here that Wagner's notorious *Judaism in Music* was reissued in 1869 in a slightly revised version—this time with his authorship fully acknowledged.

The one late nineteenth-century commentator who did mention Wagner by name was the little-known American music historian Arthur M. Little, who completed a dissertation on Mendelssohn's *Antigone* at the University of Leipzig sometime in the early 1890s. Published in the United States in 1893, Little's work devotes fully half of one chapter to discussing the relationship between Greek tragedy and Wagnerian music drama.[10] As Little explains, the purpose of this inquiry is to attain a firmer grasp of Greek drama and thereby to better understand Mendelssohn's task of composing music for *Antigone*. In a subsequent chapter, he arrives at the following conclusion: "The modern world looked eagerly for a music-drama at Mendelssohn's hands; it found only an enrichment, however wonderful, of concert music, suggested to the gifted composer by the beautiful choruses of *Antigone*."[11]

According to Little, Mendelssohn's music had failed precisely because it came to assume a life of its own, divorced from the drama for which it was composed. Echoing what by now had become a familiar criticism, Little complained that the music was "not in the right style." He maintained that Mendelssohn was more concerned with writing beautiful music than with creating a score that served both poetry and plot. As he explained: "There is something radically wrong in any music for a Greek tragedy which may be detached from its vital connection with the drama, and find an independent life of its own when transplanted into a concert hall."[12] Whereas Little regarded Wagner's later operas as a synthesis of music and drama not unlike that of Greek tragedy itself—hence the section comparing the two—he viewed Mendelssohn's *Antigone* as little more than a series of pleasing choral numbers loosely connected to Sophocles' play.

Ending the present study with a discussion of Mendelssohn's *Antigone* seems fitting for at least two reasons. First, it brings us back to the work that initially sparked the nineteenth-century trend of reviving ancient drama with music. Second, of all the music to Greek tragedy discussed in this book, only *Antigone* continued to be heard with any regularity into the final decades of the nineteenth century and the opening decades of the twentieth.[13] Moreover, the legacy of the Mendelssohn-Tieck *Antigone* was reflected in productions of Greek tragedy that occurred on the European stage even after Mendelssohn's work had begun to fade from view.

In England, the practice of staging Greek plays in the original language at Cambridge University began in 1882 with a production of Sophocles' *Ajax*. Inspired most immediately by performances of *Agamemnon* at Oxford and *Oedipus the King* at Harvard University in 1880 and 1881, respectively, the Cambridge tradition continues to this day with productions given triennially.[14] The music for the inaugural production was composed by George Macfarren, who had known Mendelssohn and had conducted the London premiere of *Antigone* at Covent Garden in 1845.

The use of music in these early Cambridge performances appears to have raised many of the same questions and presented many of the same challenges that had confronted Mendelssohn some forty years earlier. As the classicist H. J. Edwards wrote in an essay for the *Cambridge Review* in 1900:

> Was [the musical treatment of the choruses] to be an archaeological attempt to reproduce a music of which little enough was known and scarcely nothing had survived—or an arrangement upon modern lines, with choral and orchestral numbers? The new order, in this as in other details, prevailed over the old.... Under these conditions the composer

upon whom it falls to set the ancient choruses is an interpreter of paramount importance, for to many of the audience his work supplies a link by which alone, or almost alone, they may come at the spirit of the play which they are witnessing.[15]

Among those who wrote music during the first two decades of the series are some of the most celebrated names in English composition of the late nineteenth and early twentieth century, including Hubert Parry, Charles Villiers Stanford, and Ralph Vaughan Williams.[16] Although these works utilize an up-to-date "modern" idiom that makes them appear quite different in nature from Mendelssohn's Greek stage works, they nonetheless feature many of the same key elements, including the frequent use of melodrama and unison choral textures. Vaughan Williams, who wrote music for the 1909 production of Aristophanes' comedy *The Wasps*, paid homage to Mendelssohn by including a blatant quotation of the *Lied ohne Worte*, Op. 62, No. 6 ("Spring Song"), at the beginning of one of his melodramatic numbers. Ultimately, the fact that such productions were performed both in Greek and within the confines of the school theater affirms that the practice of staging Greek tragedy with music had by then become a largely academic, somewhat esoteric pursuit.

In Germany of the twentieth century, the rapprochement of music and Greek tragedy continued along both operatic lines, as in the case of a work like Richard Strauss's *Elektra* (1909), and in connection with a more broadly conceived theatrical tradition, such as the radical stage experiments by Carl Orff, *Antigonae* (1949), *Oedipus der Tyrann* (1958), and *Prometheus desmotes* (1967). Although a discussion of such works is beyond the scope of this study, it is worth noting some basic similarities and differences between these undertakings and those explored in the above pages.

Strauss's music for *Elektra*—and the libretto by Hofmannsthal upon which it was based—can be said to represent a decisive break with the prevailing nineteenth-century German view of ancient Greece. Whereas Mendelssohn and Tieck were primarily concerned with restoring elements of the Sophoclean original, Strauss and Hofmannsthal were engaged in a self-consciously modernist rewriting of the ancient work—one that, in the eyes of many contemporaries, constituted nothing less than an assault on the original and its governing aesthetic.[17]

Orff's Greek works, while ostensibly a more radical "assault" on antiquity, are ultimately more closely aligned with the Mendelssohnian tradition. Like Mendelssohn, Orff employed restricted instrumentation along with the pervasive use of repeated-note, speech-like singing in what appears to represent an attempt at evoking aspects of ancient Greek practice. Moreover, for all of the obvious differences among Orff's Greek works, they are united by an experimental approach to reconciling modern music and ancient drama through a distinctive blend of elements both past and present, as the composer's use of translations by Friedrich Hölderlin (1770–1843) and the original Greek in *Prometheus* clearly attest.

Although neither the Greek-inspired works of Strauss nor those of Orff appear to be direct descendants of Mendelssohn's Sophoclean settings, their mere existence points to the continued significance of ancient Greece within German culture of the twentieth century. As we have seen, the nineteenth-century manifestation of this cultural affinity in works such as Mendelssohn's *Antigone* combined the spheres of art, scholarship, and politics into a single endeavor. We have also seen how this endeavor was fraught with questions surrounding the relationship of a glorious yet idealized classical past to an emerging modern Germany with an increasingly strong sense of national identity rooted in a common history and shared cultural heritage. Along with the radical ideas of Wagner that were formulated against its backdrop, this development of staging Greek tragedy with music stands as a testament to the enduring legacy of ancient Greece, while reminding us of the degree to which this legacy left its lasting imprint on German music of the nineteenth century.

NOTES

Introduction

1. For a reproduction and detailed description of this medallion, see Flashar, *Mendelssohn und die griechische Tragödie*, 27–28.
2. Friedrich Wilhelm IV to Prince Johann of Saxony, July 8, 1846. Georg, *Briefwechsel*, 225–26.
3. Butler, *Tyranny of Greece*; and Rehm, *Griechentum und Goethezeit*.
4. For a good overview, see the chapters on Germany in Dover, *Perceptions*.
5. Steinberg, "Incidental Politics."
6. One of the most articulate statements of this view is found in Bourdieu, *Field of Cultural Production*, esp. 29–73.
7. Flashar, *Mendelssohn und die griechische Tragödie*. Among other works by this author, see esp. Flashar, *Inszenierung der Antike*, 60–81.
8. Boetius, *Wiedergeburt*.
9. Flashar, "Mendelssohn-Bartholdys Vertonung antiker Dramen."
10. See Wagner, *Judaism in Music*, GS 5:66–85 (PW 3:79–122).
11. See Geary, "Incidental Music."

Chapter 1

1. Schiller, *Über die aesthetische Erziehung*, 20:322.
2. See Behler, "Force of Classical Greece."
3. Quoted in *Die schönsten Aufsätze Goethes*, ed. Horst Oppel (Recklinghausen: Bitter, 1948), 493. Unless otherwise noted, translations are my own.
4. Hegel, *Geschichte der Philosophie*, 117.
5. On this topic, see Vick, "Greek Origins," esp. 495–97; and Walter Rüegg, "Die Antike als Begründung des deutschen Nationalbewußtseins," in *Antike in der Moderne*, ed. Wolfgang Schuller (Konstanz: Universitätsverlag Konstanz, 1985), 267–87.

6. Fragment no. 137. Quoted and translated by Andrew Knight in Dover (ed.), *Perceptions*, 195.

7. The most comprehensive accounts of German Hellenism, albeit from a literary perspective, remain Butler, *Tyranny*; Rehm, *Griechentum*; and Hatfield, *Aesthetic Paganism*.

8. On Winckelmann's influence, see especially Potts, *Flesh*; and Uhlig, *Griechenland*.

9. Winckelmann, *Thoughts on Imitation*, 33.

10. Ibid., 42.

11. See the chapter on the Middle Ages by Jan M. Ziolkowski in Kallendorf (ed.), *A Companion*, 17–29.

12. Winckelmann, *Thoughts on Imitation*, 33.

13. Winckelmann, *History of Ancient Art*, 2:179–80.

14. See Hatfield, *Winckelmann*; and Fridrich, *Sehnsucht*.

15. The sculpture of Laocoön, which dates from around 40–20 B.C., served as an important point of reference for German writers on aesthetics in the late eighteenth century.

16. This essay is reprinted in Herder, *Sämtliche Werke*, thirty-three vols., ed. Bernhard Suphan (Hildesheim: Georg Olms Verlag, 1967), 15:35–50, at 49.

17. Bruce Alan Brown, "Gluck," in *The New Grove Dictionary of Music and Musicians*, second ed., ed. Stanley Sadie (New York: Macmillan, 2001), 10:46.

18. Winckelmann, *Thoughts on Imitation*, 42.

19. Translated in *Strunk's Source Readings in Music History*, vol. 5, ed. Wye J. Allanbrook (New York: Norton, 1998), 932–34. Even if the preface was not authored by Gluck, as some have suggested, it was clearly written by someone with knowledge of Gluck's approach to the music.

20. Quoted and translated in F. J. Lamport, *German Classical Drama: Theatre, Humanity and Nation* (Cambridge: Cambridge University Press, 1990), 11.

21. G. E. Lessing, "Briefe, die neuste Literatur betreffend," in *Lessings Werke*, ed. Gunter E. Grimm (Frankfurt am Main: Deutscher Klassiker Verlag, 1997), 4:500–01.

22. See Herder, "Shakespeare," in *Selected Writings on Aesthetics*, ed. and trans. Gregory Moore (Princeton, NJ: Princeton University Press, 2006), 293–97.

23. Ibid., 296.

24. Marchand, *Down from Olympus*, 4.

25. On the nineteenth-century reception of Winckelmann, see Esther Sophia Sünderhauf, *Griechensehnsucht und Kulturkritik: die deutsche Rezeption von Winckelmanns Antikenideal 1840–1945* (Berlin: Akademie Verlag, 2004), esp. 1–20.

26. Quoted in Trevelyan, *Goethe*, 130.

27. Grair, "Antiquity," 71.

28. See Goethe's letter of March 23, 1787, which appeared as part of the *Italienische Reise*. Reprinted in *Goethes Werke: Hamburger Ausgabe in 14 Bänden*, ed. Erich Trunz (Munich: C. H. Beck, 1981), 11:219–20.

29. Quoted and translated in Grair, "Antiquity," 71.

30. Franz Schubert completed a setting of this poem in 1819.

31. Goethe, "Winckelmann," 237.

32. Schiller, *On the Naïve and Sentimental*, 34.

33. Schiller implies in thinly veiled terms that Goethe is a modern example of a naïve poet.

34. See Grair, "Antiquity," 77–78.

35. Joachim Wohlleben, "Germany, 1750–1830," in Dover (ed.), *Perceptions*, 170.

36. See, e.g., Humboldt's 1793 essay, "Über das Studium des Altertums, und des griechischen insbesondere," in *Gesammelte Schriften*, 1:255–81.

37. Humboldt, "Geschichte des Verfalls und Unterganges der Griechischen Freistaaten," in *Gesammelte Schriften*, 3:171–218, at 184.

38. McClelland, *State, Society, and University*, 119.

39. Karl-Heinz Fallbacher, *Literarische Kultur in München zur Zeit Ludwigs I und Maximilians II* (Munich: C. H. Beck, 1992), 65.

40. Behler, "Force of Classical Greece," 134.

41. Schlegel, *On the Study of Greek Antiquity*, 48.

42. Schiller, "Die Zwei Fieber," *Sämtliche Werke*, eds. Fritz and Walter Strich (Leipzig: Tempel, 1911), 1:319.

43. A. W. Schlegel, *Course of Lectures*, 24.

44. Quoted in Butler, *Tyranny of Greece*, 264.

45. Hegel, *Aesthetics*, 1:303 ff.

46. Ibid., 1:517.

47. See Marchand, *Down from Olympus*, 32–35.

48. See Bergdoll, *Schinkel*, 46–48.

49. Anthony Grafton, "Polyhistor into Philolog," *History of Universities* 3 (1983): 159–92.

50. Quoted in Anthony Grafton, "Prolegomena to Friedrich August Wolf," *Journal of the Warburg and Courtauld Institutes* 44 (1981): 101–29, at 103.

51. Marchand, *Down from Olympus*, 40–51.

52. Ibid., xvii–xviii.

53. See Vick, "Greek Origins."

54. Marchand, *Down from Olympus*, 21.

55. Pfeiffer, *History of Classical Scholarship*, 181.

56. Vick, "Greek Origins," 488–94.

57. Marchand, *Down from Olympus*, 33–34.

58. See Gilbert Highet, *The Classical Tradition: Greek and Roman Influences on Western Literature* (Oxford: Oxford University Press, 1957), 375.

59. Quoted and translated in Stoneman, "A Crazy Enterprise," 310–11.

60. See Christian Wagenknecht, *Deutsche Metrik: Eine historische Einführung* (Munich: C. H. Beck, 1981), 78–91.

Chapter 2

1. Donner, *Sophokles*, 153–210.

2. The actual task of reconstructing the stage appears to have been led by the painter Johann Karl Jakob Gerst. See Boetius, *Wiedergeburt*, 205. Also worth noting is that, for this and other Potsdam (and Berlin) productions of Greek tragedy, the program lists Karl Stawinski as the stage director. In reality, however, Stawinski served a role subordinate to Tieck concerning both the overall conception and realization of the production, and thus he was left to contend with matters of a more practical nature.

3. E.. H. Toelken, "Über die Eingänge zu dem Proscenium und der Orchestra des alten Griechischen Theaters," *Allgemeine preußische Staats-Zeitung*, November 6, 1841.

4. Devrient, *Geschichte*, 5:157.

5. Flashar, *Inszenierung der Antike*, 60–81.

6. Hall and Macintosh, *Greek Tragedy*, 320.

7. Ranke used this phrase in his *Geschichte der romanischen und germanischen Völker von 1494 bis 1514*, published in 1824.

8. See, e.g., Barclay, *Frederick William*; Toews, *Becoming Historical*; and Bußmann, *Zwischen Preussen*.

9. Parts of this argument have been explored in Geary, "Reinventing the Past."

10. On the early years of the king's reign, see Barclay, *Frederick William*, 52 ff.

11. Barclay, *Fredrick William*, 51.

12. Quoted in Barclay, *Frederick William*, 50.

13. Ibid.

14. Toews, *Becoming Historical*, 20–21.

15. Ibid., xvii–xx, quotation at xix.

16. Ibid., 27.

17. See Barclay, *Frederick William*, 24–48.

18. Bunsen to Schelling, August 1, 1840. Bunsen, *Aus seinen Briefen*, 2:133–34.

19. Prutz, *Zehn Jahre*, 1:209.

20. For a discussion of Mendelssohn's time in Berlin, see Brodbeck, "Winter of Discontent"; and Dinglinger, "General-Musik-Direktor."

21. Humboldt to Bunsen, October 19, 1840. Humboldt, *Briefe*, 38–39.

22. Ibid., 39–40.

23. Bunsen to Friedrich Wilhelm IV, October 30, 1840. Bunsen, *Aus seinen Briefen*, 2:142.

24. Ludwig von Massow to Mendelssohn, November 23, 1840. GB-Ob, M. Deneke Mendelssohn d. 38, vol. 12, no. 141.

25. See the letter from Felix to Paul Mendelssohn, March 3, 1841. Mendelssohn, *Briefe 1833–47*, 278–80.

26. See Mendelssohn's undated draft response to the Prussian court official Ludwig von Massow. GB-Ob, M. Deneke Mendelssohn d. 38, vol. 12, no. 250. Also see Massow's letter of December 11, 1840. GB-Ob, M. Deneke Mendelssohn c. 42, no. 26, folios 43–44.

27. See the letter from Felix to Paul Mendelssohn, January 2, 1841. Mendelssohn, *Briefe 1833–47*, 256–60; and Mendelssohn to Karl Klingemann, March 10, 1841. Klingemann, *Briefwechsel*, 258.

28. Mendelssohn to Klingemann, July 15, 1841. Ibid., 264. Mendelssohn ultimately received the title in September of that year.

29. Mendelssohn's memorandum of May 1841. Mendelssohn, *Briefe 1833–47*, 289.

30. See Botstein, "Aesthetics of Assimilation."

31. On the importance of such institutions for Mendelssohn, see Peter Mercer-Taylor, "Mendelssohn and the Institution(s) of German Art Music," in Mercer-Taylor (ed.), *Cambridge Companion*, 11–25.

32. Mendelssohn to Falkenstein, April 8, 1840. Mendelssohn, *Briefe 1833–47*, 228.

33. See Großmann-Vendrey, *Musik der Vergangenheit*, 138–72.

34. James Garratt, "Mendelssohn and the Rise of Musical Historicism," in Mercer-Taylor (ed.), *Cambridge Companion*, 55–70, esp. 60–65.

35. See the discussion in Botstein, "Neoclassicism."

36. See Fischer, "Ludwig Tieck," 107 ff.; and Köpke, *Ludwig Tieck*, 2:103–05.

37. Fischer, "Ludwig Tieck" 112.

38. Flashar, *Inszenierung der Antike*, 66.

39. Cabinet Order dated June 22, 1842. Reprinted in Fischer, "Ludwig Tieck," 116.

40. Ibid.

41. Schneider, *Aus meinen Leben*, 2:222–23.

42. Schuster, *Jugend des Königs*, 1:142, 202.

43. The discussion that follows is heavily indebted to Flashar, *Inszenierung der Antike*, 35–59.

44. See Macintosh, "Tragedy in Performance," 286; and Flashar, *Inszenierung der Antike*, 57.

45. Quoted in Flashar, *Inszenierung der Antike*, 53.

46. Rochlitz indicated in his text where music might be used, and he did so in a way that conforms to conventional notions of incidental music. See Boetius, *Wiedergeburt*, 45–48. Boetius also suggests, on the basis of correspondence between Rochlitz and Goethe, that music may indeed have played some limited role in the 1809 Weimar production.

47. Fischer, "Ludwig Tieck," 112.

48. Devrient mentions a reading by Tieck in September and implies that at least one additional reading occurred at some point. See Devrient, *Meine Erinnerungen*, 223.

49. This often repeated claim was initially made by the nineteenth-century theologian and historian Friedrich Nippold in his commentary to the published memoirs and correspondence of K. J. von Bunsen, one of the king's trusted advisors. It should be noted, however, that Nippold's account is often inaccurate and must be approached with caution. See Bunsen, *Aus seinen Briefen*, 2:261.

50. This claim is made in Paulin, *Ludwig Tieck*, 336. Also see Werner, *A New Image*, 374. Relying on information from Friedrich Nippold, Werner erroneously reports that Tieck used the translation by August Böckh. This translation, however, was not completed until well after the court premiere of *Antigone* and was not published until 1843.

51. See Tieck, *Kritische Schriften*, 4:371; and Friedrich Förster, foreword to Böckh, Toelken, and Förster, *Über die Antigone*, viii.

52. Devrient, *Meine Erinnerungen*, 218.

53. Heinrich Eduard Jacob reports Tieck as having said: "Antigone is a Christian, a 'Christian martyr.' What she does may be likened to the act of the Blessed Virgin and Mary Magdelene when they took Jesus from the cross and 'tended him with spices.'" Jacob cites as his source W. Krägenbrink, *Tieck als Vorleser* (Königsberg, n.d.). After an exhaustive search, I have been unable to locate this source. Tieck's reported statement does resonate with claims made by Devrient, though it should be noted that Jacob's account of *Antigone* contains many factual errors. See Heinrich Jacob, *Felix Mendelssohn and His Times*, trans. Richard and Clara Winston (London: Barrie and Rockliff, 1963), 290–91.

54. To cite just two examples, Friedrich Schlegel referred to Sophocles as the leader of a "chorus" of Greek tragedians in a fragment from 1795 and A. W. Schlegel, in his *Lectures on Dramatic Art and Literature*, described Sophocles as foremost among his peers.

55. Hegel, *Aesthetics*, 2:464.
56. Steiner, *Antigones*, 2.
57. See Steiner, *Antigones*, 19–42.
58. Hegel, *Philosophy of Religion*, 2:264.
59. Ibid.
60. Steiner, *Antigones*, 39.
61. Ibid., 41–42.
62. Ibid., 182.
63. Böckh, "Über die Antigone" (1824, 1828). Not unlike Hegel, whom he never mentions, Böckh argues against simply viewing Antigone as an innocent victim and dismissing Creon as a tyrant.
64. Steinberg, "Incidental Politics," 141. Portions of this essay also appear in Steinberg's more recent book, *Listening to Reason: Culture, Subjectivity, and Nineteenth-Century Music* (Princeton, NJ: Princeton University Press, 2004), 106–22.
65. Ibid., 140.
66. See Nipperdey, *Germany*, 280–91.
67. Todd, *Mendelssohn*, 422.
68. Marx, *Nineteenth-Century*, 67.
69. D-B, ms. autogr. 56 [2].
70. Boetius, "Kompositorische Urschrift," 169.
71. Steinberg, "Incidental Politics," 154.
72. Ibid., 152.
73. Böckh, "Über die Darstellung," 78.
74. Universitätsbibliothek Leipzig, Rep. IX, 16, fol. 10r. Hellmut Flashar, who brought this sketch to light, maintained that Mendelssohn was responsible for it (see Flashar, *Mendelssohn und die griechische Tragödie*, 16). Although the composer cannot be definitively ruled out as the artist, the possibility seems remote. As Ulrich Konrad has pointed out, the letter from Mendelssohn to the Leipzig official Wilhelm Demuth that this drawing was found with includes language that would appear to belie the existence of any such sketch. Demuth himself notes only that the drawing was sent to him by an "acquaintance." Moreover, the writing that appears on the sketch is not in Mendelssohn's hand. See Konrad, "*König Oedipus*," 257.
75. Most scholars now believe that the use of such a raised stage was characteristic of Greek tragedy not in the fifth-century B.C. but in the somewhat later Hellenistic period (ca. 300–31 B.C.). For a more detailed description of the staging, see Böckh, "Über die Darstellung," 78–83.
76. For a good description of the stage, see Förster, foreword to Böckh, Toelken, and Förster, *Über die Antigone*, ix.
77. Ludwig Rellstab, "Darstellung der Antigone des Sophokles, auf dem königlichen Theater des neuen Palais zu Potsdam," *Vossische Zeitung*, October 30, 1841. On the use of "authentic" costumes, see Boetius, *Wiedergeburt*, 230–34.
78. Böckh, "Über die Darstellung," 83.
79. Mendelssohn to David, October 21, 1841. Mendelssohn, *Briefe aus Leipziger Archiven*, 169.
80. Böckh, "Über die Darstellung," 91. Contrary to what Douglass Seaton has suggested, Böckh's description of the chorus in formations of three rows of five does

not refer specifically to the Prussian court production, but rather provides what he believed to have been formations common to ancient Greek tragedy. Concerning the 1841 performance, Böckh notes only that the chorus entered "in half choruses, one man after the other" (91–92). See Seaton, "Mendelssohn's Dramatic Music," 194, 242, n. 165.

81. See "Koryphaeos," in Drieberg, *Wörterbuch*, 78–79.

82. On the choreography, see Boetius, *Wiedergeburt*, 255–58.

83. Mendelssohn to Macfarren, December 8, 1844. K. Mendelssohn, *Goethe and Mendelssohn*, 131. The translation is lightly emended; the emphasis is Mendelssohn's.

84. Toelken, "Über die Eingänge zu dem Proscenium und der Orchestra des alten griechischen Theaters," in Böckh, Toelken, and Förster, *Über die Antigone*, 49.

85. See "Tragödie," in Drieberg, *Wörterbuch*, 178.

86. Mendelssohn to Klingemann, September 6, 1841. Klingemann, *Briefwechsel*, 266.

87. Felix Mendelssohn, *Das Mädchen von Andros: Eine Komödie des Terentius in den Versmassen des Originals übersetzt von F****. Mit Einleitung und Anmerkungen herausgegeben von K. W. L. Heyse* (Berlin: Ferdinand Dummler, 1826).

88. Botstein, "Neoclassicism," 6 ff.; also see Kes, *Rezeption*, 45–49.

89. Devrient, *Meine Erinnerungen*, 218–19.

90. Ibid., 220.

91. Roger Savage, "Incidental Music," in *New Grove Dictionary of Music*, second ed., ed. Stanley Sadie (New York: Macmillan, 2001), 12:139.

92. See Aristotle, *Poetics*, 67–69. For a concise discussion concerning the formal construction of Greek tragedy, see Zimmermann, *Greek Tragedy*, 15–20.

93. West, *Greek Music*, 105.

94. Pickard-Cambridge, *Dramatic Festivals*, 156–67; 245–46.

95. Böckh, "Über die Darstellung," 93.

96. D-B, N. Mus. ms. 7. For a reproduction of the page in question, see Boetius, "Kompositorische Urschrift," 171.

97. Ibid., 172.

98. Rellstab, "Darstellung der Antigone."

99. This manuscript draft is dated September 27, 1841. D-B, MA Depos. Berlin ms. 4

100. Sophocles, *Four Dramas* (trans. Ewans), 84.

101. Todd, *Mendelssohn*, 424.

102. Mendelssohn to David, October 21, 1841. Mendelssohn, *Briefe aus Leipziger Archiven*, 169.

103. Böckh, "Über die Darstellung," 96.

104. See Devrient, *Meine Erinnerungen*, 221–22; and Rellstab, "Darstellung der Antigone."

105. Unless otherwise noted, translations from the play are my own and are based upon the 1839 Donner translation.

106. See the discussion in Burton, *The Chorus*, 135–36.

107. Quoted in Weiss, "Unbekannte Zeugnisse," 56.

108. Böckh, "Über die Darstellung," 93.

109. See Flashar, "August Böckh."

110. Seaton, "Mendelssohn's Dramatic Music," 200.

111. Wilhelm von Humboldt, introduction to *Agamemnon*, in *Gesammelte Schriften*, ed. Königlich Preussischen Akademie der Wissenschaft (Berlin: Behr, 1909), 8:135.

112. Böckh, "Über die Darstellung," 95.

113. Mendelssohn to Droysen, December 2, 1841. Wehmer, *Tief gegründet Herz*, 72.

114. To cite but two examples, see Andraschke, "Mendelssohns *Antigone*," 150; and Flashar, "Mendelssohn und die griechische Tragödie," 19–20.

115. Seaton, "Mendelssohn's Dramatic Music," 200–01.

116. Raven, *Greek Metre*, 72. It should be noted, however, that definitions of aeolic meter frequently vary among modern-day scholars.

117. West, *Greek Metre*, 19.

118. Seaton, "Mendelssohn's Dramatic Music," 200.

119. Schlegel, *Lectures on Dramatic Art*, 71. The translation is lightly emended.

120. To cite one example of this tendency, an anonymous reviewer for the *Vossische Zeitung* noted in the wake of the 1842 Berlin production of *Antigone* that the majority of the public could understand Sophocles' work only in a superficial sense. "Königliches Theater," *Vossische Zeitung*, April 15, 1842.

121. For a somewhat different notion of translation as it relates to Mendelssohn's music, see Garratt, "Mendelssohn's Babel."

122. Mendelssohn to David, October 21, 1841. Mendelssohn, *Briefe 1833–47*, 309.

123. Wehmer, *Tief gegründet Herz*, 72.

124. See Cooper, "Of Red Roofs"; and Seaton, "The Problem."

125. It is perhaps worth noting that this strophic pair has been the subject of much scholarly attention because of the composer's instructions to use Böckh's translation at only this point in the score. See Flashar, "August Böckh."

126. Dahlhaus, *Nineteenth-Century Music*, 47.

127. Sophocles, *Four Dramas* (trans. Ewans), 55.

128. Schiller, "Use of the Chorus," 243–44.

129. See the discussion of this ode in Scott, *Musical Design*, 37–41.

130. *Allgemeine musikalische Zeitung* 44 (1842): 437; and August Schmidt, "Die Chöre von Sophokles *Antigone*," *Wiener allgemeine Musik-Zeitung* 6 (1846): 133.

131. Böckh, "Über die Darstellung," 90.

132. See Christoph-Hellmut Mahling, "Berlin: Music in the Air," in *The Early Romantic Era between Revolutions: 1789 and 1848*, ed. Alexander Ringer (Englewood Cliffs, NJ: Prentice Hall, 1991), 132–33.

133. Quoted and translated in Mahling, "Music in the Air," 133.

134. *Allgemeine musikalische Zeitung* 42 (1840): 890.

135. Peter Mercer-Taylor, "Mendelssohn's 'Scottish' Symphony and the Music of German Memory," *19th-Century Music* 19 (1995): 68–82.

136. Much has been written on this topic. See, e.g., Mosse, *Nationalization*, esp. 73–99; and Düding, Friedemann, and Münch (eds.), *Öffentliche Festkultur*.

137. G. W. Fink, "Musik zur Sekularfeier der Erfindung der Buchdruckerkunst," *Allgemeine musikalische Zeitung* 42 (1840): 610–611.

138. Ibid., 611.

139. Förster, "Über die Antigone des Sophokles," in Böckh, Toelken, and Förster, *Über die Antigone*, 9.

140. Mercer-Taylor, "Mendelssohn's 'Scottish' Symphony," 77.

Chapter 3

1. "Aufführung der Antigone auf dem Hoftheater zu Potsdam," *Allgemeine preussische Staats-Zeitung*, November 5, 1841; Rellstab, "Dartstellung der Antigone."
2. Rellstab, "Darstellung der Antigone."
3. *Vossische Zeitung*, November 8, 1841.
4. Ludwig Rellstab, "Noch ein Wort zu *Antigone*," *Vossische Zeitung*, November 15, 1841.
5. "Aufführung der Antigone."
6. E.. H. Toelken, "Über die Eingänge zu dem Proscenium und der Orchestra des alten Griechischen Theaters," *Allgemeine preussische Staats-Zeitung*, November 6, 1841; and E. H. Toelken, "Die Wiederbelebung der Griechischen Tragödie," *Allgemeine preussische Staats-Zeitung*, December 4, 1841.
7. Toelken, "Die Wiederbelebung."
8. Ibid.
9. All references to this essay are to the subsequently published Böckh, "Über die Darstellung."
10. Böckh, "Über die Darstellung," 75.
11. Friedrich Förster, foreword to Böckh, Toelken, and Förster, *Über die Antigone*, iii (emphasis original).
12. Ibid.
13. Mendelssohn to Klingemann, September 6, 1841. Klingemann, *Briefwechsel*, 267.
14. Boetius, *Wiedergeburt*, 85–86.
15. For a more detailed discussion of this performance, see Weiss, "Unbekannte Zeugnisse"; and Boetius, *Wiedergeburt*, 83–91, 264–75.
16. C. F. B., *Allgemeine musikalische Zeitung* 44 (1842): 211.
17. Droysen, "Aufführung der Antigone," 146.
18. Brennglass, "Antigone in Berlin."
19. For further discussion, see Flashar, *Mendelssohn und die griechiche Tragödie*, 36–44.
20. Edgar Allan Poe, "The Antigone at Palmo's," *Broadway Journal*, April 12, 1845. Reprinted in *The Complete Works of Edgar Allen Poe*, seventeen vols., ed. James A. Harrison (New York: AMS Press, 1965), 12:134.
21. "The Antigone of Sophocles," *Times* (London), January 3, 1845.
22. "Antigone," *The Musical World* 20 (1845): 33.
23. Mendelssohn to Macfarren, December 8, 1844. K. Mendelssohn, *Goethe and Mendelssohn*, 131–32.
24. *Punch, or the London Charivari*, "Antigone Analysed," January 18, 1845, 42.
25. Mendelssohn to Fanny Hensel, March 25, 1845, Hensel, *Mendelssohn Family*, 2: 317.
26. [Hermann], *Über Sophokles Antigone*.
27. Quoted in [Hermann], *Über Sophokles Antigone*, 4 (footnote).
28. Ibid., 44.
29. Ibid., 46.
30. Droysen, "Aufführung der Antigone," 149.
31. Ibid.

32. Ibid., 152.
33. Ibid., 147.
34. Droysen was actually the first to use the term "Hellenism" to denote Greek culture between roughly the time of Alexander and the emergence of Christianity.
35. See Southard, *Droysen*, esp. 1–31.
36. Quoted in Southard, *Droysen*, 11.
37. "Königliche Hof- und Nationaltheater," *Der bayerische Landbote*, December 1, 1851.
38. Drieberg, *Wörterbuch*, 178.
39. Robert to Clara Schumann, March 24, 1842. Boetticher, *Robert Schumann*, 259.
40. Hebbel, *Tagebücher*, 4:25.
41. Droysen, "Aufführung der Antigone," 148.
42. Böckh, "Über die Darstellung," 90.
43. Devrient, *Meine Erinnerungen*, 224–25.
44. Schlegel, *Lectures on Dramatic Art*, 47. The translation is lightly emended.
45. Droysen, "Aufführung der Antigone," 149.
46. Förster, foreword to Böckh, Toelken, and Förster, *Über die Antigone*, x–xi.
47. Droysen, "Aufführung der Antigone," 148.
48. Steinberg, "Incidental Politics," 152.
49. See the discussion in Burton, *The Chorus*, 132–34.
50. On ancient Dionysian worship, see Pickard-Cambridge, *Dramatic Festivals*, 30 ff.
51. Mendelssohn to Macfarren, December 8, 1844. K. Mendelssohn, *Goethe and Mendelssohn*, 132 (translation emended).
52. Heinrich Schmidt, "Erste Aufführung der Antigone," *Neue Zeitschrift für Musik* 16 (1842): 95.
53. *Allgemeine musikalische Zeitung* 44 (1842): 437.
54. *Berlinische Nachrichten von Staats- und gelehrten Sachen*, April 15, 1842.
55. [Hermann], "Über Sophokles Antigone," 21–22.
56. Becker, "Über die Bearbeitung," 14.

Chapter 4

1. *Vossische Zeitung*, August 9, 1843.
2. Förster, foreword to Böckh, Toelken, and Förster, *Über die Antigone*, xi.
3. Ibid.
4. See the discussion in chapter 3.
5. D-B, mus. ms. autogr. Commer, 24.
6. An essay on the German revival of Greek tragedy that appeared in the *Allgemeine musikalische Zeitung* in 1864 mentions a production of Sophocles' *Philoctetes* at the Französisches Gymnasium in Berlin. No date for this performance is given, and I have been unable to find any other record of it.
7. Flashar, *Inszenierung der Antike*, 33–46.
8. Mendelssohn to Bunsen, May 4, 1844. Mendelssohn, *Briefe 1833–47*, 404–08.
9. Bunsen to Mendelssohn, April 28, 1844. Mendelssohn, *Briefe 1833–47*, 403.

10. Mendelssohn to the Geheim Cabinetsrath Müller, March 12, 1845. Mendelssohn, *Briefe 1833–47*, 436.

11. This performance was for invited guests only and was followed two days later by one for the general public.

12. Ludwig Rellstab, *Vossische Zeitung*, April 29, 1851.

13. There is some question as to the first production date of *Oedipus at Colonus*. See Gesine Schröder, "Gymnasiasten-Theater: Heinrich Bellermanns Musik zu Sophokles," in Stuber and Beck, *Theater und 19. Jahrhundert*, 35–57, at 37.

14. See the preface to Bellermann, *Chöre aus Aias*.

15. Todd, *Mendelssohn*, 442.

16. Mendelssohn to Tieck, October 15, 1842. Holtei, *Briefe*, 2:337.

17. For biographical information on Taubert, which is fairly limited, see especially Carl Freiherrn von Ledebur, *Tonkünstler-Lexicon Berlins von den ältesten Zeiten bis auf die Gegenwart* (Berlin: Ludwig Rauh, 1861), 583–92.

18. Donner, *Euripides*.

19. Boetius, *Wiedergeburt*, 92–94.

20. Drach, *Bühnenreform*, 64–65 (footnote 2).

21. D-B, mus. ms. autogr. W. Taubert, 84 N.

22. See Boetius, *Wiedergeburt*, 180.

23. On the reception of *Medea* in nineteenth-century Germany, see Hall, Macintosh, and Taplin, *Medea*, 12 ff.

24. See Zimmermann, "Seiner Zeit," 110–11.

25. Ewans, *Opera from the Greek*, 56–58.

26. Euripides, *Medea* (trans. Kovacs), 317.

27. Ewans, *Opera from the Greek*, 60–66.

28. On Seneca's portrayal of Medea as witch and its subsequent influence, see Fiona Macintosh, "The Performer in Performance," in Hall, Macintosh, and Taplin, *Medea*, 7–9.

29. Lü, *Medea*, 21–46.

30. Gebel also wrote music—now lost—to several other librettos that Klest had adapted from ancient Greek and Roman drama, including an *Oedipus* of 1751.

31. Lü, *Medea*, 47.

32. Ewans, *Opera from the Greek*, 66–67.

33. Ibid. On *Medea* and the operatic tradition, see McDonald, "Medea è mobile: The Many Faces of Medea in Opera," in Hall, Macintosh, and Taplin, *Medea*, 100–18.

34. Mendelssohn to Rebeckah Dirichlet, August 10, 1843. Hensel, *Mendelssohn Family*, 2:197.

35. Tieck, *Kritische Schriften*, 4:373. It is also possible that assessments of *Medea* were colored by a widespread belief at the time that the works of Euripides were somehow inferior to those of Aeschylus and Sophocles. On this notion, see Mastronarde, *Art of Euripides*, 11–12.

36. "Euripides' Medea," *Allgemeine preussische Staats-Zeitung*, 670.

37. "Feuilleton," *Allgemeine musikalische Zeitung* 45 (1843): 640.

38. *Vossische Zeitung*, October 17, 1843.

39. *Vossische Zeitung*, August 9, 1843.

40. *Allgemeine musikalische Zeitung* 45 (1843): 848.

41. Dr. L., *Berliner musikalische Zeitung* 1 (1844).

42. See the discussion in Mastronarde, *Medea*, 103–05.

43. Michael R. Halleran, "Episodes," in *A Companion to Greek Tragedy*, ed. Justina Gregory (Malden, MA: Blackwell, 2005), 181.

44. Ewans, *Opera from the Greek*, 56.

45. Mastronarde, *Medea*, 24.

46. Ewans, *Opera from the Greek*, 57.

47. Ibid., 58.

48. Although modern scholars agree that all of the lines for Medea and the nurse constitute anapests, Donner labeled only a portion of them as such. It is worth noting that Taubert refrained from setting those lines not indicated by Donner as anapestic, suggesting that the former was relying heavily on information gleaned from the latter's translation.

49. Of significance here is Medea's physical location. See the discussion in Mastronarde, *Art of Euripides*, 252–53.

50. On Euripides' portrayal of female characters, see Rabinowitz, *Anxiety Veiled*.

51. Chong-Gossard, *Gender and Communication*, 164.

Chapter 5

1. See Brodbeck, "Winter of Discontent."

2. Quoted in Ibid., 3.

3. Mendelssohn to Ludwig von Massow, October 23, 1842. Mendelssohn, *Briefe 1833–47*, 339–41.

4. Dinglinger, "General-Musik-Direktor," 23–26.

5. See Mendelssohn to Klingemann, November 23, 1842. Klingemann, *Briefwechsel*, 274–75.

6. Ibid., 275. Shakespeare's *The Tempest* is one of several proposed court productions that never came to fruition.

7. Felix to Lea Mendelssohn, November 28, 1842. Mendelssohn, *Briefe 1833–47*, 351.

8. Felix to Lea Mendelssohn, December 11, 1842. Mendelssohn, *Briefe 1833–47*, 356.

9. Felix to Paul Mendelssohn, July 21, 1843. Mendelssohn, *Briefe 1833–47*, 384.

10. Mendelssohn to Klingemann, June 12, 1843. Klingemann, *Briefwechsel*, 282.

11. Mendelssohn to Droysen, December 2, 1841. Wehmer, *Tief gegründet Herz*, 217.

12. Mendelssohn to Geheim Cabinetsrath Müller, March 12, 1845. Mendelssohn, *Briefe 1833–47*, 436.

13. Franz Fritze, *Sämmtliche Tragödien des Sophokles* (Berlin: Förstner, 1845). Fritze was a jurist and a personal friend of Tieck, who wrote the foreword to this edition.

14. "Oedipus in Kolonos," *Allgemeine preußische Staats-Zeitung*, November 3, 1845; and Ludwig Rellstab, "Oedipus in Kolonus," *Vossische Zeitung*, November 3, 1845.

15. *Allgemeine musikalische Zeitung* 48 (1846): 178–79.

16. Ibid., 178.

17. Rellstab, "Oedipus in Kolonos."

18. "Königliches Theater," *Vossische Zeitung*, November 12, 1845.

19. *Allgemeine preußische Staats-Zeitung*, November 3, 1845.

20. Mendelssohn to Rebecka Dirichlet, March 25, 1845. Hensel, *Mendelssohn Family*, 2:317.

21. The piano-vocal edition was issued simultaneously by Ewer in England, where it featured an English text by William Bartholomew.

22. Tieck, *Kritische Schriften*, 4:379.

23. *Allgemeine musikalische Zeitung* 48 (1846):178.

24. Ibid., 179.

25. Schlegel, *Lectures on Dramatic Art*, 97.

26. Scott, *Musical Design*, 196.

27. Ibid., 210.

28. Burton, *The Chorus*, 253.

29. Todd, *Mendelssohn*, 501–02.

30. Scott, *Musical Design*, 224.

31. Ibid.

32. See Scott, *Musical Design*, 233–35.

33. Hall, *Suffering*, 324.

34. Scott, *Musical Design*, 243.

35. Ibid., 248.

36. Seaton, "Mendelssohn's Dramatic Music," 213.

37. For a discussion of the religious overtones in Mendelssohn's *Athalie*, see Seaton, "Mendelssohn's Dramatic Music," 216–19.

38. Gardiner, *Sophoclean Chorus*, 111.

39. Sophocles, *Theban Plays* (trans. Fagles), 376.

40. Schlegel, *Lectures on Dramatic Art*, 103. The translation is lightly emended.

41. "Oedipus in Kolonos," *Allgemeine preußische Staats-Zeitung*, November 3, 1845.

42. Klingemann to Mendelssohn, March 7, 1845. Klingemann, *Briefwechsel*, 305.

43. See Köpke, *Ludwig Tieck*, 213.

44. See, e.g., Georg Feder, "On Felix Mendelssohn Bartholdy's Sacred Music," trans. Monika Hennemann, in Seaton (ed.), *The Mendelssohn Companion* (Westport, CT: Greenwood Press, 2001), 272. For his part, Charles Rosen has described Mendelssohn as the inventor of "religious kitsch" because of his use of the chorale in concert music. See Charles Rosen, *The Romantic Generation*, (Cambridge, MA: Harvard University Press, 1995), 590–94.

45. Scott, *Musical Design*, 239.

46. Botstein, "Neoclassicism," 3.

47. Bergdoll, *Schinkel*, 87.

48. Botstein, "Neoclassicism," 10.

Chapter 6

1. "Königliche Hof- und Nationaltheater," parts 1–5, *Der bayerische Landbote*, November 28, 29 and December 1, 2, and 4, 1851.

2. *Der bayerische Landbote*, December 2, 1851, supplement.

3. *Allgemeine Zeitung*, November 30, 1851.

4. *Allgemeine Zeitung*, December 2, 1851.

5. *Neueste Nachrichten aus dem Gebiete der Politik*, December 4, 1851.

6. On Dingelstedt's appointment at the Munich court theater, see Dirrigl, *Maximilian*, bk. 2, 1025–77.

7. *Neueste Nachrichten*, December 3, 1851.

8. *Neueste Nachrichten*, December 4, 1851.

9. *Der bayerische Landbote*, December 2, 1851, supplement.

10. Dirrigl, *Ludwig*, 166.

11. On Ludwig's architectural projects, see Watkin and Mellinghoff, *German Architecture*, 141–70.

12. See the discussion in Kathleen Curran, *The Romanesque Revival: Religion, Politics, and Transnational Exchange* (University Park: Pennsylvania State University Press, 2003), 36–93.

13. Dirrigl, *Ludwig*, 137.

14. Quoted in Watkin and Mellinghoff, *German Architecture*, 142.

15. Quoted in Dirrigl, *Ludwig*, 147.

16. Watkin and Mellinghoff, *German Architecture*, 157–62.

17. Quoted in Eda Sagarra, *Germany in the Nineteenth Century: History and Literature* (New York: Peter Lang, 2001), 102.

18. Dirrigl, *Ludwig*, 163–65.

19. See Gollwitzer, *Ludwig*, 156–61.

20. For a translation and discussion of this work, see *In What Style Should We Build? The German Debate on Architectural Style*, trans. Wolfgang Hermann (Santa Monica, CA: Getty Center for the History of Art and Humanities, 1992).

21. See Garratt, "Rise of Musical Historicism," 59–60.

22. Quoted in ibid., 60.

23. Dirrigl, *Ludwig*, 149.

24. See Watkin and Mellinghoff, *German Architecture*, 156.

25. Quoted in Dirrigl, *Ludwig*, 137.

26. See the discussion of philhellenism in chapter 1.

27. On Ludwig's philhellenism, see Gollwitzer, *Ludwig*, 472–74.

28. Altmann, *Maximilianeum*, 7.

29. Ibid., 34–35.

30. On Dingelstedt's appointment, see Zenger, *Geschichte*, 345–413.

31. Quoted in ibid., 346.

32. Quoted in Dirrigl, *Maximilian*, bk. 2, 1025–26.

33. Ibid., 1039.

34. Ibid., 1038.

35. Quoted in Zenger, *Geschichte*, 349.

36. Dirrigl, *Maximilian*, bk. 2, 1027–35.

37. Quoted in ibid., 1040.

38. See the discussion in Konrad, "*König Oedipus*," 255–56.

39. Boetius, *Wiedergeburt*, 291.

40. Dingelstedt confirms in a letter to Maximilian II that it was indeed the king's decision to commission Lachner for music to Sophocles' play. See Konrad, "*König Oedipus*," 254.

41. Ibid.

42. Lachner divided the score into two parts, and in some manuscript versions of the work included an entr'acte to be played in between the two halves (i.e., immediately following No. 7). It is also worth noting here that the copyist manuscript of the score (D-Mbs, St. th. 718/1) indicates a change (made in a second hand) as to where No. 14 begins. This same hand has crossed out the heading "No. 15" and replaced it with "No. 16" but, oddly enough, includes no reference to what would necessarily have been No. 15.

43. *Allgemeine Zeitung*, December 1, 1852.

44. Burton, *The Chorus*, 138.

45. Scott, *Musical Design*, 139.

46. *Allgemeine Zeitung*, December 1, 1852.

47. *Allgemeine Zeitung*, December 5, 1852, supplement.

48. See Burton, *The Chorus*, 168.

49. On questions concerning the authenticity of these lines, see Burton, *The Chorus*, 182–184.

50. *Allgemeine Zeitung*, January 19, 1854.

Chapter 7

1. Wrassiwanopulos-Braschowanoff, *Wagner und die Antike*, 9.

2. Ibid., 10.

3. See, e.g., Houston Stewart Chamberlain, *Richard Wagner*, trans. G. Ainsle Hight, rev. ed. (Philadelphia: J. B. Lippincott, 1897), 370. Depicting Wagner as a kind of modern-day Sophocles with unique insight into Greek art, Chamberlain asserts that "[t]he man who built [Bayreuth] carried Greek art within himself, as part of his own soul."

4. Wrassiwanopulos-Braschowanoff, *Wagner und die Antike*, 53.

5. Petsch, "Der Ring."

6. See Meinck, *Die sagenwissenschaftlichen Grundlagen der Nibelungendichtung Richard Wagners* (Berlin: Felber, 1892); and Wolfgang Golther, *Die sagengeschichtlichen Grundlagen der Ringdichtung Richard Wagners* (Berlin: Verlag der Allgemeine Musik-Zeitung, 1902).

7. Wilson, *Wagner's Dramas*; and Drews, *Ideengehalt*.

8. Schadewaldt, "Wagner und die Griechen."

9. See Deathridge, *Wagner Beyond*, 107–09.

10. Ibid., 102.

11. See Wagner's account of this period in Wagner, *My Life*, 342–43.

12. For a detailed inventory of Wagner's library, see Westernhagen, *Wagners Dresdener Bibliothek*.

13. Wagner, *My Life*, 342.

14. Ibid.

15. See Lloyd-Jones, *Blood for the Ghosts*, 126–42; and Müller, "Wagner and Antiquity."

16. As a recent example, see Foster, *Wagner's Ring Cycle*. Foster argues that each of the *Ring*'s operas articulate a particular phase of Greek poetic and political development as filtered through Wagner's Hegelian-inspired understanding of ancient Greek

culture. Also see M. Owen Lee, *Athena Sings: Wagner and the Greeks* (Toronto: University of Toronto Press, 2003). This work is less scholarly in nature but nonetheless reveals a continued interest in the theme of Wagner and the Greeks.

17. Wagner, *Art and Revolution*, GS, 3:9 (PW, 1:32). Unless otherwise noted, the translations of Wagner's writings are my own and are based on the edition of the composer's prose works that initially appeared between 1871 and 1883. See Wagner, *Gesammelte Schriften* (abbreviated as GS). For ease of reference, citations also refer to the readily available, if not always ideal, English translation by William Ashton Ellis. See Wagner, *Prose Works* (abbreviated as PW).

18. Wagner, "What is German?" GS, 10:41 (PW, 4:103).

19. Wagner, *Art and Revolution*, GS, 3:28 (PW, 1:51).

20. Cited in Jürgen Kühnel, "The Prose Writings," trans. Simon Nye, in Müller and Wapnewski (eds.), *Wagner Handbook*, 565–651, at 583.

21. Wagner, *Art and Revolution*, GS, 3:24 (PW, 1:48).

22. Ibid., 3:29 (1:53).

23. Ibid., 3:34–35 (1:57–58).

24. For a discussion of Wagner's political sympathies, see Mitchell Cohen, "To the Dresden Barricades:the Genesis of Wagner's Political Ideas," in *The Cambridge Companion to Wagner*, ed. Thomas S. Grey (Cambridge:Cambridge University Press, 2008), 47–64.

25. Wagner, *Art and Revolution*, GS, 3:30 (PW, 1:54).

26. Ibid., 3:26 (1:50).

27. Ibid., 3:30–35 (PW, 1:54–58).

28. Wagner, *Artwork of the Future*, GS, 3:48 (PW, 1:75).

29. Ibid., 3:50–53 (1:77–81).

30. Borchmeyer, *Theory and Theatre*, 65–66.

31. Ibid., 66.

32. Wagner, *Opera and Drama*, GS, 4:29 (PW, 2:150)

33. Ibid., 4:14 (2:133).

34. Ibid., 4:29 (2:150).

35. Wagner, *A Communication to My Friends*, GS, 4:236 (PW, 1:275).

36. Wagner, *Art and Revolution*, GS, 3:30 (PW, 1:54).

37. Ibid., 3:29 (1:53). The emphasis is Wagner's.

38. Carl Dahlhaus, "Wagner's Place in the History of Music," in Müller and Wapnewski (eds.), *Wagner Handbook*, 99–117, at 104.

39. Wagner, *Art and Revolution*, GS, 3:28–29 (PW, 1:52–53).

40. Ibid., 3:30 (1:54).

41. Ibid., 3:18 (1:41).

42. See the discussion in Boetius, *Wiedergeburt*, 276–80.

43. Wagner, *My Life*, 289.

44. Wagner, "To Friedrich Nietzsche," GS, 9:296 (PW, 5:293).

45. Wagner, *Judaism in Music*, GS, 5:78 (PW, 3:92).

46. Ibid., GS, 5:81 (PW, 3:95).

47. Ibid., GS, 5:79 (PW, 3:93–94).

48. Ibid., GS, 5:73 (PW, 3:87).

49. See, e.g., the composer's unfavorable comments on Mendelssohn's aesthetic in Wagner, *Opera and Drama*, GS, 4:116–117 (PW, 2:253).

50. Cooper, "Mendelssohn Received," 241–42.
51. On Wagner's anti-Semitism, see especially Weiner, *Wagner and the Anti-Semitic Imagination*; Rose, *Race and Revolution*; and Katz, *Darker Side*.
52. This argument is made compellingly in Katz, *Darker Side*, 40–41.
53. Wagner, *Judaism in Music*, GS, 5:83 (PW, 3:97).
54. Ibid., GS, 5:75–76 (PW, 3:89–90).
55. Ibid., GS, 5:68 (PW, 3:82). The term "art-commodity-exchange" [*Kunstwarenwechsel*] is borrowed from Katz, *Darker Side*.
56. Wagner, *Opera and Drama*, GS, 4:65 (PW, 2:191).
57. Ibid., GS, 4:54. (PW, 2:179).
58. Ibid., GS, 4:56 ff. (PW, 2:182 ff.).
59. See especially Borchmeyer, *Theory and Theatre*, 290–91; and Rather, *The Dream*, 55–56.
60. Wagner to Theodor Uhlig, November 12, 1851. Wagner, *Selected Letters*, 233.
61. Wagner, *Opera and Drama*, GS, 4:60 (PW, 2:186).
62. Ibid., GS, 4:61 (PW, 2:187).
63. Ibid., GS, 4:63 (PW, 2:189).
64. Ibid., GS, 4:63–64 (PW, 2:190).
65. Ewans, *Wagner and Aeschylus*, esp. 63–66.
66. Borchmeyer, *Theory and Theatre*, 290.
67. Ibid., 297.
68. Rather, *The Dream*, 47–63.
69. Ibid., 56.
70. Wagner to August Röckel, January 25/26, 1854. Wagner, *Selected Letters*, 308. The emphasis is Wagner's.
71. Rather, *The Dream*, 59.
72. Ibid., 61–62.
73. Berry, *Treacherous Bonds*, 195.
74. Ibid., 113.
75. Ibid., 265.
76. Wagner, *Cosima Wagner's Diaries*, 138.
77. Sophocles, *Theban Plays* (trans. Fagles), 86.
78. Cooke, *I Saw the World*, 53.

Chapter 8

1. Marx, *Music of the Nineteenth Century*, 66.
2. *Allgemeine musikalische Zeitung* 5 (1870): 143.
3. Friedrich Chrysander, "Mendelssohn's Antigone," *Allgemeine musikalische Zeitung* 11 (1876): 165.
4. See the discussion in Borchmeyer, *Theory and Theatre*, 65–68.
5. *Allgemeine musikalische Zeitung* 5 (1870): 143.
6. *Musikalisches Wochenblatt* 3 (1872): 787.
7. *Allgemeine musikalische Zeitung* 5 (1870): 143.

8. *Allgemeine musikalische Zeitung* 8 (1873): 220.

9. "Die Wiener Hofoper," *Allgemeine musikalische Zeitung* 16 (1881): 733. It is worth noting that I have been unable to find any late nineteenth-century reviews of *Antigone* in the *Neue Zeitschrift für Musik*, which beginning around the middle of the century had become an organ of the progressive musical movement associated above all with Wagner and Liszt.

10. See esp. the chapter entitled "The Relation of Greek Tragedy to the Italian Opera and the Wagnerian Music-Drama" in Little, *Mendelssohn's Music*, 17–28.

11. Little, *Mendelssohn's Music*, 36.

12. Ibid., 37.

13. The last known production of the work prior to its 1979 Berlin revival appears to have occurred in 1918 at the Burgtheater in Vienna.

14. See Easterling, "Early Years."

15. Cited in Dent, "Cambridge Greek Plays," 27.

16. See Dent, "Cambridge Greek Plays."

17. On the reception of Strauss's *Elektra*, see Bryan Gilliam, *Richard Strauss's Elektra* (Oxford: Oxford University Press, 1991), 1–17. See also the discussion in Ewans, *Opera from the Greek*, 81–103.

BIBLIOGRAPHY

Altmann, Lothar. *The Maximilianeum in Munich.* Translated by Margaret Marks. Regensburg: Schnell and Steiner, 1993.

Andraschke, Peter. "Felix Mendelssohns *Antigone.*" In *Felix Mendelssohn Bartholdy Kongreß-Bericht Berlin 1994,* edited by Christian Martin Schmidt, 141–66. Leipzig: Breitkopf und Härtel, 1997.

Aristotle. *Poetics.* Edited and translated by Stephen Halliwell. Cambridge, Mass: Harvard University Press, 1995.

Barclay, David E. *Frederick William IV and the Prussian Monarchy 1840-1861.* Oxford: Oxford University Press, 1995.

Becker, Julius. "Über die Bearbeitung der antiken Dramen: Antigone und Medea, für unsere Bühnen." Parts 1 and 2. *Neue Zeitschrift für Musik* 20 (1844): 9–10, 14–15.

Behler, Ernst. "A. W. Schlegel and the Nineteenth-Century Damnatio of Euripides." *Greek, Roman, and Byzantine Studies* 27 (1986): 335–67.

———. "The Force of Classical Greece in the Formation of the Romantic Age in Germany." In *Paths from Ancient Greece,* edited by Carol G. Thomas, 118–39. New York: Brill, 1988.

Bellermann, Heinrich. *Chöre, Sologesänge und Melodramen aus dem Aias des Sophokles,* op. 32. Berlin: Schlesinger, 1883.

Bergdoll, Barry. *Karl Friedrich Schinkel: An Architecture for Prussia.* New York: Rizzoli, 1994.

Berry, Mark. *Treacherous Bonds and Laughing Fire: Politics and Religion in Wagner's Ring.* Burlington, VT: Ashgate, 2006.

Böckh, August. "Über die Antigone des Sophokles." In *Abhandlungen der historisch-philologischen Klasse der königlichen Akademie der Wissenschaften zu Berlin aus dem Jahre 1824* (1824): 41–88.

———. "Über die Antigone des Sophokles." In *Abhandlungen der historisch-philologischen Klasse der königlichen Akademie der Wissenschaften zu Berlin aus dem Jahre 1828* (1828): 49–112.

———. "Über die Darstellung der Antigone." In *Über die Antigone des Sophokles und ihre Darstellung auf dem königlichen Schloßtheater im neuen Palais bei Sanssouci*. Berlin: E. Schroeder, 1842.

Böckh, August, E. H. Toelken, and Friedrich Förster. *Über die Antigone des Sophokles und ihre Darstellung auf dem königlichen Schloßtheater im neuen Palais bei Sanssouci*. Berlin: E. Schroeder, 1842.

Boetius, Susanne. "'…da componirte ich aus Herzenslust drauf los…' Felix Mendelssohn Bartholdys kompositorische Urschrift der Schauspielmusik zur 'Antigone' des Sophokles, op. 55," *Musikforschung* 55 (2002): 162–83.

———. *Die Wiedergeburt der griechischen Tragödie auf der Bühne des 19. Jahrhunderts: Bühnenfassungen mit Schauspielmusik*. Tübingen: Max Niemeyer Verlag, 2005.

Boetticher, Wolfgang. *Robert Schumann: Einführung in Persönlichkeit und Werk*. Berlin: Bernhard Hahnfeld, 1941.

Borchmeyer, Dieter. *Richard Wagner: Theory and Theatre*. Translated by Stewart Spencer. Oxford: Oxford University Press, 1991.

Botstein, Leon. "The Aesthetics of Assimilation and Affirmation: Reconstructing the Career of Felix Mendelssohn." In *Mendelssohn and His World*, edited by R. Larry Todd, 5–42. Princeton: Princeton University Press, 1991.

———. "Neoclassicism, Romanticism, and Emancipation: The Origins of Felix Mendelssohn's Aesthetic Outlook." In *The Mendelssohn Companion*, edited by Douglass Seaton, 1–23. Westport, Conn.: Greenwood Press, 2001.

Bourdieu, Pierre. *The Field of Cultural Production: Essays on Art and Literature*. Edited by Randal Johnson. Cambridge: Polity Press, 1993.

Brennglas, Adolf. "Antigone in Berlin." In *Berlin wie es ist und—trinkt*. 3d ed., vol. 23. Leipzig: Ignaz Jackowitz, 1846.

Brodbeck, David. "A Winter of Discontent: Mendelssohn and the Berliner Domchor." In *Mendelssohn Studies*, edited by R. Larry Todd, 1–32. Cambridge: Cambridge University Press, 1992.

Bruford, W. H. *The German Tradition of Self-Cultivation: Bildung from Humboldt to Thomas Mann*. Cambridge: Cambridge University Press, 1975.

Bunsen, Christian Carl Josais Friherr von. *Aus seinen Briefen und nach eigener Erinnering geschildert von seiner Witwe*. Edited by Friedrich Nippold. 3 vols. Leipzig: Brockhaus, 1869.

Burton, R. W. B. *The Chorus in Sophocles' Tragedies*. Oxford: Oxford University Press, 1980.

Bußmann, Walter. *Zwischen Preußen und Deutschland: Friedrich Wilhelm IV. Eine Biographie*. Berlin: Siedler, 1990.

Butler, E. M. *The Tyranny of Greece over Germany*. New York: Macmillan, 1935.

Chong-Gossard, J. H. Kim On. *Gender and Communication in Euripides' Plays: Between Song and Silence*. Boston: Brill, 2008.

Cooke, Deryck. *I Saw the World End: A Study of Wagner's Ring*. Oxford: Oxford University Press, 1979.

Cooper, John Michael. "Mendelssohn Received." In *The Cambridge Companion to Mendelssohn*, edited by Peter Mercer-Taylor, 233–50. Cambridge: Cambridge University Press, 2004.

———. "Of Red Roofs and Hunting Horns: Mendelssohn's Song Aesthetic, with an Unpublished Song Cycle (1830)." *Journal of Musicological Research* 21 (2002): 277–317.

Dahlhaus, Carl. *Nineteenth-Century Music.* Translated by J. Branford Robinson. Berkeley and Los Angeles: University of California Press, 1989.

Deathridge, John. *Wagner Beyond Good and Evil.* Berkeley and Los Angeles: University of California Press, 2008.

Dent, Edward J. "Music for the Cambridge Greek Plays." In *Edward J. Dent: Selected Essays*, edited by Hugh Taylor, 26–36. Cambridge: Cambridge University Press, 1979.

Devrient, Eduard. *Meine Erinnerungen an Felix Mendelssohn-Bartholdy und seine Briefe an mich.* Leipzig: J. J. Weber, 1869.

———. *Geschichte der deutschen Schauspielkunst.* 5 vols. Leipzig: Weber, 1848–74.

Dinglinger, Wolfgang. "Mendelssohn: General-Musik-Direktor für kirchliche und geistliche Musik." In *Felix Mendelssohn Bartholdy Kongreß-Bericht Berlin 1994*, edited by Christian Martin Schmidt, 23–36. Leipzig: Breitkopf und Härtel, 1997.

Dirrigl, Michael. *Ludwig I. König von Bayern, 1825-1848.* Munich: Hugendubel, 1980.

———. *Maximilian II: König von Bayern, 1848-1864.* Munich: Hugendubel, 1984.

Donner, Johann Jakob Christian. *Sophokles.* Heidelberg: C. F. Winter, 1839.

———. *Des Euripides Medeia.* Heidelberg: C. F. Winter, 1841.

Dover, K. J., ed. *Perceptions of Ancient Greece.* Cambridge, Mass.: Blackwell, 1992.

Drach, Erich. *Ludwig Tiecks Bühnenreformen.* Berlin: R. Trenkel, 1909.

Drews, Arthur. *Der Ideengehalt von Richard Wagners dramatischen Dichtungen im Zusammenhange mit seinem Leben und seiner Weltanschauung, nebst einem Anhang: Nietzsche und Wagner.* Leipzig: E. Pfeiffer, 1931.

Drieberg, Friedrich von. *Wörterbuch der griechischen Musik.* Berlin: Schlesinger, 1835.

Droysen, Johann Gustav. "Die Aufführung der Antigone des Sophokles in Berlin." In *Kleine Schriften zur alten Geschichte von Johann Gustav Droysen*, edited by E. Hübner, 2:146–152. Leipzig: Veit und Co., 1894. Originally published in *Die Spenersche Zeitung*, 25 April 1842.

Düding, D., P. Friedemann, and P. Münch, eds. *Öffentliche Festkultur: politische Feste in Deutschland von der Aufklärung bis zum ersten Weltkrieg.* Reinbeck bei Hamburg: Rowohlt Taschenbuch, 1988.

Easterling, Pat. "The Early Years of the Cambridge Greek Play: 1882-1912." In *Classics in 19th and 20th Century Cambridge: Curriculum, Culture and Community*, edited by Christopher Stray, 27–48. Cambridge: Cambridge Philological Society, 1999.

Ewans, Michael. *Wagner and Aeschylus: The Ring and the Oresteia.* London: Faber and Faber, 1982.

———. *Opera from the Greek: Studies in the Poetics of Appropriation.* Burlington: Vt.: Ashgate, 2007.

Euripides. *Medea.* Edited and translated by David Kovacs. Cambridge, Mass.: Harvard University Press, 1994.

Feder, Georg. "Felix Mendelssohns Briefe an Pauline und Julius Hübner." In *Festschrift Rudolf Elvers zum 60. Geburtstag*, edited by Ernst Herttrich and Hans Schneider, 157–198. Tutzing: Hans Schneider, 1985.

Ferris, David S. *Silent Urns: Romanticism, Hellenism, Modernity.* Stanford: Stanford University Press, 2000.

Fischer, L. H. "Ludwig Tieck am Hofe Friedrich Wilhelms IV." In Fischer, *Aus Berlins Vergangenheit: Gesammelte Aufsätze zur Kultur- und Litteraturgeschichte Berlins*, 107–41. Berlin: L. Oehmigke, 1891.

Flashar, Hellmut. "F. Mendelssohn-Bartholdys Vertonung antiker Dramen." In *Berlin und die Antike. Aufsätze: Architektur—Kunstgewerbe—Malerei—Skulptur—Theater und Wissenschaft vom 16. Jahrhundert bis heute*, edited by Willmuth Arenhövel and Christa Schreiber, 351–61. Berlin: Deutsches Archeologisches Institut, 1979.

——. "August Böckh und Felix Mendelssohn Bartholdy." In *Disiecta membra: Studien, Karl Gründer zum 60. Geburtstag*, edited by W. Schmidt-Biggemann, 66–81. Basel: Schwabe, 1989.

——. *Inszenierung der Antike: das griechische Drama auf der Bühne von der frühen Neuzeit bis zur Gegenwart*. Munich: C. H. Beck, 1991.

——. *Felix Mendelssohn-Bartholdy und die griechische Tragödie: Bühnenmusik im Kontext von Politik, Kultur, und Bildung*. Leipzig: Hirzel, 2001.

Foster, Daniel H. *Wagner's* Ring *Cycle and the Greeks*. Cambridge: Cambridge University Press, 2010.

Fridrich, Raimond M. *"Sehnsucht nach dem Verlorenen": Winckelmanns Ästhetik und ihre frühe Rezeption*. New York: P. Lang, 2003.

Gardiner, Cynthia P. *The Sophoclean Chorus: A Study of Character and Function*. Iowa City: University of Iowa Press, 1987.

Garratt, James. "Mendelssohn's Babel: Romanticism and the Poetics of Translation." *Music & Letters* 80 (1999): 23–49.

——. "Mendelssohn and the Rise of Musical Historicism." In *The Cambridge Companion to Mendelssohn*, edited by Peter Mercer-Taylor, 55–70. Cambridge: Cambridge University Press, 2004.

Geary, Jason. "Mendelssohn's Antigone and the Creation of an Ancient Greek Musical Language." *Journal of Musicology* (2006): 187–226.

——. "Incidental Music and the Revival of Greek Tragedy from the Italian Renaissance to German Romanticism." In *Ancient Drama in Music for the Modern Stage*, edited by Peter Brown and Suzana Ograjensek, 47–66. Oxford: Oxford University Press, 2010.

Georg, Johann, Herzog zu Sachsen, ed. *Briefwechsel zwischen König Johann von Sachsen und den Königen Friedrich Wilhelm IV. und Wilhelm I. von Preußen*. Leipzig: Quelle und Meyer, 1911.

Goethe, J. W. "Winckelmann." In *German Aesthetic and Literary Criticism: Winckelmann, Lessing, Hamann, Herder, Schiller, Goethe*, edited by H. B. Nisbet, 233–58. Cambridge: Cambridge University Press, 1985.

Gollwitzer, Heinz. *Ludwig I. von Bayern, Königtum im Vormärz: Eine politische Biographie*. Munich: Süddeutscher Verlag, 1987.

Grafton, Anthony. "Polyhistor into Philolog: Notes on the Transformation of German Classical Scholarship, 1780-1850." In *History of Universities*, 3:159–212. Amersham, England: Avebury, 1983.

Grair, Charles A. "Antiquity and Weimar Classicism." In *The Literature of Weimar Classicism*, edited by Simon Richter, 63–88. Rochester: Camden House, 2005.

Grey, Thomas S. *Wagner's Musical Prose: Texts and Contexts*. Cambridge: Cambridge University Press, 1995.

Großmann-Vendrey, Susanna. *Felix Mendelssohn Bartholdy und die Musik der Vergangenheit.* Regensburg: Gustav Bosse, 1969.
Güthenke, Constanze. *Placing Modern Greece: The Dynamics of Romantic Hellenism, 1770-1840.* Oxford: Oxford University Press, 2008.
Hall, Edith and Fiona Macintosh. *Greek Tragedy and the British Theatre, 1660-1914.* Oxford: Oxford University Press, 2005.
Hall, Edith, Fiona Macintosh, and Oliver Taplin, eds. *Medea in Performance, 1500-2000.* Oxford: Oxford University Press, 2000.
Hall, Edith. *Greek Tragedy: Suffering under the Sun.* Oxford: Oxford University Press, 2010.
Hatfield, Henry. *Winckelmann and his German Critics, 1755-1781: A Prelude to the Classical Age.* New York: King's Crown Press, 1943.
———. *Aesthetic Paganism in German Literature From Winckelmann to the Death of Goethe.* Cambridge: Harvard University Press, 1964.
Hebbel, Friedrich. *Friedrich Hebbels Tagebücher.* 4 vols. Leipzig: Hesse und Becker, [1904].
Hegel, Georg Wilhelm Friedrich. *Vorlesungen über die Geschichte der Philosophie.* Edited by G. J. P. J. Bolland. Leiden: Adriani, 1908.
———. *Aesthetics: Lectures on Fine Art.* 2 vols. Translated by T. M. Knox. Oxford: Clarendon Press, 1974–75.
———. *Phenomenology of Spirit.* Translated by A. V. Miller. Oxford: Oxford University Press, 1977.
———. *Lectures on the Philosophy of Religion.* 3 vols. Translated by E. B. Speirs and J. Burdon. New York: Humanities Press, 1962.
Hensel, Sebastian. *The Mendelssohn Family (1729-1847): From Letters and Journals.* 2 vols. Translated by Karl Klingemann. New York: Haskell, 1969.
Hermann, Gottfried. *Elementa Doctrinae Metricae.* Leipzig: Fleischer, 1816.
[Hermann, Gottfried]. *Über Sophokles Antigone und ihre Darstellung auf dem deutschen Theater* Leipzig: Wilhelm Engelmann, 1842.
Hiller, Ferdinand. *Mendelssohn: Letters and Recollections.* Translated by M. E. von Glehn. New York: Vienna House, 1972.
Hoffmann, Max. *August Böckh: Lebensbeschreibung und Auswahl aus Seinem Wissenschaftlichen Briefwechsel.* Leipzig: B. G. Teubner, 1901.
Holtei, Karl von, ed. *Briefe an Ludwig Tieck.* 4 vols. Breslau: Eduard Trewendt, 1864.
Humboldt, Alexander von. *Alexander von Humboldt und das preußische Königshaus: Briefe aus den Jahren 1835-1857.* Edited by Conrad Müller. Leipzig: K. F. Koehler, 1928.
Humboldt, Wilhelm von. *Briefe von Alexander von Humboldt an Christian Carl Josias Freiherr von Bunsen.* Leipzig: F. A. Brockhaus, 1869.
———. *Gesammelte Schriften,* 17 vols. Edited by the Königlich Preussischen Akademie der Wissenschaft. Berlin: Behr, 1903–36.
———. *Humanist without Portfolio: An Anthology of the Writings of Wilhelm von Humboldt.* Edited and translated by Marianne Cowan. Detriot: Wayne State University, 1963.
Jones, Peter Ward. "The Library of Felix Mendelssohn Bartholdy." In *Festschrift Rudolf Elvers zum 60. Geburtstag,* edited by Ernst Herttrich and Hans Schneider, 289–328. Tutzing: Hans Schneider, 1985.

Kallendorf, Craig W., ed. *A Companion to the Classical Tradition*. Malden, Mass.: Blackwell, 2007.

Katz, Jacob. *The Darker Side of Genius: Richard Wagner's Anti-Semitism*. Hanover, NH: University Press of New England, 1986.

Kes, Barbara R. *Die Rezeption der Komödien des Plautus und Terenz im 19. Jahrhundert*. Amsterdam: B. R. Grüner, 1988.

Klingemann, Karl, ed. *Felix Mendelssohn-Bartholdys Briefwechsel mit Legationsrat Karl Klingemann in London*. Essen: Baedeker, 1909.

Konold, Wulf. *Felix Mendelssohn Bartholdy und Seine Zeit*. Regensburg: Laaber, 1984.

Konrad, Ulrich. "*König Oedipus*: Franz Lachners Münchner Bühnenmusik zur Tragödie des Sophokles (1852)." In *Franz Lachner und seine Brüder: Hofkapellmeister zwischen Schubert und Wagner*, edited by Stephan Hörner and Hartmut Schick, 247–80. Tutzing: Hans Schneider, 2006.

Köpke, Rudolf. *Ludwig Tieck: Erinnerungen aus dem Leben des Dichters nach dessen mündlichen und schriftlichen Mittheilungen*. Leipzig: Brockhaus, 1855.

Little, Arthur M. *Mendelssohn's Music to the Antigone of Sophocles*. Washington, D. C.: Gibson Bros., 1893.

Lloyd-Jones, Hugh. *Blood for the Ghosts: Classical Influences in the Nineteenth and Twentieth Centuries*. London: Duckworth, 1982.

Lü, Yixu. *Medea unter den Deutschen: Wandlungen einer literarischen Figur*. Freiburg im Breisgau: Rombach Verlag, 2009.

Maas, Paul. *Greek Metre*. Translated by Hugh Lloyd-Jones. Oxford: Oxford University Press, 1962.

Macintosh, Fiona. "Tragedy in Performance: Nineteenth- and Twentieth-Century Productions." In *The Cambridge Companion to Greek Tragedy*, edited by P. E. Easterling, 284–323. Cambridge: Cambridge University Press, 1997.

Marchand, Suzanne L. *Down from Olympus: Archaeology and Philhellenism in Germany, 1750-1970*. Princeton: Princeton University Press, 1996.

Marx, A. B. *The Music of the Nineteenth Century and its Culture*. Translated by August Heinrich Wehrhan and C. Natalia Macfarren. London: Robert Cocks, [1855].

Mastronarde, Donald J., ed. *Euripides: Medea*. Cambridge: Cambridge University Press, 2002.

———. *The Art of Euripides: Dramatic Technique and Social Context*. Cambridge: Cambridge University Press, 2010.

May, Gabrielle Schmoll. *Tradition im Umbruch: zur Sophokles-Rezeption im deutschen Vormärz*. New York: P. Lang, 1989.

McClelland, Charles E. *State, Society, and University in Germany, 1700-1914*. Cambridge: Cambridge University Press, 1980.

Mendelssohn Bartholdy, Felix. *Musik zur Tragödie Antigone von Sophokles*, op. 55 (Klavierauszug vom Komponisten). Edited by Joachim Draheim. Wiesbaden: Breitkopf und Härtel, n.d.

———. *Oedipus in Kolonos des Sophokles*, op. 93. Vollständiger Klavierauszug. Leipzig: Breitkopf und Härtel, [1851].

———. *Briefe aus den Jahren 1833 bis 1847 von Felix Mendelssohn Bartholdy*. Edited by Carl and Paul Mendelssohn Bartholdy. Leipzig: Hermann Mendelssohn, 1863;

Letters of Felix Mendelssohn Bartholdy from 1833 to 1847. Translated by Lady Wallace. Boston: Oliver Ditson, 1863.

———. *Musik zu Antigone von Sophokles*, op. 55 (Partitur). In *Felix Mendelssohn Bartholdy's Werke: Kritisch durchgesehene Ausgabe*. Edited by Julius Rietz. Vol. 15/1. Leipzig: Breitkopf und Härtel, 1874–77.

———. *Musik zu Oedipus in Kolonos von Sophokles*, op. 93 (Partitur). In *Felix Mendelssohn Bartholdy's Werke: Kritisch durchgesehene Ausgabe*. Edited by Julius Rietz. Vol. 15/3. Leipzig: Breitkopf und Härtel, 1874–77.

———. *Felix Mendelssohn Bartholdy: Briefe an deutsche Verleger*, edited by Rudolf Elvers. Berlin: Walter de Gruyter, 1968.

———. *Briefe aus Leipziger Archiven*. Edited by Hans-Joachim Rothe and Reinhard Szeskus. Leipzig: VEB Deutscher Verlag für Musik, 1972.

———. *Briefe*. Edited by Rudolf Elvers. Frankfurt am Main: Fischer, 1984.

Mendelssohn-Bartholdy, Karl. *Goethe and Mendelssohn*. Translated by M. E. von Glehn. London: Macmillan, 1872.

Mercer-Taylor, Peter, ed. *The Cambridge Companion to Mendelssohn*. Cambridge: Cambridge Univ. Press, 2004.

Mosse, George. *Nationalization of the Masses: Political Symbolism and Mass Movements in Germany from the Napoleonic Wars Through the Third Reich*. New York: Howard Fertig, 1975.

Müller, Ulrich. "Wagner and Antiquity." In *Wagner Handbook*, edited by Ulrich Müller and Peter Wapnewski. Translated by Stewart Spencer and edited by John Deathridge, 227–35. Cambridge, MA: Harvard University Press, 1992.

Müller, Ulrich and Peter Wapnewski, eds. *Wagner Handbook*. Translation edited by John Deathridge. Cambridge, MA: Harvard University Press, 1992.

Nietzsche, Friedrich. *The Birth of Tragedy and Other Writings*. Edited by Raymond Geuss and Ronald Speirs and translated by Ronald Speirs. Cambridge: Cambridge University Press, 1999.

Nipperdey, Thomas. *Germany from Napoleon to Bismarck, 1800-1866*. Translated by Daniel Nolan. Dublin: Gill and Macmillan, 1996.

Paulin, Roger. *Ludwig Tieck: A Literary Biography*. Oxford: Oxford University Press, 1985.

Petsch, Robert. "Der Ring des Nibelungen in seinen Beziehungen zur griechischen Tragödie." *Richard Wagner-Jahrbuch* 2 (1909): 284–330.

Pfeiffer, Rudolf. *History of Classical Scholarship from 1300 to 1850*. Oxford: Oxford University Press, 1976.

Pickard-Cambridge, Arthur. *The Dramatic Festivals of Athens*. Rev. ed. by John Gould and D. M. Lewis. Oxford: Oxford University Press, 1988.

Potts, Alex. *Flesh and the Ideal: Winckelmann and the Origins of Art History*. New Haven: Yale University Press, 1994.

Prutz, Robert. *Zehn Jahre: Geschichte der neusten Zeit, 1840–1850*. Vol. 1. Leipzig: J. J. Weber, 1850.

Rabinowitz, Nancy. *Anxiety Veiled: Euripides and the Traffic in Women*. Ithaca: Cornell University Press, 1993.

———. *Greek Tragedy*. Malden, MA: Blackwell, 2008.

Rather, L. J. *The Dream of Self-Destruction: Wagner's Ring and the Modern World.* Baton Rouge: Louisiana State University Press, 1979.

Raven, D. S. *Greek Metre: An Introduction.* London: Faber and Faber, 1962.

Rehm, Walther. *Griechentum und Goethezeit: Geschichte eines Glaubens.* Leipzig: Dieterich, 1936.

Rellstab, Ludwig. "Dartstellung der Antigone des Sophokles." *Vossische Zeitung,* 30 October 1841.

Rochow, Caroline and Marie de la Motte-Fouqué. *Vom Leben am preußischen Hofe, 1815-1852.* Berlin: Ernst Siegfried Mittler und Sohn, 1908.

Rose, Paul Lawrence. *Wagner: Race and Revolution.* New Haven: Yale University Press, 1992.

Schadewaldt, Wolfgang. "Richard Wagner und die Griechen." In *Hellas und Hesperien: Gesammelte Schriften zur Antike und zur neueren Literatur in zwei Bänden,* 2:341–405. Zürich: Artemis, 1970.

Schiller, Friedrich. "On the Use of the Chorus in Tragedy." Preface to *The Bride of Messina. In Historical Dramas.* Translated by Samuel Taylor Coleridge, E.A. Aytoun, and A.J.W. Morrison, 2:241–46. London, New York, and Chicago: The Anthological Society, 1901.

———. Über die aesthetische Erziehung des Menschen in einer Reihe von Briefen. In *Schillers Werke,* edited by Benno von Wiese, 20:309–412. Weimar: Hermann Böhlaus, 1962.

———. *On the Naive and Sentimental in Literature.* Translated by Helen Watanabe-O'Kelly. Manchester: Carcanet New Press, 1981.

Schlegel, August Wilhelm. *Course of Lectures on Dramatic Art and Literature.* Translated by John Black. New York: AMS Press, 1965.

Schlegel, Friedrich. *On the Study of Greek Antiquity.* Edited and translated by Stuart Barnett. Albany: State University of New York, 2001.

Schneider, Louis. *Aus meinem Leben,* 2 vols. Berlin: Ernst Siegfried Mittler und Sohn, 1879.

Schuster, Georg, ed. *Die Jugend des Königs Friedrich Wilhelm IV. von Preußen und des Kaisers und Königs Wilhelm I. Tagebuchblätter ihres Erziehers Friedrich Delbrück (1800-1809).* 3 vols. Berlin: A. Hofmann, 1907.

Scott, William C. *Musical Design in Sophoclean Theater.* Hanover, N. H.: University Press of New England, 1996.

Seaton, Douglass. "The Problem of the Lyric Persona in Mendelssohn's Songs." In *Felix Mendelssohn Bartholdy Kongreß-Bericht Berlin 1994,* edited by Christian Martin Schmidt, 167–86. Leipzig: Breitkopf und Härtel, 1997.

———. "Mendelssohn's Dramatic Music." In *The Mendelssohn Companion,* edited by Douglass Seaton, 143–256. Westport, Conn.: Greenwood Press, 2001.

Sheehan, James J. *German History 1770-1866.* Oxford: Oxford University Press, 1989.

Sophocles. *Four Dramas of Maturity: Aias, Antigone, Young Women of Trachis, Oidipous the King.* Edited by Michael Ewans and translated by Michael Ewans, Graham Ley, and Gregory McCart. London: J. M. Dent, 1999.

———. *The Three Theban Plays.* Translated by Robert Fagles. New York: Viking Penguin, 1982.

Sorkin, David. *The Transformation of German Jewry, 1780-1840.* Oxford: Oxford University Press, 1987.
Southard, Robert. *Droysen and the Prussian School of History.* Lexington: University Press of Kentucky, 1995.
Steinberg, Michael P. "The Incidental Politics to Mendelssohn's Antigone." In *Mendelssohn and His World*, edited by R. Larry Todd, 137–57. Princeton: Princeton University Press, 1991.
Steiner, George. *Antigones.* Oxford: Oxford University Press, 1984.
Stolberg-Wernigerode, Otto Graf zu. *Anton Graf zu Stolberg-Wernigerode: Ein Freund und Ratgeber König Friedrich Wilhlems IV.* Munich and Berlin: R. Oldenbourg, 1926.
Stoneman, Richard. "'A Crazy Enterprise': German Translators of Sophocles from Opitz to Böckh." In *Sophocles Revisited: Essays Presented to Sir Hugh Lloyd-Jones*, edited by Jasper Griffin, 307–29. Oxford: Oxford University Press, 1999.
Stuber, Petra and Ulrich Beck, eds. *Theater und 19. Jahrhundert.* Hildesheim: Georg Olms, 2009.
Taubert, Wilhelm. *Chöre zur Medea des Euripides*, op. 57 (piano-vocal score). Berlin: T. Trautwein, [1845].
Tieck, Ludwig. *Kritische Schriften.* 4 vols. Leipzig: F. A. Brockhaus, 1848–52.
Todd, R. Larry. *Mendelssohn: A Life in Music.* Oxford: Oxford University Press, 2003.
Toews, John. *Becoming Historical: Cultural Reformation and Public Memory in Early Nineteenth-Century Berlin.* Cambridge: Cambridge University Press, 2004.
Trevelyan, Humphrey. *Goethe and the Greeks.* Cambridge: Cambridge University Press, 1941.
Uhlig, Ludwig, ed. *Griechenland als Ideal: Winckelmann und seine Rezeption in Deutschland.* Tübingen: Gunter Narr, 1988.
Vick, Brian. "Greek Origins and Organic Metaphors: Ideals of Cultural Autonomy in Neohumanist Germany from Winckelmann to Curtius." *Journal of the History of Ideas* 63 (2002): 483–500.
Wagner, Cosima. *Cosima Wagner's Diaries.* Edited by Martin Gregor-Dellin and Dietrich Mack and translated by Geoffrey Skelton. 2 vols. New York: Harcourt Brace Jovanovich, 1977–80.
Wagner, Richard. *Richard Wagner's Prose Works.* Translated by William Ashton Ellis. 8 vols. 1892–99. Reprint, St. Clair Shores, MI: Scholarly Press, 1972.
———. *Gesammelte Schriften und Dichtungen von Richard Wagner.* 3d ed. 10 vols. Leipzig: C. F. W. Siegel, [1903].
———. *My Life.* Translated by Andrew Gray and edited by Mary Whittall. Cambridge: Cambridge University Press, 1983.
———. *Selected Letters of Richard Wagner.* Edited by Stewart Spencer and Barry Millington. London: J. M. Dent and Sons, 1987.
Watkin, David and Tilman Mellinghoff. *German Architecture and the Classical Ideal.* Cambridge, Mass.: MIT Press, 1987.
Wehmer, Carl, ed. *Ein tief gegründet Herz: Der Briefwechsel Felix Mendelssohn-Bartholdys mit Johann Gustav Droysen.* Heidelberg: Lambert Schneider, 1959.
Weiner, Marc A. *Richard Wagner and the Anti-Semitic Imagination.* Lincoln: University of Nebraska Press, 1995.

Weiss, Hermann F. "Unbekannte Zeugnisse zu den Leipziger Aufführungen von Felix Mendelssohn Bartholdys Bühnenmusik zur 'Antigone' in den Jahren 1841 und 1842." *Musikforschung* 51 (1998): 50–7.

Werner, Eric. *Mendelssohn: A New Image of the Composer and His Age*. Translated by Dika Newlin. London: Free Press of Glencoe, 1963.

West, M. L. *Ancient Greek Music*. Oxford: Oxford University Press, 1992.

———. *Greek Metre*. Oxford: Oxford University Press, 1982.

Westernhagen, Curt von. *Richard Wagners Dresdener Bibliothek 1842-1849: Neue Dokumente zur Geschichte seines Schaffens*. Wiesbaden: Brockhaus, 1966.

Wilamowitz-Moellendorff, Ulrich von. *Griechische Verskunst*. Darmstadt: Wissenschaftlicher Buchgesellschaft, 1975.

———. *History of Classical Scholarship*. Translated by Alan Harris. London: Gerald Duckworth, 1982.

Wilson, Pearl Cleveland. *Wagner's Dramas and Greek Tragedy*. New York: Columbia University Press, 1919.

Winckelmann, Johann Joachim. Thoughts on the Imitation of the Painting and Sculpture of the Greeks. In *German Aesthetic and Literary Criticism*, edited by H. B. Nisbet, 29–54. Cambridge: Cambridge University Press, 1985.

———. *The History of Ancient Art*. 2 vols. Translated by G. Henry Lodge. Boston: J. R. Osgood, 1880.

Wiora, Walter, ed. *Die Ausbreitung des Historismus über die Musik*. Regensburg: Gustav Bosse, 1969.

Wrassiwanopulos-Braschowanoff, George. *Richard Wagner und die Antike: Ein Beitrag zur kunstphilosophischen Weltanschauung Richard Wagners*. Bayreuth: Lorenz Ellwanger, 1905.

Zenger, Max. *Geschichte der Münchener Oper*. Edited by Theodor Kroyer. Munich: F.X. Weizinger, 1923.

Zimmermann, Bernhard. *Greek Tragedy: An Introduction*. Translated by Thomas Marier. Baltimore: Johns Hopkins University Press, 1991.

———. "Seiner Zeit voraus—Euripides *Medea*." In *Mythische Wiederkehr: Der Ödipus- und Medea-Mythos im Wandel der Zeiten*, edited by Bernhard Zimmermann, 103–19. Freiburg in Breisgau: Rombach, 2009.

INDEX

Aeschylus, 39, 88, 199, 218
  Agamemnon, 61, 231
  Eumenides, 102, 138, 156
  Oresteia, 102, 200, 219
  Prometheus Bound, 219
  Prometheus trilogy, 198–99, 218
  Seven against Thebes, 214, 216
  and Wagner's *Ring des Nibelungen*,
    198–99
Altertumswissenschaft, 23–24
ancient Greece
  as aesthetic model, 2, 10, 11–12, 14, 23,
    175, 202–03
  concept of freedom in, 13, 88, 204
  German affinity with, 3, 10, 23, 26, 29,
    173, 202, 209, 233
  historicist view of, 7, 11, 13, 208
  ideal of, 4, 11, 13, 16–17, 19, 21–22, 26,
    70–71, 167, 172, 204–05, 230
  national character of, 15, 26
  as pedagogical tool, 19–20, 25
  superiority of, 12–13, 25
Antigone, 7, 41–43
  and Creon, 44–45
  in opposition to the state, 216–18,
    221, 224
  parallels with Brünnhilde, 201,
    220–24
  parallels with Siegfried, 215, 219–20
Antigone (*see* Mendelssohn *and see* Sophocles)
Aristophanes, 101, 199, 232

Aristotle,
  dramatic unities of, 15
  on the structure of Greek tragedy, 53
  Poetics, 53

Bach, Johann Sebastian, 8, 34, 163, 211
  St. Matthew Passion, 37, 58
Bakunin, Mikhail, 203
Bayreuth Festival, 198
Bayreuth Festspielhaus, 197
Becker, Julius, 97
Beethoven, Ludwig van, 34, 37, 89,
    172, 211
  legacy of, 212, 214
Bellermann, Heinrich
  Ajax, 103
  Oedipus at Colonus, 103
  Oedipus the King, 103
Bellermann, Johann Friedrich, 84
Benda, Georg, 108
Berlin
  and cultural revitalization of, 29, 33–34,
    38–39, 70, 78
  Mendelssohn in, 34–36, 136–38
  neoclassical architecture in, 23, 167
  royal court at, 2, 21
  as seat of royal power, 70
  and stage revivals of Greek
    tragedy, 100–03
  University of, 20, 24, 33
Bildung, 19, 37, 177, 227

Böckh, August, 1, 47, 49, 70, 88, 103
  assessment of Mendelssohn's *Antigone*, 56, 58, 60–61, 70, 82–83, 90
  and historicism, 25, 71, 208
  and the rise of classical philology, 24
  as scholarly advisor to *Antigone*, 28, 46, 48
  views on *Antigone*, 43
Boetius, Susanne, 5–6, 45, 57, 84, 105
Borchmeyer, Dieter, 204–05, 219, 220
Bothe, Friedrich Heinrich, 105
Brünnhilde, 219–20
  and parallels with Antigone, 201, 220–24
Bunsen, Karl Josias von, 33, 34, 102

Cherubini, Luigi, 108–09, 124
choral recitative, 30, 54, 55, 56, 65
Chrysander, Friedrich, 228
classical philology, 11, 20, 23–25
Commer, Franz, 101
Congress of Vienna, 31
Corneille, Pierre, 14, 15, 108, 207, 209
Crelinger, Auguste, 58, 105

Dahlhaus, Carl, 207
David, Ferdinand, 47, 58, 64
Devrient, Eduard, 28, 41, 49–50, 59, 90
Dingelstedt, Franz von, 168, 170, 176
  and Greek tragedy in Munich, 179, 180, 193, 195
  and theater reform, 169, 177–79
Donner, Johann Jakob, 26, 200
  translation of *Antigone*, 28, 40–41, 46, 54, 56, 60–62, 63, 68–69, 76–77, 84, 92–93, 225
  translation of *Medea*, 105, 115–16, 118, 122–23
  translation of *Oedipus at Colonus*, 138–39, 154, 160, 163, 165
  translation of *Oedipus the King*, 168, 179, 183, 187
Drieberg, Friedrich von, 48, 89
Droysen, Johann Gustav, 49, 62, 64, 96, 103, 138, 199, 208
  reconstruction of Prometheus trilogy, 198, 200
  review of Mendelssohn-Tieck *Antigone*, 84, 88–92
Dürer, Albrecht, 172

Eichhorn, J. A. F., 136
Euripides, 14, 39, 40, 99, 105, 200
  Medea (*see also* Taubert)
    adaptations of, 107–09
    plot, 105–06
Ewans, Michael, 107, 124, 219

Falkenstein, J. P. von, 36, 84
Fasch, Johann Friedrich, 37
Fink, G. W., 73
Flashar, Hellmut, 5–6, 29, 60
Förster, Friedrich, 74, 83, 91, 99–100
Franz, Johann, 101
Friedrich Wilhelm III, King of Prussia, 31
Friedrich Wilhelm IV, King of Prussia, 1, 3, 26, 28
  and Greek tragedy, 38–39, 40, 48, 49, 78, 137, 141, 208
  as crown prince, 33, 35, 38
  as patron of the arts, 33, 35, 81
  cultural and political reforms of, 29, 31–33, 38–39, 135–36
  desire for Christian-German state, 31, 32, 41, 69, 157, 163
  "monarchical project" of, 33, 67, 78
Fritze, Franz, 101, 139

Gabrieli, Andrea, 9
Gärtner, Friedrich von, 171–73
Genelli, Hans Christian, 46
German Hellenism, 2, 3, 10–12
  changing nature of, 23
  key aspects of, 18
Germany
  as *Kulturstaat*, 20, 73, 78
  national identity of, 1, 3, 4, 10, 16, 20, 23, 30, 32, 67, 73, 78, 169, 173, 233
Gesamtkunstwerk (*see* Richard Wagner)
Glasbrenner, Adolf, 84
Gluck, Christoph Willibald, 14, 45
Goethe, Johann Wolfgang von, 10, 11, 26, 34, 172, 177
  essay on Winckelmann, 18, 21
  Faust, 59, 218
  Iphigenie auf Tauris, 16, 179
  and staging of Greek tragedy, 29, 39–40
  and Weimar Classicism, 11, 16–19
Gottsched, Christoph, 15
Graecomania, 21, 26, 83, 85

Greek chorus, 46–48, 63, 66, 68
Greek meter, 61
   imitation of in German literary works, 26
   in German translations, 28, 40, 56, 60–61
   in Mendelssohn's *Antigone*, 60, 62–63, 74, 76
   in music, 30, 46, 58–59, 61–62
Greek tragedy
   and Christianization, 3, 58
   and connection to Wagnerian opera, 198
   otherness of, 64, 77
   stage revivals of, 28, 46, 100–03
   structure of, 53
   use of music in, 48–49, 63–64, 100–104
   use of recitative in, 53
Greek War of Independence, 23, 173, 175
Griechenveriene, 23
Grillparzer, Franz, 105, 109
Grimm, Jakob, 33
Grimm, Wilhelm, 33
Gutenberg, Johannes, 172
Gutenberg festival, 72–73, 76
Gymnasium
   and performances of Greek tragedy, 85, 101–03

Handel, George Frederick, 37, 172
   Messiah, 3, 165
Hebbel, Friedrich, 90, 178
Hegel, Georg Wilhelm Friedrich, 10, 33, 88, 202
   Aesthetics, 22, 41
   interpretation of *Antigone*, 41–43, 217, 221
Heine, Heinrich, 22, 178, 210
Hellenism (*see* German Hellenism)
Herder, Johann Gottfried, 13, 14, 15
Hermann, Gottfried, 24, 60, 87, 97, 103
Heyse, Karl, 49
historicism
   emergence of, 29, 32
   in architecture, 174
   in music, 37, 174
Hitler, Adolf, 198
Hölderlin, Friedrich, 26, 233
Homer, 24, 39, 61, 198, 199, 200
   Nausicaa, 12
   Odyssey, 26
Humboldt, Alexander von, 33, 34, 72
Humboldt, Wilhlem von, 11, 19–20, 25, 61

incidental music, 9, 52–53, 100

Klenze, Leo von, 168, 171–73 175, 180
   Glyptothek, 2, 171–72
Klingemann, Karl, 49, 137, 138, 156, 163
Klopstock, Friedrich, 26
kommos (defined), 58

Lachner, Franz
   background of, 180–81
   and Munich court production of *Antigone*, 102, 168, 180–81
   Oedipus the King
      compositional approach to, 170, 181, 187, 190
      Mendelssohn's influence on, 180–81, 184
      Munich production of, 2, 5, 170, 179, 180, 193
      music of, 181–86, 190–95
      overall style of, 186, 190
      reception of, 195
Laube, Heinrich, 87–88, 100, 178
Lehrs, Samuel, 199
Lessing, Gotthold Ephriam, 13, 15, 202
Loewe, Carl, 85
Lortzing, Albert
   Der Wildschütz, 84–85
Louis XIV, King of France, 207, 209
Ludwig I, King of Bavaria, 5
   and Bavarian identity, 172, 174
   and political ties to Greece, 175
   cultural reforms of, 169–74
   philhellenism of, 175
Luther, Martin, 163

Macfarren, George, 48, 86, 96, 231
Männergesangverein, 66
marching anapests, 54
Marx, Adolph Bernhard, 45, 227
Marx, Karl, 212
Massow, Ludwig von, 35
Maximilian II, King of Bavaria, 168, 176
   and Bavarian identity, 177
   and Greek tragedy, 170, 180
   and the Munich court theater, 177–78
   cultural reforms of, 5, 170, 176–77
Medea, 105–09, 123–25
Medea (*see* Euripides *and see* Taubert)
melodrama, 30, 57, 58–60
Mendelssohn, Abraham, 34, 45

Mendelssohn, Felix
  aesthetic views of, 167
  and attacks on by Wagner, 209–14
  Antigone, Op. 55
    compositional approach to, 4, 30, 37, 49–52, 53, 62–65, 230
    as compositional model, 110–11, 120, 123, 128, 134, 181, 184
    critique of, 87, 89–90, 97
    Dresden production of, 209–10
    Kassel production of, 85
    later reception of, 227–31
    London production of, 48, 85–86, 231
    Munich production of, 102, 168–69, 179
    music of, 43–45, 48–49, 54–59, 65–72, 76–78, 92–96
    as new musical genre, 99–100
    New York production of, 85
    "Ode to Man," 67–71, 98, 230
    overall style of, 45–46, 63–66, 74, 92–93, 97–98
    Prussian court production of, 1, 28, 45, 57, 58
    reception of, 4, 8–9, 70
    Stettin production of, 85
  as Prussian court composer, 33, 34, 35–36, 136–38
  Athalie, Op. 74, 137, 138, 155
  education of, 49, 60, 210
  Elijah, Op. 70, 95, 163
  Die Erste Walpurgisnacht, Op. 60, 65
  family background of, 34
  Festgesang (Gutenberg), 72–73, 76–77
  interest in music of the past, 37–38, 212
  Lied ohne Worte, Op. 62, No. 6 ("Spring Song"), 232
  Lobgesang [Symphony No. 2 in B-flat Major], Op. 52, 45, 76, 163
  A Midsummer Night's Dream, op. 61 (incidental music), 135, 137, 138
  Oedipus at Colonus, Op. 90
    compositional approach to, 135–36, 141, 144–45, 154–55
    music of, 145–55, 157–66
    overall style of, 144, 155, 163, 165
    Prussian court production of, 2, 135, 138–39
    reception of, 135, 139–40
  political views of, 35, 45–46, 70
  professional career of, 34–35
  religious views of, 45
  Symphony No. 3 in A Minor ("Scottish"), Op. 56, 76, 165
  St. Paul (Paulus), Op. 36, 35, 65, 163
Mendelssohn, Moses, 34, 45
Mendelssohn-Tieck *Antigone*
  Berlin production of, 57, 84, 209
  choreography, 48
  Christian dimension of, 41
  groundbreaking nature of, 1–2, 29, 40, 46, 80, 85, 101
  influence of, 2, 4, 80, 83
  Leipzig production of, 46, 57, 84
  modern assessments of, 43
  music to (*see* Mendelssohn)
  Potsdam premiere of, 28
  reception of, 79–83, 87–88, 227
  role of music in, 48–49
  royal commission of, 1, 29, 35, 38, 48, 81
  staging of, 46–48, 81–82
  and Wagner's assessment of (*see* Wagner)
Meyerbeer, Giacomo, 102, 209, 212–14
Minckwitz, Johannes, 179
Mozart, Wolfgang Amadeus, 37, 172
Müller, Karl Ottfried, 208
Munich
  architecture of, 171–76
  court theater of, 17, 177–78
  royal court of, 2, 5, 21

Napoleon, 20, 23, 32, 173
neoclassicism
  in architecture, 167
  French, 14–15, 207–08
  in the visual arts, 17
neo-humanism, 19, 23, 167
Neues Palais Theater, 28, 38, 46–47, 104, 138
Niebuhr, Barthold Georg, 199
Nietzsche, Friedrich, 197, 210
  Birth of Tragedy, 8, 228, 230

orchestra (Greek), 46, 53
Orff, Carl, 232–33

parados (defined), 53
Palladio, Andrea, 16, 171
Petsch, Robert, 197–98, 218
Philhellenism, 23, 175,
Plato, 199
Plautus, 39, 101

Poe, Edgar Allan, 85
Potsdam (*see* Berlin)
Proudon, Pierre-Joseph, 203
Prussia, 23, 31, 70, 167, 170 (*see also* Berlin)
    Academy of Arts in, 34
    and German nationalist aims, 33, 78, 88, 174
    neo-humanist reforms in, 19–20, 25
    as kingdom, 32
    and Napoleonic Wars, 20
Prutz, Robert, 33

Racine, Jean, 14, 39, 179, 206, 207, 209, 211
    Athalie, 137, 155
Radziwill, Prince Anton, 59
Ranke, Leopold von, 29
Rellstab, Ludwig, 57, 59, 79, 80, 102, 139
Ring des Nibelungen (*see* Wagner)
Rochlitz, Friedrich, 39–40
Röckel, August, 220
Romanticism, 11, 21–22, 26
Rott, Karl Moritz, 58

Schadewaldt, Wolfgang, 198–200
Schelling, Friedrich, 33, 177
Schiller, Friedrich, 21, 26, 72, 172, 177, 179, 202
    "Die Götter Griechenlands," 17–18
    on the Greek chorus, 68
    Letters on Aesthetic Education, 10, 18
    and Weimar Classicism, 11, 16, 17–19
Schinkel, Karl Friedrich, 23, 33
    Altes Museum, 2, 23, 167, 172
    neoclassical outlook of, 167
Schlegel, August Wilhelm, 22, 39, 42, 63–64, 90–91, 141
Schlegel, Friedrich, 11, 21–22, 26, 42, 156
Schmidt, August, 70
Schmidt, Heinrich, 97
Schneider, Louis, 38–39
school theaters, 39, 101–03, 134, 227, 232
Schopenhauer, Arthur, 205, 219
Schröder-Devrient, Wilhelmine, 210
Schulz, Adolf, 102
Schumann, Clara, 89
Schumann, Robert, 89
Seaton, Douglass, 6, 60, 62–63, 155, 240n8
Semper, Gottfried, 210

Seneca, 107–09
Shakespeare, 15, 39, 135, 179, 206
Siegfried, 219–20, 222–23
Sillig, Julius, 199
Solger, Karl Wilhelm, 41
Sophocles, 1, 15, 41, 70, 80, 90, 101, 200, 239n54, 245n35
    Ajax, 103, 231
    Antigone, 49, 89, 221 (*see also* Mendelssohn)
    Hegel's interpretation of, 42–43, 217
    parallels with Wagner's *Ring* cycle, 219
    plot, 41–42
    idea of state versus individual in, 4, 41–43, 45, 70
    significance of for Germany, 41
    structure of, 51–52
    Weimar production of, 29, 39–40
    Elektra, 101
    Oedipus at Colonus, 103, 141, 214 (*see also* Mendelssohn)
    lyric dialogue in, 144, 149
    plot, 140–41
    religious underpinnings of, 141, 155–57
    structure of, 142–43
    Oedipus the King, 103, 214 (*see also* Lachner)
    idea of fate in, 192–94
    plot, 179–80
    religious associations of, 186
    structure of, 187–88
    Wagner's interpretation of, 215
    Philoctetes, 244n6
    Theban trilogy, 138, 169, 179, 195–96
Spohr, Louis, 85
Spontini, Gaspare, 210
stasimon (defined), 53
Stabreim, 225
Steinberg, Michael P., 4, 6, 43, 45–46, 92
Strauss, Richard, 232–33

Taubert, Wilhelm
    background of, 104
    Medea, Op. 57
    Berlin production of, 104
    compositional approach to, 105, 110–11, 115–17, 120, 122–23, 134
    music of, 111, 115–22, 124–34
    overall style of, 111, 123–28, 130–31

Taubert, Wilhelm (*Cont.*)
    Prussian court production of, 2,
        99, 104
    reception of, 109–10
Terence, 39, 49, 101
Thiersch, Friedrich, 20, 168, 179
thymele, 46
Tieck, Ludwig, 1, 33, 206
    and staging of Greek tragedy, 28, 40, 43,
        46–47, 49, 105, 157, 163
    as Prussian court poet, 33, 38–39, 40–41
    as stage director, 104
Todd, R. Larry, 6, 44, 58, 145, 147
Toelken, E. H., 28, 48, 81–83

Vaughn Williams, Ralph, 232
Virgil, 12, 13
Voss, Johann Heinrich, 26, 39, 61

Wagner, Adolf, 199
Wagner, Cosima, 221
Wagner, Richard, 26
    interpretation of Oedipus myth, 201,
        214–18, 219, 221
    negative assessment of Mendelssohn's
        Antigone, 7–8, 201, 205–11,
        213–14, 218
    and Mendelssohn's *Antigone*, 221,
        224–25
    and music drama, 204, 207, 228
    and Sophocles' *Antigone*, 214, 221
    anti-Semitism of, 8, 201, 209,
        211–14, 230
    "artwork of the future," 204, 208
    Gesamtkunstwerk, 7, 8, 12, 197, 202, 204,
        207, 213, 228
    ideas on *das Volk*, 204, 209, 213
    influence of Greek tragedy on, 22, 200,
        207, 221–24, 230
    interest in ancient Greece, 197, 199–200
    interest in Greek tragedy, 7
    library of, 199–200
    operas:
        Der fliegende Holländer, 198, 209
        Götterdämmerung, 219, 222
        Lohengrin, 199
        Die Meistersinger, 199
        Das Rheingold, 223
        Siegfried, 220
        Siegfrieds Tod, 214, 219
        Tannhäuser, 199
        Die Walküre, 215, 219, 222
        Ring des Nibelungen, 8, 197–98, 214, 215
            and Aeschylus' Prometheus
                trilogy, 198
            and Greek mythology, 198
            incest motif in, 215, 219, 220
            and Oedipus myth, 201, 215, 218,
                220, 224
            parallels with Sophocles'
                Antigone, 219–20
    views on Greek tragedy, 202, 208–09
    views on the character of
        Antigone, 216–17
    views on society and the state,
        216–17, 219
    writings:
        Art and Revolution, 202–04, 207, 213
        Artwork of the Future, 203
        A Communication to My Friends, 206
        Judaism in Music, 211–14, 230
        Mein Leben, 199, 210
        Opera and Drama, 204–06,
            214–18, 220–21
        "What is German?", 202
Wagner, Wieland, 198
Weimar Classicism (*see* Goethe *and see*
    Schiller)
Wolf, Friedrich August, 23–24, 25
Winckelmann, Johann Joachim, 11, 12–14,
    15, 24, 25, 70, 202, 204, 208,
    211, 230

Young Germany, 22, 178

Zelter, Karl Friedrich, 34, 37